The Early Slavs

The Early Slavs

Eastern Europe from the Initial Settlement
to the Kievan Rus

Pavel M. Dolukhanov

LONGMAN
London and New York

Addison Wesley Longman Limited,
Edinburgh Gate,
Harlow, Essex CM20 2JE, England
and Associated Companies throughout the world.

*Published in the United States of America
by Addison Wesley Longman, New York*

© Addison Wesley Longman Limited 1996

First published 1996

ISBN 0 582 23627 4 CSD
ISBN 0 582 23618 5 PPR

British Library Cataloguing-in-Publication Data

A catalogue record for this book is available from the British Library

Library of Congress Cataloging-in-Publication Data

Dolukhanov, Pavel Markovich.
    The early Slavs: Eastern Europe from the initial settlement to the
    Kievan Rus / Pavel M. Dolukhanov.
        p. cm.
    Includes bibliographical references and index.
    ISBN 0-582-23627-4 (casebound). – ISBN 0-582-23618-5 (pbk.)
    1. Slavs – History. 2. Europe, Eastern – History. I. Title.
    DJK27.D65 1996   95-45474
                                                      CIP

Set by 7.00 in 10/12 Sabon
Produced by Longman Singapore Publishers (Pte) Ltd.
Printed in Singapore

Contents

List of Illustrations

Preface

I am beginning this book with apologies, and my first apology concerns the title. The Slavs, as a distinct ethnicity, were first mentioned by Greek writers only in the second century AD whereas I begin my story with the initial appearance of tool-making hominids in Russian territory, which occurred *c.* 500 thousand years before that.

During the millennia which have left no written documents, the succeeding generations of people who lived in the vast spaces of the Russian Plain could hardly be described as belonging to any ethnic entity; they had no common name, whether it was 'Slavs' or anything else. The same is true for large groups of early humans in any other part of the world. Yet I am convinced that I am right in choosing this time dimension for my story. The origins and early development of peoples known as the Slavs could be rightly understood only if viewed from a wide temporal perspective.

My second apology follows directly from the first. Having chosen to write a wide panorama of Slavic pre- and proto-history, I necessarily transgressed into areas less familiar to me professionally.

At this moment, it is inevitable that I must say a few words about myself. I was trained as a geomorphologist and Quaternary geologist at the University of Leningrad (now St Petersburg) in Russia (formerly the USSR). Immediately after graduating in 1960, I joined the staff of the Leningrad Institute of Archaeology, Academy of Sciences of the USSR. Since then I have conducted palaeoenvironmental and geochronological investigations of archaeological sites in more or less all parts of the former USSR. These studies were mainly concerned with Mesolithic and Neolithic Age sites and pivoted around the problem of the Mesolithic–Neolithic transition. I was especially interested in the study of the emergence of agriculture and stock-breeding in their environmental context, and in the various social, cultural and linguistic implications of this. Yet, being one of the few environmental scientists directly involved in archaeology, I was obliged from time to time to work on archaeological sites of various ages, not necessarily belonging to the Mesolithic or Neolithic. I also took part in excavations of Palaeolithic sites. For a number of years I was involved in several projects related to the study of Bronze Age sites, particularly in the Caucasus and Central Asia. On several occasions I took part in field investigations of 'classical' sites containing Greek and Scythian strata, on the shores of the Black Sea.

Investigations of sites in the area of Usvyaty played a particularly important role in my early archaeological career. In the early 1960s, Dr A.M. Miklyayev from the State Hermitage Museum in St Petersburg found a group of lake dwellings of Neolithic and Early Bronze Age in that area of western Russia. He invited me to take part in his studies. Miklyayev, being a broad-minded scholar, at a later stage widened the scope of his research which eventually covered the entire archaeological sequence from Final Palaeolithic to the Middle Ages. The project, which is still in progress, enabled me to collect an immense volume of data on the geomorphology, geochronology and stratigraphy of sites of various age in this particular area. The premature death of Dr Miklyayev in 1993 temporarily interrupted the project but it has now been resumed by his students.

Our fruitful discussions with Dr Miklyayev were at the base of yet another project, which was later initiated by myself and Dr E.N. Nosov, the medieval archaeologist from the Institute of Archaeology in St Petersburg. This project was especially targeted at early Medieval sites, allegedly associated with the Early Slavs. During the four consecutive seasons (1980–84), we surveyed a great number of sites ranging in age from the sixth to the eleventh centuries AD. These sites, found in various environmental settings, were located in the heartland of Early Slavic settlement in northwestern Russia, in and around Novgorod, and included the catchment of Lake Ilmen, the fringes of the Valdai Heights and the southern shores of Lake Ladoga. In the last chapters of this book I will discuss some of the results of these studies, that so far have not been published in full.

The bulk of the information used in this book came from various publications. When I came to the West, I was lucky enough to be able to bring the greater part of my library, and these books and articles enabled me to write the essential part of this work. A great many of the other books necessary for my research were obtained via the interlibrary exchange network. I received several recent publications, otherwise unattainable here, from my friends and colleagues in Russia. (With sadness I have to remark that the quantity and quality of these publications severely suffered in recent years: one of the adverse side-effects of post-*perestroika* developments.)

In conclusion, I wish to express deep gratitude to all my colleagues, both in St Petersburg and Newcastle-upon-Tyne, who in various ways assisted me in completing this work. I am especially indebted to Dr Yuri Chistov from the Institute of Anthropology (Kustkammer) in St Petersburg for valuable advice in the field of physical anthropology and to Dr Kira Ogorodnikova from the

Department of Russian, University of Maryland (USA), who corrected the linguistic and phonological terminology. Special gratitude is due to my friend James Bickel, who kindly agreed to read several chapters of this work, and, being a professional musician, has introduced a harmony into my heavily syncopated English.

The publishers would like to thank the following for their permission to reproduce illustrative material: Nauka Publishers, Moscow, for Figures 9, 10, 12, 13, 15, 18, 19, 23, 25, 28, 29, 31, 33, 40, 41 and 46; Naukova Dumka Publishers, Kiev, for Figures 14 and 47; Oxford University Press for Figure 38; Akademie Verlag, Berlin, for Figures 43 and 45; Archäologisches Landesmuseum der Christian-Albrechts-Universität, Schleswig for Figure 32.

Transliteration of Cyrilic Names

Cyrilic	Latin spelling	Pronunciation
Аа	a	a (as in *far*)
Бб	b	b, p (at the end)
Вв	v	v, f (at the end)
Гг	g	g, k (at the end)
Дд	d	d, t (at the end)
Ее	e	ye
Ёё	yo	yo
Жж	zh	ž, š (at the end)
Зз	z	z, s (at the end)
Ии	i	i (as in *fit*)
Кк	k	k
Лл	l	l
Мм	m	m
Нн	n	n
Оо	o	o
Пп	p	p
Рр	r	r
Сс	s	s
Тт	t	t
Уу	u	oo
Фф	f	f
Хх	h, x	kh
Цц	c	ts
Чч	ch	ch
Шш	sh	sh
Щщ	shch	shch
Ъъ	'	nonpalatized sound
Ыы	y	ee

Cyrilic	Latin spelling	Pronunciation
Ьь	'	palatized sound
Ээ	e	e (as in *get*)
Юю	yu, ju	you
Яя	ya, ja	ya

The Slavs and Archaeology in Russia

Addressing over and over again the Soviet archaeological publications of past years, I could not fail to be captivated by the magnitude and high standards of archaeology in the former Soviet Union. At the height of its development (particularly from the 1950s to the 1980s), the network of archaeological institutions established in the USSR had no direct analogies anywhere in the world. Several hundred professional archaeologists in Russia and other Soviet republics, gathered in centralized and adequately budgeted institutions, carried out systematic archaeological investigations in all parts of that huge country. The results of these studies were regularly published in numerous periodicals and monographs. One of the last achievements of Soviet archaeology was the publication, in numerous volumes, of *The Archaeology of the USSR*, under the general editorship of Professor B.A. Rybakov, the long-time director of the Institute of Archaeology in Moscow. At the time when these volumes started to appear, I, like many of my former colleagues, was rather critical of their scholarly values; now, at a distance, I can truly estimate their significance as state-of-the-art summaries of the latest achievements in various areas of Russian archaeology.

Yet in dealing with Russian and Soviet archaeological publications, one should necessarily take into account the methodological and philosophical features that resulted from the specific conditions in which scholarly thought was developing in that country. Since its early stages, archaeology in Russia was strongly nationalistic. Archaeology as scholarship in Russia dates back to the early eighteenth century – the reign of Peter the Great. The policy of the czar was directed towards the 'opening up of a window to Europe', that is, the closer political and cultural integration of Russia into Europe. Hence, the interest in the cultural heritage of Russia in general, and archaeology in particular, was largely dictated by the political necessity of finding the evidence that Russia is, and always was, part of Europe.

The first archaeological excavations in Russia were carried out in 1710 by a German priest, Willhelm Tolle. He excavated burial mounds at Ladoga. This assemblage, situated east of St Petersburg, remains one of the most important Slavic sites. It provides evidence for the presence of Vikings in that part of Russia from at least the ninth century AD. It may not be by chance that, by comparing the excavated material with the antiquities of Northern Germany and Scandinavia, the excavator concluded that these materials belonged to 'Gothic tribes'.

Peter the Great was the first Russian ruler to comprehend the importance of archaeological finds. In one of his decrees, the czar stipulated that 'all ancient objects . . . found in the ground or under water' should be collected and handed over to the authorities. These collections served as a base for the first museum to be opened in Russia in 1715, the *Kunstkammer* (now the Museum for Anthropology, Russian Academy of Sciences). Acquisitions made by Peter the Great formed the first archaeological assemblage to be recorded in Russia. These were 'golden objects' from the Scythian barrows in Siberia which formed the famous 'Siberian collection' (Rudenko 1962). Since that time, the Scythian (and Sarmatian) antiquities have remained one of the main priorities in Russian archaeology.

For a long time, in the nineteenth and early twentieth centuries, the efforts of Russian archaeologists concentrated on the classical sites in the Black Sea area. These were Greek colonies on the Black Sea coast. Their excavators included L.E. Stefani, V.V. Latyshev, M.I. Rostovtseff and many other scholars. No less impressive were the excavations of Scythian and Sarmatian mounds (kurgans) by I.E. Zabelin, S.A. Zhebelev and others. The excavations of these sites enjoyed considerable official support; there was no shortage of funds. The most spectacular finds were displayed at the Hermitage Museum in St Petersburg, as well as in Moscow and provincial museums. These finds were included in the curricula of classical colleges (*gimnazii*). Implicitly, official support for classical archaeology in Old Russia stemmed from the 'Third Rome' ideology, according to which Muscovy regarded herself as the legitimate successor to the Byzantine heritage and, therefore, the spiritual leader of the Orthodox world.

The next important area of pre-Revolutionary archaeology in Russia (or even the main priority, according to the Russian Archaeological Society, established in 1851) was the excavation of Slavic antiquities. The first excavations, mostly of burial mounds, were conducted in the early 19th century in the Novgorod district (N.A. Ushakov, A.I. Kulzhinsky), near Moscow (A.D. Chertkov, F.N. Kitaev) and near Ryazan' (M.N. Makarov, A. Tikhomirov). Later, in the 1870s, N.E. Brandenburg excavated Slavic barrows south of the Ladoga Lake. A.A. Samokvasov, and particularly D.Ya. Spizyn, studied the Slavic sites in central Russia.

Summing up the main problems dealt with by Slavic archaeology in pre-Revolutionary Russia, Lebedev (1992: 152) singled out the following:

- territories, held by various Slavic tribes, as evidenced by the particulars of archaeological finds, and, especially, burial rites;
- the level in the development of material culture;
- spiritual culture, as evidenced by archaeological materials and supplemented by the data of language and folklore;
- cultural, economic and political links with the outside world (both in the west and the east).

Implicitly, Slavic archaeology in Russia was influenced by pan-Slavic nationalism, particularly since the 1860s. At that time, Russian intellectuals who adhered to the Slavophile movement, for example, N.Ya. Danilevsky, (1822–65) often expressed the views that Slavic peoples belonged to a 'new and superior type of world culture, which would eventually result in their unification and domination over the rest of Europe'. The nationalist implications stood out particularly strongly in the *ethno-cultural* approach which became a leading paradigm in pre-Revolutionary Russian archaeology. It is highly significant that, as Klejn (1991) notes, the concept of *archaeological culture,* as an equivalent of *ethnicity,* emerged both in Russia and Germany at about the same time – in the mid-nineteenth century. In the latter case, this concept stemmed from the 'romanticist–nationalist school' of German philosophy. Philosophical foundations of a similar concept in Russia are less obvious.

The ethno-cultural concept was introduced in Russia by two prominent archaeologists: V.A. Gorodtsov (1860–1945) and A.A. Spitzyn (1858–1931). Both scholars played a positive role in the history of Russian archaeology. In his study on the prehistoric pottery, Gorodtsov (1901) was the first to put forward the principles of numerical taxonomy. He was equally well ahead of his time when he advocated a 'deductive-classificatory approach', which included the 'type' as a basic unit. Applying his methodology to Bronze Age burial sites of southern Russia, Gorodtsov identified three chronologically consecutive 'cultures': Pit-Grave, Catacomb and Timber Grave. These concepts remain in use to this day. Later, in his synthetic works (Gorodtsov 1908), he suggested a universal model of cultural development viewed as a succession of 'archaeological cultures'. At about the same time, A.A. Spitzyn (1899) identified several archaeological cultures in the Eneolithic, Bronze and Iron Ages of European Russia: Volosovian, Tripolian, Zarubintsian and Chernyakhovian.

It should be stressed that neither Gorodtsov nor Spitzyn ever abused the ethno-cultural paradigm. They used it primarily as an instrument for the classification of vast amounts of archaeological material accumulated by that time. Only later did both scholars attempt to interpret cultural units in ethnic terms. Spitzyn identified two types of Slavic burial site in northwestern Russia ('long barrows' and 'conic mounds') that he ascribed to two 'cultural groups' of early Slavs. He also singled out the sites that he viewed as belonging to the Finns.

3

Gorodtsov, in his synthesis of the south Russian Iron Age, identified the Scythian, Sarmatian and Gothic antiquities. He regarded the cultural area of 'urnfield' in central and eastern Europe as belonging to a hypothetical 'Slavic-Germanic family'. Discussing the origins of Slavonic ethnicity, Gorodtsov rightly stressed the importance of urban centres which had not been properly studied at that time. He viewed the Dyakovian Iron Age culture as being at the heart of the central Russian cultural tradition. He also identified Finnish antiquities, where he saw the cultural elements traceable in the ethnographical records of Finland and Estonia. In all cases these concepts were in line with the contemporary level of European archaeology and were devoid of pronounced nationalistic bias.

In contrast, the nationalistic underpinnings were more obvious in the pronouncements made by V.V. Chvojka (Khvoika), a Ukrainian archaeologist of Czech origin (1850–1914). At the turn of the century, he (Chvojka 1901, 1913) discovered the Tripolye culture, as well as the so-called *'polya pogrebenij'* (urnfields), later recognized as Zarubintsian and Chernyakhovian Iron Age cultures, in forest-steppic Ukraine. Chvojka interpreted the entire cultural sequence of Tripolye–Zarubintsian–Chernyakhovian as reflecting consecutive stages in the development of Slavic ethnicity. Thus he laid a foundation for the discussion which flared up much later, in the 1950s–1970s that had strong nationalistic undertones.

Since the 1920s, Marxist historical materialism became the leading epistemology of Soviet archaeology. The preoccupation with social problems greatly determined the concentration of Soviet archaeologists on social problems. The Marxist ideology was introduced to Russian archaeology by N.Ya. Marr (1864–1934), who was a prominent linguist and archaeologist even before the Revolution. Based on his original interpretation of the linguistic evidence, Marr put forward a 'Japhetic theory', according to which all languages passed through identical stages of evolution. He argued that languages belonged to an ideological superstructure and were, therefore, class-related.

In the 1920s and 1930s, Soviet archaeologists (Ravdonikas, Efimenko, Boriskovsky and other scholars) proclaimed the identification of 'socio-economic formations based on the study of the material remains' as a principle aim of archaeology. In accordance with the 'stadial concept', Prehistory and Early History were viewed as a sequence of 'socio-economic formations'. At that time, the Japhetic theory was considered as a Marxist ideological basis of Soviet archaeology: the stages in the evolution of language were broadly equated with social changes.

One of the immediate consequences of the adoption of the Marxist ideology by young Soviet archaeologists was the total rejection of the cultural-ethnic concept. All interpretative theories of Soviet archaeologists at that time were based on the autochthonous development, both 'migrationism' and 'diffusionism' being denounced as 'bourgeois nationalism' and 'racism'. The problems of ethnicity were generally ignored, primitive and often naive social reconstructions being suggested instead. For example Krichevsky (1940) viewed the early agricultural Tripolye society as featuring matriarchal clan society and primordial communism, while Bronze Age burial mounds in southern Russia were seen as indices of patriarchal pastoral societies (Kruglov and Podgaetsky 1935).

Soon after the war, Soviet archaeologists gradually abandoned the stadial theory. Stalin inflicted the final blow when he denounced Marrism as a 'vulgar Marxism' (Stalin 1950). The cultural-ethnic concept was gradually rehabilitated. At that stage, the equation of archaeological entities with ethnicities became even more straightforward than in the earlier Gorodtsov and Spitzyn works. Thus Bryusov, one of the leading Soviet archaeologists, wrote: 'archaeological cultures . . . reflect the originality of technology, economy, mode of life and other aspects of certain ethnic tribes or, rather, groups of related tribes, in their specific historic development' (Bryusov 1956: 20). Yu.N. Zakharuk took a step further when he equated archaeological cultures not only with ethnic, but also with linguistic entities. He wrote: 'an archaeological culture is an aggregation of chronologically and spatially inter-related archaeological sites (assemblages) of a certain type, which reflect the spread and a certain stage in the historical development of a group of related tribes speaking dialects of the same language' (Zakharuk 1964: 39). Another Ukrainian archaeologist, Braichevsky, was still more categorical when he wrote: 'we regard archaeological culture as an association of archaeological phenomena which correspond to a certain ethnic identity. And we cannot identify as a culture an assemblage which does not correspond to a definite ethnic entity' (Braichevsky 1965). In the 1960s, Soviet archaeologists totally abandoned concepts of autochthonic development. Step by step, they returned to the ideas of diffusions and migrations. But, as Klejn (1993) notes, it is significant that both diffusions and migrations were mostly centrifugal.

Based on the direct equation of archaeological 'cultures' with ethnicities, Soviet archaeologists hypothesized on the origins of the Slavs, Scythians, Sarmatians and other major ethnicities in the area of the former Soviet Union. Very often these hypotheses had a strong nationalistic underpinning.

In recent years, particularly since the political collapse of the Soviet Union, one may witness a total rejection of Marxism by Russian archaeologists. The side-effect of this was the rise of nationalism that was tacitly omnipresent in Russian archaeology since the 1950s. The ethnic-cultural paradigm is a convenient instrument commonly used in the nationalistic-oriented concepts.

The popularity of L.N. Gumilev's works is a typical and dangerous phenomenon in the Russia of the late twentieth century. These works, where literary fantasies substitute hard archaeological evidence, are often openly racist. Gumilev (1980) views *ethnos* as a part of the biosphere, which passes though the stages of development depending on the presence or absence of a 'passionate personality'. The interaction of two 'positive ethnical systems' may lead to the emergence of 'destructive anti-systems'. Particularly harmful, according to Gumilev (1980: 474–5), were the contacts between the Jews and the Greeks in the Hellenistic world. Equally destructive were the interactions of the Kushans with the Indian civilization, the Hunnu with the Chinese civilization, etc. Gumilev's concepts are now widely exploited by ultra-chauvinistic groups in Russia.

National archaeological schools in non-Russian republics of the USSR, in Leo Klejn's words, were constantly manoeuvering between 'Scylla of indictment in nationalism and Charybdis of submission to Russification'. The cultural-ethnical approach remained the leading paradigm in these national archaeological schools. This often takes naive forms: local archaeologists tend to identify their nations with 'glorious peoples' of the past, for example the Moldavians seek to identify themselves with the Dacians, and the Azeris with the ancient Albanians (Klejn 1993). Archaeological arguments in the cultural-ethnic sense were, and are, often used in ethnical conflicts, substantiating the claims on the territories under dispute. Thus, both Georgian and Armenian archaeologists assert claims to the 'Urartian heritage'. The cultural and political significance of the Turcic expansion are differently viewed in the neighbouring Middle Asian republics.

In contrast to the cultural-ethnic paradigm, the present writer, following the lead of several British colleagues, notably John Chapman, prefers to use different units of analysis with less straightforward ethnical connotations (Chapman and Dolukhanov 1993). The use of elements of network analysis developed in sociology proves to be particularly instrumental. Networks, which are viewed as unbounded fields of social relations, in which inter-personal links are more important than any definition of group membership, provide a flexibility essential in the analysis of social groupings. The following advantages of network analysis are especially noted: (Noble 1973)(1) it is applicable to any groupings of males and females; (2) it permits an infinite series of interconnected relationships; (3) it allows the emergence of foci of relationships over time but does not treat them as static; (4) it treats humans as operating in broad fields of social relationships rather than in culture-determined analytical contexts. Network analysis is further strengthened by Michael Mann's theory of social power (Mann 1986). He viewed society as a multitude of overlapping and intersecting socio-spatial networks of power, through which individuals and groups mobilize social power to effect control over people and resources. Mann identified four interdependent sources of social power: (1) ideological; (2) economic; (3) military and (4) political. The most significant implication is that all these networks or arenas of social power in proper circumstances may result in the formation of archaeologically perceptible entities which Russian and many western archaeologists still prefer to call 'cultures'. Ethnicity is but one of the multiple variants of arenas of power which emerge under specific conditions and include social networks of varying intensity. In my previous work (Dolukhanov 1994) I defined ethnicity as a dynamic socio-cultural system which develops at a certain level of social complexity and features peculiarities in transmission and storage of cultural information, social behaviour, psychology, ideology and in corresponding semiotic and symbolic systems.

The reconstruction of past languages forms an essential element in the studies of past ethnicities. In this respect the definition of language, as primarily a semiotic system, which I found in the works by Roman Jakobson, the Russian-born linguist (1896–1982), seems to me highly instrumental. Jakobson wrote: 'Evidently, language is a constituent of culture, but in the ensemble of cultural phenomena it functions as their superstructure, groundwork and universal medium of communication'(1973: 34–5). In the same paper Jakobson went still further and made yet another significant observation. He found analogies in linguistics and economics: 'Talcott Parsons treats the monetary system as "a code" in the grammatical-syntactical sense. He avowedly applies to the economic interchange the theory of code and message developed in linguistics'(1973: 43). In other words, Jakobson, using the terms of modern information theory, viewed the communication of verbal messages as a part of semiotic information transmitted in social networks. These are basic theoretical premises on which the present work is based.

Chapter 2 ....

Geographical Setting

Geology and landforms

The events which will be the subject of this book occurred mainly within the confines of the East European (or Russian) Plain. This geographical unit corresponds to one of the main stable blocks of the planet Earth – the East European platform (Fig. 1). Like similar structures in other parts of the world, the East European platform comprises two stages: an ancient crystalline basement and the cover of sedimentary rocks of various thickness deposited during the course of more recent epochs of its geological history.

The crystalline basement is made up of Pre-Cambrian granite and gneiss, in most cases exceeding 1 billion years in age. In most parts of the Plain, crystalline rocks are hidden beneath a cover of sedimentaries. The massive outcrops of this crystalline basement lie in the extreme north of the Plain – in Finland, neighbouring Karelia and the Kola peninsula. They form a part of the Baltic or Fennoscandian shield which occupies the northern cap of Europe. In other parts of the platform, the crystalline basement lies at a considerable depth. Crustal movements resulted in several undulations of the basement, detectable in the thickness of sedimentary deposits. One of the depressions, the Baltic synclise, lies immediately south of the Baltic shield. Its basement plunges to a depth of about 2000 metres. Another major depression, the Pripet synclise, lies further to the south. The maximum depression of the basement is situated in the central part of the platform. Known as the Moscow synclise, its basement plunges to 2800 metres. The second crystalline outcrop, the Ukrainian shield, is situated further to the south. It crosses the middle stretches of the Dniepr in an area of the famous Dniepr Rapids. The Rapids, which for centuries prevented navigation in that area, played an important role in the later history of the Russian and the Ukrainian peoples.

The upper stage of the platform consists of sedimentary rocks formed during the last 500 million years. Their more or less horizontally lying strata

8

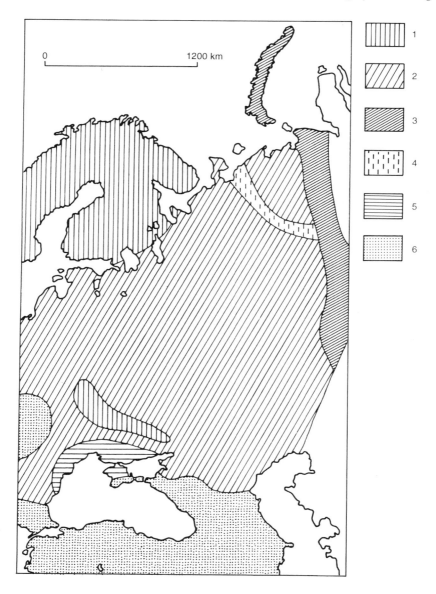

Fig. 1 Tectonic zones.
Key. 1 – Archaean plates exposed (Baltic and Ukrainian shields); 2 – Archaean plate overlain by younger deposits (Russian plate); 3 – Hercynian orogenic belt (Uralian); 4 – Hercynian belt concealed (Timan); 5 – Hercynian plate (Pontic depression); 6 – Alpine orogenic belt.

9

were deposited in the shallow parts of the seas which repeatedly transgressed into the platform. The undisturbed deposition of the sedimentary cover resulted in the widespread flatness of the relief. The greater part of the Russian Plain lies between 100 and 150 metres above sea, rarely reaching an altitude beyond 300 metres (Fig. 2). These were Late Quaternary glaciations that greatly shaped the relief of the northwest part of the Plain during the last 300,000 years. The region, stretching from the Middle Dniepr to the Smolensk-Moscow Ridge, was an arena of the Middle Pleistocene (the Dniepr and Moscow) glaciations. Morainic till, which is normally less than 15 metres thick, lies directly on Pre-Quaternary deposits, and is often overlain by loess. Large terraced river valleys are particularly typical of this area.

Intensive water erosion, which dissected the uplifted surface of the carbonate Palaeogenic deposits, has formed the relief of the central Russian upland, where morainic deposits of the Moscow (Late Middle Pleistocene) glaciation are found only on the watersheds.

The impact of the Late Pleistocene (or Valdai) glaciation was much stronger. Its limit stretches from Grodno and Vilnius in the west, to the Mologo-Sheksna lowland in central Russia, and further northeast to Vologda and the Northern Dvina catchment. Its central or morainic section consists of closely set morainic hills alternating with deep furrows usually taken up by the lakes. The highest hills, building the Valdai Heights, reach in places 300–350 metres and form an important watershed where the greatest rivers of the Russian Plain, the Volga and Western Dvina, have their sources. The starting point of the third major river, the Dniepr, is not far away. Huge areas to the north of the main morainic belt are taken up by endless sandy plains that were formed in the ice-dam lakes during the final stages of Valdai glaciation, alternating with the terminal moraines built up during the ultimate transgressions of ice. A major escarpment (the Glint), developed on the northern limits of the Silurian limestone plateau, runs south of the Gulf of Finland and goes further to the east. It separates a system of major waterways which include the Gulf of Finland, the River Neva and Lake Ladoga. Via the Volkhov river and Lake Ilmen this waterway led from the Baltic Sea into the Russian interior. Throughout later Prehistory and Early History this was a window through which the inner areas of the Russian Plain had an access to the west. The low-lying littoral zone of the Baltic Sea consists of dune-crowned marine terraces, alternating with in-shore coastal lagoons that were formed during various stages of the post-glacial history of the Baltic Sea.

The southern part of the East European platform includes several major geological structures which are reflected in the present-day relief: the Ukrainian shield, with its major outcrops of the crystalline basement, is the most important. It forms a major fold, and a system of faults separates it from the surrounding areas. Morphologically it is an elevated plateau, which consists of separate blocks, the highest one reaching 472 metres. These blocks were cut by deep terraced river valleys.

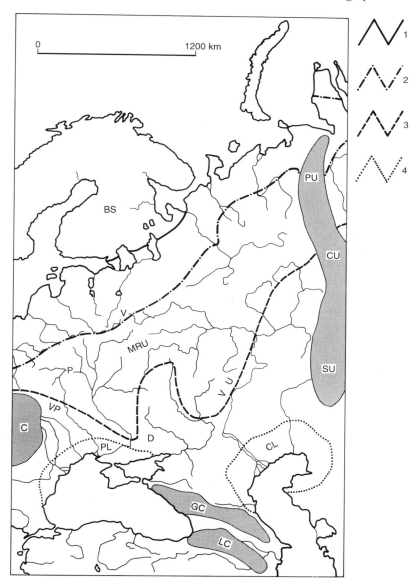

Fig. 2 Surface configurations.
    Key. 1 – Limits of the Baltic shield; 2 – Limits of the Last glaciation; 3 –
Limits of the Middle Pleistocene glaciations; 4 – Limits of the Pontic and Caspian
depressions. BS – Baltic Shield; MRU – Middle Russian Upland; V – Valdai
Heights; P – Poless'e; VP – Volyno-Podolia; D – Donets Heights; PL – Pontic
Lowland; CL – Caspian Lowland; VU – Middle Volga Upland; PU – Polar
Urals; CU – Central Urals; SU – Southern Urals; C – Carpathian Mountains;
GC – Greater Caucasus; LC – Little Caucasus.

11

The Volyno-Podolia highland joins the Ukrainian shield in the west. Here the crystalline basement lies hidden beneath sediments of the Lower Palaeozoic Age. Erosional surfaces formed in that area during the Tertiary were later incised by numerous river valleys, many of them deep and canyon-like.

The Donets Heights lie to the east, reaching the Middle Dniepr loop. This is a folded system which has been essentially formed during the Hercynian orogenic event. Repeated upliftings which lasted until the Quaternary epoch, formed an elevation consisting of several deeply eroded denudation surfaces on the folded basement. Its altitude reaches 200–350 metres.

Undulating, intensively eroded hills contrive a typical relief of the Moldavian Plate, restricted to the Dniepr-Prut interfluve. Its most elevated central uphills (Kodry) consist of erosional surfaces incised by numerous valleys and ravines.

The southern edge of the Russian Plain forms the Pontic depression: a gigantic trough or a foreland, separating the 'young' Alpine-type mountains, the Crimean and Carpathian from the Russian Plain. Morphologically, this is an accumulative plain, with an altitude of less than 200 metres, evenly tilted towards the sea. The plain is incised by the broad terraced valleys of major rivers (Prut, Dniepr, Southern Bug, Dniepr and Don), often with well-developed estuaries. A system of in-shore lagoons with off-shore bars and spits is notable along the sea coast. This area was an arena of the Greek colonization in the first millennium BC.

One of the peculiarities of the natural setting of the South Russian Plain is loess deposits which are developed predominantly on the watersheds and reach, in places, the thickness of over 100 metres. According to the widely accepted theory, these deposits were formed during the colder episodes of the Quaternary epoch.

Another major trough, the Manych, separates the Russian Plain from the largest system of folded mountains of eastern Europe – the Greater Caucasus. In the northern Caucasus, north of the Greater Caucasus Ridge, two major lowlands, the Azov-Kuban and the Terek-Kuma, flank the hilly Stavropol plateau, correspondingly, from the west and the east. The Terek-Kuma lowland gradually transforms into the Caspian depression in the east. The greater part of the latter lies less than 20 metres below sea-level. The present level of the Caspian Sea is 27 metres; this land-locked lake, the largest in the world, has no access to the ocean.

The elevation of the Middle Volga forms an uplifted and intensively eroded surface of the tectonic origin. It resulted from the rise of a dome in the early Tertiary times.

The comparatively low (300–800 metres) Ural mountains mark the eastern limit of the Russian Plain, separating it from the West Siberian Lowland. The Urals are the remains of a huge Hercynian mountain system. Subjected to a prolonged sub-aerial denudation, the Urals were reduced to a system of peneplanes, which follow the north-southern direction. Its highest peak (Mount Narodnaya, 1894 metres) lies in the north. The elevated Polar Urals form the eastern pillar of the north Russian façade which is open to the Arctic Ocean. It includes the much-eroded Timan range. The remaining part consists of near-horizontal marine sediments, predominantly of Permian Age. In places, the glacial and fluvio-glacial deposits partly enliven the monotony of the relief.

Summing up the geomorphology of the Russian Plain one should stress the territorial immensity on the one hand, and the flatness of its relief on the other. This huge and predominantly even block of dry land is situated at a considerable distance from the major oceans. Notwithstanding important changes in the environment, these essential characteristics of relief remained constant throughout the Prehistory and Early History of the Russian Plain.

Hydrology

Several major rivers cross the East European Plain. These rivers were always of great importance as major waterways linking together various parts of the huge land-mass and giving them an access to the outer world. These rivers drain into the Arctic ocean (the Northern Dvina, Pechora), the Baltic Sea (the Western Dvina, Nieman, the Neva-Ladoga system), and the Black Sea (the Prut, Dniestr, Southern Bug, Dniepr, Don). Both the Baltic and Black Seas are the gulfs of the Atlantic Ocean transgressing deep inland. The Volga, the longest river in Europe (3530 km), the mother of Russian rivers, flows into the land-locked Caspian Sea, which has no outlet to the ocean.

Rivers in the morainic area are comparatively young (although their valleys in most cases were inherited from much older times) and have few terraces. In contrast, the rivers in the extra-glacial area have had a much longer history. Their valleys are often well developed and contain numerous terraces (particularly notable along the high right bank). Many rivers flowing in a southerly direction (for example, the Dniepr and its tributaries; the Don and the Volga) were the channels through which the meltwater from the glaciers was drained into the southern seas during the Ice Age. Consequently, these rivers have developed vast terraces accumulated over that period of time. In some cases (for example, in the Pripet river valley) these terraces are 20–30 km wide. As we shall see later, numerous Upper Palaeolithic sites in central Russia and Ukraine are usually located on these terraces. The rivers of the Russian Plain are generally snow-fed; melting snow in the spring often causes high water and even floods. During warmer seasons in the Ice Age these rivers often turned into chains of lakes.

Climate

The climate of the Russian Plain is, and always was, predominantly continental; it results from its geographical position, far away from the humid air-masses forming above the oceans. The main features of the climate are a large annual range of air temperature with hot summers and cold winters, considerable diurnal variations, and insufficient rainfall (the maximum usually falls in summer). Another peculiarity of the climate is the latitudinal zonality. It follows from the geographical position of the Russian Plain – a huge land-mass stretching from 75°N in the north to 45°N in the south.

During the winter the atmospheric circulation over the Russian Plain is severely affected by a high-pressure system which develops over northern Asia (Siberian anticyclone) and pushes the masses of cold air over the entire Russian Plain. During the coldest months (January–February) the temperature there may drop below 20–25°C (Fig. 3). Occasionally, the Siberian air may reach western Europe (particularly eastern England), often causing havoc. Precipitation markedly increases with the intrusions of the westerlies (particularly common in the northwestern areas), and these winds bring thaws with wet snow and mists.

Although precipitation in winter is usually relatively light, a stable snow cover persists in the greater part of the Russian Plain from December until March (longer in the north and east). The depth of snow reaches 20–30 cm in the Baltic countries, 50 cm near Moscow and over 70 cm in northeastern Russia. The depth of frozen soil may reach 50–100 cm. Some areas of the north are affected by 'permafrost': the upper layers of the ground are permanently frozen. During the coldest stage of the Last glaciation, 22,000–15,000 years ago, the permafrost affected the entire Russian Plain. Traces of permanently frozen ground were found near the city of Rostov, in the low stretches of the River Don. An area of low pressure envelops the greater part of the Russian Plain in summer. At that time, the Atlantic cyclonic circulations often bring rainy weather, the total amount of rainfall reaching 500 mm in the western areas but rapidly diminishing to the east and, particularly, the southeast. Mean July temperatures in western and central Russia vary between 15 and 20°C. The temperature is considerably higher in the southeast. The highest temperature in southern Ukraine may reach 37–38°C. These high temperatures, combined with shortage of moisture, often cause severe droughts in that area.

Vegetation and soils

Contemporary vegetation of the Russian Plain generally follows climatic zonality (Fig. 4). *Tundra*, or arctic waste, occupies the northernmost part of

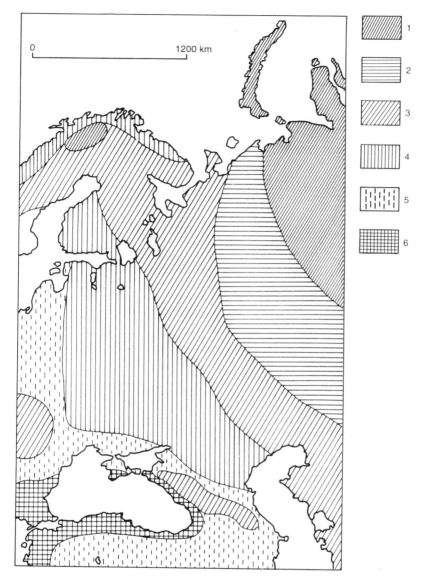

Fig. 3 Climate – Mean January temperature (C°)
Key. 1 – <–20°; 2 – –20 – –15°; 3 – –15 – –10°; 4 – –10 – –5°; 5 – –5–0°; 6 – 0– +5°.

the Plain: the swampy shores of the Arctic Ocean and its islands. This vegetation consists of strong cold-resistant plants, mostly mosses and lichens. It includes perennial herbs (grasses, sedges and rushes) as well as shrub-like trees (such as *Betula nana* or dwarf-birch). We shall encounter many of these

15

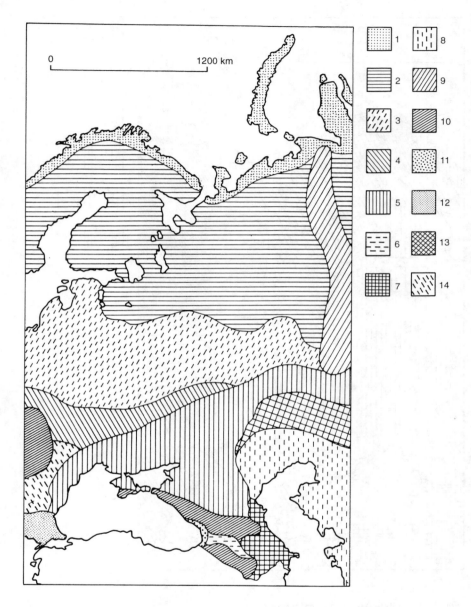

Fig. 4 Vegetation.
Key. 1 – Tundra; 2 – Tayga forest; 3 – Mixed deciduous forests; 4 – Forest-steppe; 5 – Steppe; 6 – Mountain steppe; 7 – Mountain semi-desert; 8 – Desert; 9 – Mountain tayga forest; 10 –Mountain mixed forest; 11 – Sub-tropical forest and grassland; 12 – Mediterranean grassland; 13 – Semi-desert; 14 – Mountain deciduous forests.

plants when discussing the environment of the groups of Stone Age hunters which lived in various parts of the Russian Plain during the Last Ice Age.

The greater part of the Russian Plain is taken up by forests. The northern part of the forested area is referred to as *Taiga* or boreal coniferous forests. The dominant needle-leaf species are fir, pine, spruce and larch. The taiga also includes some deciduous species, particularly light-loving birch and aspen. The former is a pioneer tree which is usually the first to replace the conifers destroyed by fires or felling.

Mixed coniferous-broad-leaved deciduous forests dominate in the area to the south and southwest of the taiga. As the special geobotanic investigations in northwestern Russia have shown, these forests are of a complex character. Until the later Middle Ages, oak forests grew predominantly on the clay soils of morainic hills and on the upper terraces of rivers. Mixed forests consisting of oak, hornbeam, ash and alder were restricted to the river floors. Spruce forests occupied wet areas in the depressions of the morainic relief. Pine forests to this day dominate poor sandy soils of the fluvio-glacial plains. This type of vegetation, which is sufficiently rich in biomass, was particularly common during the warmer episodes of recent geological history. It was able to support large groups of prehistoric hunters and fishers. At a later stage, these forests saw the initial stages of the agricultural revolution in that area.

In the south, the mixed forests gradually transform into *deciduous forests*, essentially similar in their composition to forests of central and western Europe. They consist of elm, oak and lime, with beech and hornbeam, the latter being more common in the southwest.

The forests gradually rarify in the southern direction, giving way to the *forest-steppe*: a narrow belt stretching across central Ukraine and southeastern Russia, where open treeless (steppic) areas alternate with deciduous woodlands (mostly oak).

Further to the south, the forest-steppe gradually passes into the true *steppe*. The natural steppe vegetation consists of drought-resistant perennial and annual herbaceous plants. These are various species of grass and their composition changes from place to place. The steppes are richest in the north where they include meadows, in which grasses are mixed with legumes, daisies and irises. In the southern, and dryer areas, the vegetation is dominated by narrow-leaved feather grasses. Halophytes, or salt-resistant plants, are restricted to some areas along the coast of the Black Sea.

The steppes played a particularly important role throughout the later Prehistory and Early History of Russia. In the Ice Age, the steppe supported considerable groups of Stone Age hunters. Later, in post-glacial times, a dramatic rise, followed by an equally spectacular demise, of an early agricultural civilization took place in the area of the present-day forest-steppe. Still later, the steppe became an arena for various groups of nomadic herdsmen. The steppe turned into a major corridor along which the groups of nomads moved between Central Asia and Europe. It was a major sphere of human, cultural and social interaction. The dichotomy between the forested north and the steppic south was of critical importance for the peoples of the Russian Plain in the later times.

The soil mantle (Fig. 5) in the greater part of the forested area of the Russian Plain consists of various types of *podzolic* soil. These soils form under the specific conditions when the loss of moisture through evaporation is much less than the input from precipitation. The downward movement of moisture transfers the surface mineral material to the lower layers and results in the ashy-coloured bleached upper layer (hence the name *zola* meaning 'ashes' in Russian). The agricultural productivity of such soils is generally low. In normal conditions, the application of organic and mineral fertilizers and intensive liming are essential. In the Russian northwest the most fertile soils have developed on the carbonate till; they belong to the 'sod-carbonate variety'. Yet, in all cases, the successful cultivation of these soils necessitated the use of sufficiently sophisticated iron tilling implements together with a farming system that included animal husbandry.

The soils in the steppes and forest-steppes include the famous *chernozems* (or 'black earth' in Russian) which are the richest in Europe. The layer of dark-grey or black (hence the name) organic matter is the product of the decay of plant roots due to the intense activity of bacteria. This soil develops from the parent material of loess which is a reservoir of nutrients. The natural fertility of the chernoziom is often reduced by droughts which are common here. Thus, notwithstanding the natural fertility of the soils, the southern Russian steppe and forest-steppe were always high-risk areas in the agricultural sense.

The poorest soils in the steppe are the *solonchaks* and *solonets* (from the Russian *'sol'* for salt). These soils usually develop in the depressions deprived of continuous drainage. Ground-water rich in salt rises by capillarity to the surface and forms the crusts of salt. The agricultural value of these soils is minimal.

Population and ethnic groups

The present population of the Russian Plain is more than 182 million[1]. The general characteristics of the population are a relative low density and an uneven distribution. The average population density in the Russian Plain is 53 per sq. km (for the entire former USSR: 11.7 per sq. km). The corresponding figures for other parts of the world are: UK – 229; India –

---

[1] This figure is based on the 1979 Census and does not take into account the recent displacements of population. The population includes: European Russia (including the Urals) – 110 million; Ukraine – 50 million; Belarus – 10 million; Baltic States – 8 million; Moldavia – 4 million.

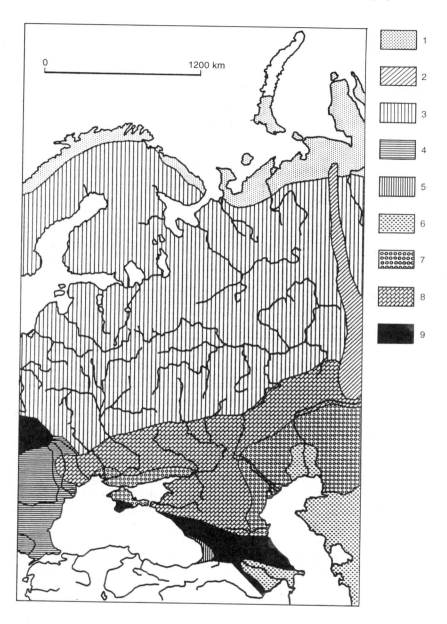

Fig. 5   Soils.
     Key. 1 – Tundra soil; 2 – Mountain tundra soil; 3 – Podzol soil; 4 – Brown
soil; 5 – Red soil; 6 – Solonchak; 7 – Chestnut soil; 8 – Chernozem; 9 – Mountain
soil.

182; China – 88; USA – 23 per sq. km). Nowadays, due to the industrialization and urbanization of the last seventy years, the most densely populated areas cluster around the major cities and industrial centres: Moscow, St Petersburg, Kiev and the Donets basin. In the latter area the population density is the highest – 195 people per sq. km. A comparatively high population density is recorded in the predominantly agricultural areas of Ukraine. A typical example is the Cherkassy district in western Ukraine where the population density is 74.1 people per sq. km. The densities in the northern part of the Russian Plain are extremely low. The average density north of the line running from St Petersburg to Perm is below 10, and in some areas is less than 1 person per sq. km. The latter figure suggests an average density of population which bases its subsistence on predominantly non-agricultural activities.

The present population of the Russian Plain belongs to different ethnic and linguistic groups (Fig. 6). The majority of them belong to the Indo-European family. The *Eastern Slavs* are by far the largest groups. They include 137 million *Russians* (in the entire former Soviet Union), 42 million *Ukrainians* and 9.4 million *Belorussians*. The *Poles*, another Slav group, form a considerable minority in the western districts of Ukraine, Belorussia and Lithuania. Other groups belonging to the Indo-European family are the *Balts*, which include the *Lithuanians* (2.8 million) and *Latvians* (1.4 million). A considerable number of Baltic groups existed in various parts of the Upper Dniepr in the seventh to fourteenth centuries and later were assimilated by the Slavs. The Prussians existed in the historical area of Prussia until the beginning of the eighteenth century; later they were absorbed by the Germans. Nearly three million *Moldavians*, the main ethnic group in Moldova, speak the Moldavian language (often considered as a dialect of Romanian), belonging to the Romance family. The *Armenians*, an ancient and independent Indo-European group, live mostly in large cities and in the northern Caucasus (previously numerous Armenian colonies were scattered in Ukraine). The *Ossetians*, whose language belongs to the East-Iranian group and is considered as similar to that of the Scythians and Sarmatians, live on both sides of the Great Caucasian Ridge, in the Russian Federation and Georgia, and their total population is 542,000.

Peoples belonging to the *Uralic* numerically take the next position. This family includes the Finno-Ugrians. According to the widely accepted linguistic classification, the Finno-Ugrian entity consists of two groups: Finno-Ugric and Samoyedic. The latter, totalling about 28,000 people, consists of small, largely nomadic, groups scattered in the extreme north of the Russian Plain and neighbouring western Siberia. The former includes two branches: the Finnic and Ugric. The *Finns* (5 million) and *Karelians* (138,000 only in the Karelian Republic of Russia) are the most numerous. It may be significant that both of these closely related (both linguistically and culturally) groups are confined to the Baltic shield with its numerous outcrops of the crystalline basement. The *Lapps* (30–40,000) live in the

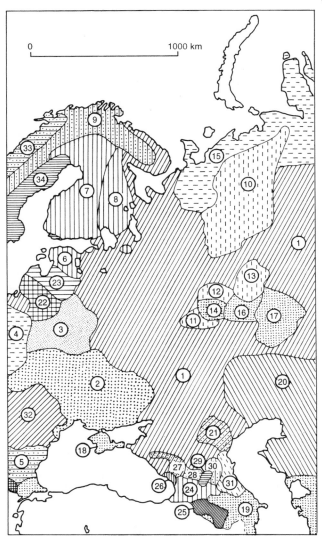

Fig. 6 Languages and linguistic groups.

Key. INDO-EUROPEAN FAMILY. SLAV GROUP: 1 – Russians; 2 – Ukrainians; 3 – Belorussians; 4 – Poles; 5 – Bulgarians; FINNO-UGRIC FAMILY: 6 – Estonians; 7 – Finns; 8 – Karelians; 9 – Saami; 10 – Komi; 11 – Mordovians; 12 – Mariyans; 13 – Udmurts; TURCIC FAMILY: 14 – Chuvash; 16 – Tatars; 17 – Bashkirs; 18 – Crimean Tartars; 19 – Azerbaijanis; 20 – Kazakhs; 21 – Kalmyks; SAMOYEDIC FAMILY: 15 – Nenets; INDO-EUROPEAN FAMILY. BALTIC GROUP: 22 – Lithuanians; 23 – Latvians; CAUCASIAN FAMILY: 24 – Georgians; INDO-EUROPEAN FAMILY: 25 – Armenians; CAUCASIAN FAMILY: 26 – Abkhazians; 27 – Adygians, Cherkessians, Kabardynians; 28 – Kabardinians; Balkarians; INDO-EUROPEAN FAMILY. IRANIAN GROUP: 29 – Osetians; CAUCASIAN FAMILY: 30 – Chechens, Ingush; 31 – Dagestanian group. INDO-EUROPEAN FAMILY. ROMANCE GROUP. 32 – Romanians, Moldavians; GERMANIC GROUP. 33 – Norwegians; 34 – Swedes.

extreme north of the Baltic shield, in the areas of northern Finland, northeastern Norway and the neighboring Kola peninsula. Another Finnic group, the *Estonians* (about one million), live in the southwestern coastal area of the Gulf of Finland and immediately to the south. There are smaller Finnic-speaking groups in northwestern Russia (for example, Ingrians and Veps) who were relatively numerous in the past; now they have almost lost their language and cultural identity. To the same branch there belongs the *Komy* (327,000) in the extreme northeast of Russia, as well as the groups living between the Kama and the Urals: *Udmurt, Mordvin* and *Mari* (together they number 2.5 million). The second branch includes the *Hungarians* (about 14 million, predominantly in the Hungarian Plain in Hungary and in neighbouring areas (Romanian Transylvania, Slovakia, Serbia and a small minority in Carpathian Ukraine). The second, Ob-Ugric group, includes the *Khanty* (21,000) and *Mansi* (7700); both are small ethnic groups of predominantly nomadic reindeer-herders, living in the north of the west Siberian lowland, east of the Urals.

Another branch of the Uralic family consists of the peoples who speak the languages belonging to the Turkic group. They are particularly numerous along the Middle Volga and further to the east. They include the *Tatars* (over 6 million), *Chuvashs* (1.8 million) and *Bashkirs* (1.4 million). A numerically large group of *Crimean Tartars*, who lived in the Crimea from the thirteenth century, was forcefully expelled in 1944. The *Azerbaidjanis* are common in large cities. The *Kalmyks* (147,000) are the most numerous among the Turkic-speaking peoples of Mongolian origin. They have lived in the steppic regions west of the Lower Volga since the eighteenth century.

The ethnic situation in the northern Caucasus is particularly complex. Several ethnic groups speak the languages which belong to a loose group of *Caucasian* languages. They comprise the languages belonging to the Abkhazo-Circassian group, and include *Kabardians* (323,000) and *Adyghians* (111,000). The Nakho-Daghestanian group consist of Nakh (611,000 *Chechen* and 192,000 *Ingush*) and Daghestanian ethnicities. The situation in Daghestan is ethnically especially complex. Among a great many small ethnic units, the largest are: *Avar* (483,000), *Dagwa* (247,000), *Lezgin* (383,000) and *Lakh* (*c.* 100,000) and more than twenty smaller ones.

About 1.8 million *Jews* live mostly in the towns of the Russian Plain. They are the descendants of ancient Semites who appeared within the area in the seventeenth century. Before the Russian Revolution of 1917 the Jews were restricted mostly to Ukraine and Belarus (the 'pale of settlement'). Following the German holocaust during the Second World War and recent emigration, the population of Jews has markedly diminished.

All these peoples and ethnic groups have had a lengthy and complicated history that included various forms of interactions, transformations and displacements. These and related topics will be discussed in the ensuing chapters.

Chapter 3 ....

The Initial Settlement

Palaeolithic beginnings

It is now a firmly established fact that the earliest indications of human-like activities in some areas of the Great East African Rift, as evidenced by the occurrence of archaeologically identifiable artefacts, coincided with a global cooling. According to various kinds of evidence, which include oxygen isotope information from deep-sea cores, foraminiferal records and pollen data, supported by radiometric dates, this cooling started *c.* 2.4 million years ago. At the same time, the first glaciers started to build up in the middle latitudes of both hemispheres. The mountain glaciers which had formed on the southern slopes of the Alps, reached the shores of the Mediterranean Sea. Ice-sheets covered the greater part of Scandinavia. Pollen spectra obtained from corresponding deposits show that a cold-resistant treeless vegetation spread along the southern shores of the that-time North Sea (a so-called Praetiglian cold stage: Zagwijn 1975).

During the Ice Ages, the volume of water in the oceans diminished, hence the sea-level dropped world-wide. There are indications of a considerable lowering of the sea-level at the time of the initial glaciation. The coring of the 'deep valleys' containing the pollen spectra indicative of initial cooling in the northwestern part of the Russian Plain has shown that at several points these valleys were 200 metres deep (Malachovsky and Markov 1969: p. 99). Simultaneously, the level of the land-locked Caspian Sea rose; it accumulated the meltwater from the glaciers. During the course of the Apsheronian transgression, which had occurred at that time, the Caspian sea-level rose up to 50 metres. The Caspian water had flooded the Lower Volga valley, reaching the present city of Volgograd (Stalingrad), and covered the greater part of the Turanian and Kura-Araxian lowlands.

The cooling was accompanied by the aridization of the climate in the temperate zone. Treeless steppe and prairies increasingly replaced the sub-tropic forests which had covered the greater part of Europe at the preceding stage. At about that time, a particular faunal assemblage (Villafranchian) emerged in the southern part of Europe. The Late Villafranchian assemblage included 'southern elephant' (*Elephas meriodionalis*), 'etruscan rhinoceros' (*Rhinoceros etruscus*), hippopotamus, and a new species of primitive horse, *Equus stenonis*. The occurrence of the latter presumes a wide expansion of treeless steppe. Still more arid was the climate of the South Russian Plain, where a so-called Khaprovian faunal assemblage was in existence. The southern elephant and horses were the dominant species. Among the latter, at least two species of horse are distinguishable: a small (*Equus stenonis*) and a large (*Equus major*) variety (Alexeyeva 1976).

During the subsequent Pleistocene epoch of the Quaternary era, the climate of our planet was in constant motion. The cold stages, which coincided with glaciations in the north and aridization in tropical and sub-tropical areas, alternated with warm or interglacial stages. During the latter, the climate became much warmer and wetter. No less than forty major climatic oscillations occurred during the last 2.4 million years (Kukla 1989). At the same time, a distinct palaeoclimatic trend is apparent: with time, the climate became increasingly colder and dryer.

An interglacial episode recorded in the so-called Cromer forest beds in the Crag basin in East Anglia was particularly significant. This occurrence has a precise dating. In its course, *c.* 700,000 years ago, there appeared a reversal of the Earth's magnetic field: from the Matuyama epoch of reversed polarity to the Brunhes epoch of normal polarity. The deposits, revealing similar magnetic characteristics, are easily identifiable throughout Europe. These deposits reflect a rapid extinction of the Tertiary warm-loving flora and fauna. Both animals and vegetation in Europe became increasingly modern, dominated by cold- and dry-resistant species.

The first major glaciation in the Russian Plain occurred *c.* 1.1 million years ago. Erratic pebbles, originating in the ice-sheets of Scandinavia, were found in the River Don catchment, in the deposits formed by the Upper Apsheronian transgression of the Caspian Sea. Morainic till of the same age was found further to the north, in Russian Karelia (Zubakov and Borzenkova 1983).

Another major glaciation has been established in the deposits immediately predating the Matuyama-Brunhes palaeomagnetic boundary, *c.* 750,000 years ago. At that time, the entire northern part of the Russian Plain, north of 52°N, was covered by an ice-sheet. The next major glaciation occurred *c.* 500,000 BP. At that time, the ice-sheet in the Russian Plain reached its maximum extent; it advanced southwards to the middle stretches of the Don river. This glaciation is known in Russia under various names: the Donian, Okaian or Berezanian (in Belorussia).

Thereafter, 400,000–300,000 BP, a lengthy warm episode has followed. According to the estimate based on fossil pollen records, the annual temperature at that time rose by 3–5°C above present values. The climate became wetter: annual precipitation was 1100–1300 mm higher than that of today. Forests which included such warm-loving species as hornbeam, yew, chestnut and holly, covered the greater part of the Russian Plain, and advanced far to the south, into the present forest-steppic area.

The next glacial episode is known in central Europe as the Saale glaciation. Its duration is estimated as *c*. 300,000–150,000 BP. As recent studies have shown, in reality two major glacial advances occurred at that time, the Drenthe and Warthe, and they were separated by a warm interval. During the initial glacial episode (the Dniepr glaciation) the ice-sheet advanced along the Dniepr valley far to the south and reached the area of Kanev. After a warm 'Roslavl' episode, another glacial advance (the Moscow glaciation) followed. At that time, the ice-sheet reached the area of central Russia in the vicinity of Moscow.

The ensuing warm episode was of major significance. Many scholars argue that it coincided with a major warming recorded in deep-sea cores and referred to it as the isotope sub-stage 5e (128,000–116,000 BP). This interglacial episode is known by Russian geologists as 'Mikulino'. As fossil pollen records show, during the Mikulino climatic optimum, broad-leaved forests expanded far to the north, reaching the shores of the White Sea. The great part of the Russian north has been submerged by a shallow 'Mga' Sea, which connected with another sea ('Eemian') in the north of Europe.

All these major environmental changes were to some degree witnessed by groups of primitive man. As has been said above, it is now firmly attested that, in some areas of the Old World, groups of hominids capable of producing archaeologically identifiable artefacts were in existence at least since 2.5 million years ago. Until quite recently the area of the Great East African Rift was considered as a probable cradle of mankind. There, in eastern and southern Africa, scholars were successful in tracing the fullest sequence in the evolution of the hominoids which eventually led to the emergence of tool-producing hominids. Also, in that particular area, the most ancient dates for sites with evidence of tool-making have been obtained. Based on this evidence, it was suggested that the dispersal of hominids into other parts of the world started at a much later date. However, recent finds in other parts of the world cast some doubts; it now seems increasingly certain that this dispersal proceeded much earlier than had been previously suggested.

One of the most spectacular finds was made in 1991, within the area of the former USSR. In August that year a joint German-Georgian expedition in southern Georgia, directed by Gerhard Bosinski and Medea Nioradze, discovered a mandible of *Homo erectus* near the town of Dmanisi (Dzhaparidze and Bosinski et al. 1989). The same level produced the remains of a Villafranchian-type fauna that included sabre-toothed lion, southern elephant and primitive horse. The radiometric age of the under-lying dolerite lava is *c*. 1.8 million years. Hence, the age of the finds is estimated as 1.6–1.7 million years old. Thus far, this site remains the earliest evidence for the presence of *Homo erectus* in the immediate vicinity of the Russian soil (Fig. 7).

Regarding the actual penetration of the tool-making hominids, probably also belonging to the species of *Homo erectus*, the most probable dates obtained recently in Europe and in the Near East show an age of about one million years. Although no reliable evidence for the human presence at that time on Russian territory is so far available, finds of comparable age are reported from the surrounding areas. These finds are particularly numerous in the Caucasus.

One of the most significant Old Stone Age sequences has been established in the Azykh cave. This cave site lies in Nagorny Karabakh, now the area disputed between Armenia and Azerbaidjan and the arena of fierce ethnic hostilities. The cave is situated in a valley of a small river, on the northern slopes of the Little Caucasus mountain range, about 20 km north of Araxes. The oldest pebble industry, reminiscent of the Oldowan in eastern Africa, was discovered in the lowermost levels of the cave. The palaeomagnetic measurements have shown an inverse polarity, allegedly corresponding to the Matuyama epoch. If this measurement is correct, it shows that the age of these levels is older than 735,000 years. On geological grounds, deposits containing the pebble industry are considered as belonging to the Apsheronian transgression of the Caspian Sea, thus corroborating the palaeomagnetic age (Velichko et al. 1980).

New discoveries seem to show that the area of early hominid settlement extended to the northern slopes of the Caucasus. The second (lower) level of Treugolny Grotto in Karachevo-Cherkessia includes a typical pebble industry with choppers, chopping-tools and scrapers. The composition of the fauna makes it a likely analogue of the Cromerian inter-glacial (700,000–600,000 BP) (Lyubin 1993).

Another group of sites of a comparable age was discovered in the southern part of Tadjikistan, also in the former Soviet Union. Deep deposits of loess that developed there contained numerous clusters of archaic palaeolithic tools. One of the oldest sites, Kouldoura, contained an assemblage of pebble tools. As in the case of Azykh, these deposits lay below the palaeomagnetic Matuyama-Brunhes boundary, establishing an order of antiquity beyond 735,000 years (Ranov 1993).

A more intense settlement of eastern Europe by groups of *Homo erectus* has coincided with the emergence of the Acheulean. This was an advanced stage in the development of early human technology. The Acheulean industries usually included handaxes: bifacially flaked rock nodules with a cutting edge. At a later stage, a special method of tool-making developed – the Levallois technique. This method consisted of the production of large standardized flakes by striking off small facets from the nodule. One of the best-known Acheulean sites, Korolevo, is situated in the immediate vicinity of the Russian Plain. The site is located in Transcarpathian Ukraine, on the upper terrace of the River Tisza, at the

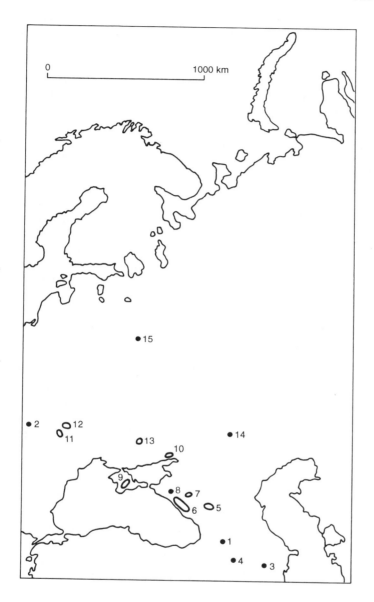

Fig. 7 The initial settlement. Lower and Middle Palaeolithic sites.
     Key. 1 – Dmanisi; 2 – Korolevo; 3 – Azykh; 4 – Erevan; 5 – Kudaro group;
6 – Black Sea coastal sites; 7 – Gub Valley sites; 8 – Il'skaya; 9 – Crimean sites;
10 – Azov Sea sites; 11 – Prut river sites; 12 – Dniestr river sites; 13 – Middle
Dniepr sites; 14 – Volgograd; 15 – Khotylevo.

point where the river left the Carpathian mountains, and entered the Great Hungarian lowland. In that area, a thick sequence of Quaternary deposits is exposed; it consists of loesses interbedded with darkish fossil soils. The sequence comprises fourteen archaeological levels; the lower seven are attested as the Acheulean. The researcher (Gladilin 1976) stressed that typologically the Transcarpathian Acheulean differed from similar industries in other parts of Europe. It includes archaic instruments – choppers and cleavers; handaxes are rare and atypical. At the same time, one notes an early appearance of the elements of the Levallois technique.

If one looks at the Russian Plain properly, the scattered Acheulean sites are located exclusively in its southern fringe. A number of Acheulean sites have been discovered by Praslov (1984) along the coast of the Azov Sea. A small collection of artefacts, including a handaxe, scrapers and flakes, presumably of the Lower Pleistocene Age, was gathered at Gerasimovka, near the town of Taganrog. Another site, Khryashchi, located on the upper terrace of the Severski Donets, has yielded a larger collection of artefacts, dominated by scrapers. Pollen analysis has shown that the deposits were raised in a cold environment, presumably during the Dniepr glaciation. Several surface finds of handaxes of the Upper Acheulean type were made at various locations of the Donets basin (Amvrosievka, Makeyevka and elsewhere). Based on the evidence of the typological similarity of these tools, one may suggest that these sites were in existence during the Mikulino interglacial.

Yet more intensely settled was the area of Caucasus. Uninterrupted Acheulean sequences were established in the cave site of Azykh in Karabakh, and also in the caves of the mountain ridges of the central Caucasus, at the altitude exceeding 3,000 metres (Kudaro I, Kudaro III and Tsona). The Acheulean layer 5 of the Azykh cave has yielded a mandible of a new species of hominid. Local specialists have baptized it an *'Azykhanthropus'*. It reveals common features with the 'anteNeanderthals' species, identified in the French Pyrenees (de Lumley 1973).

Recently, a series of thermoluminescent (TL) dating has been obtained for the samples from the Acheulean levels of the central Caucasian cave sites. The earliest date came from the Lower Acheulean level of the Kudaro III cave – 560,000±112,000 BP. The youngest dates from the same site are 360,000–350,000 BP (Lyubin 1993). Clusters of Acheulean sites were found on the marine terraces of the Black Sea; they are particularly numerous near the city of Sukhumi in Abkhazia. The probable age of these sites is 600,000–500,000 years.

Summing up the existing evidence, one may conclude that rare groups of hominids penetrated some areas of Russia soon after they appeared in Europe and the Near East. During the greater part of the Lower and Middle Pleistocene, the hominid population of the Russian Plain was extremely scarce. One may suggest that isolated groups occasionally penetrated the Plain either from the Caucasus or from southern Europe. It is true that a considerable number of Old Stone Age sites may be lost; they are either buried under more recent deposits or completely washed away. At the same time, these scattered finds clearly show that the evolution of early mankind was following a similar path in all parts of the inhabitable world, which included the Russian Plain.

The Last Ice Age

The events which occurred during the Last glaciation were of vital importance for the initial settlement of the Russian Plain. This glaciation is commonly known in Russia as 'Valdai'. In various regions of Europe the same glaciation is referred to as Würm (in the Alps); Weichselian (in Germany and Poland) or Devensian (in the British Isles). According to the modern estimate based on radiometric measurements, this glaciation has started at 117,000–115,000 and lasted until 10,000 years ago.

The history of this glaciation in the Russian Plain is sufficiently well studied, due to the efforts of many generations of Russian scholars. These studies clearly show that at least four stages are distinguishable in the course of the Valdai glaciation. The first stage corresponded to the isotope stages 5d–4 and lasted from 117,000–115,000 until 69,000 BP. At that time, a treeless Arctic tundra dominated the vegetation cover. This was interrupted by the spread of coniferous forests during the milder episodes, which were first identified in Denmark and Holland: Amersfoort, Brörup and Odderadde. The sea-level at that time dropped to at least 20 metres below the present level. Ice-sheets of moderate size formed in the northern latitudes (Zubakov and Borzenkova 1983).[1]

The next stage lasted from 69,000 until *c*. 24,000 BP. At this time, the greater part of Europe was free of glaciers. This was proven by radiocarbon dating of the layers of peat which had formed well north of the Arctic circle. Yet the climate remained generally cool. Several mild episodes are distinguishable; during their course coniferous tundra forests were widely spread. Based on detailed investigations in northwestern Russia, at least four such mild episodes were identified (Arslanov 1987): Early (34,000–35,000 BP); Middle or Kashinian (33,600–29,000 BP); Late-Shenian (33,600–29,000 BP); Late-Dunavian (32,000–24,000 BP). The maximum rise in temperature occurred at 31,000 and 26,000 BP. There are indications that during one of the warm episodes considerable areas in the Russian north were transgressed by the sea.

The coldest time-span which corresponded to isotope stage 2, lasted from 24,000 to 15,000 BP. At that time, two huge glaciers covered

---

[1] There exists a minority view (Zarrina and Krasnov 1983), according to which ice sheet reached the maximum extent during the course of the early Valdai.

considerable areas of northern and northeastern Europe. These glaciers originated from two centres: the first located in the Scandinavian mountains, and the second in the Novaya Zemlya archipelago. Sea-level at that time was at least 120 metres below that of modern times.

The area immediately to the south was taken up with the periglacial-steppic vegetation, essentially similar to that of the present-day Taimyr peninsula in northern Siberia. Rare forests survived only within river valleys. The palaeoclimatic reconstruction based on fossil pollen records shows that winter temperatures of that time were 10-14°C below those of the present day, while summer temperatures were 2-3°C cooler than now. The climate was generally dry: annual precipitation was less than 200 mm. One of the peculiarities of the glaciation maximum was an intensive formation of loesses. This process was particularly strong during the coldest and driest stage, 23,000–17,000 BP. The upper surface of the ground was affected by permafrost; these deposits contain ice wedge clasts and cryoturbation structures resulting from repeated freezing and thawing (Velichko et al. 1993). Another characteristic feature of glacial landscapes was the common occurrence of ice-dam lakes. These lakes formed in the valleys of rivers, the flow of which was barred by an ice-sheet. The rivers, through which the water of these lakes was channelled towards the southern seas (Caspian and Black Sea), turned, at least seasonally, into chains of lakes.

Soon after reaching its maximum extent, the ice-sheet started to retreat northwards. This recession took the form of an oscillation: the warm stages alternated with the cold episodes during which glaciers advanced again. This final stage of the glaciation, referred to as the Late Glacial, lasted from 15,000 to 10,000 BP. One of the first Late Glacial warm phases, Raunis, occurred *c.* 14,000–13,000 BP. After a short-lived cold stage, a new warm stage followed. This stage is known as Bölling, named after a site in Denmark, and it lasted from 13,300–11,000 BP. Another yet warmer stage, Alleröd, took place between 11,800 and 11,000 BP. During its course the July temperature rose from 8–9°C to 16–17°C. During these two warm intervals, spruce, pine and birch forests massively spread on the Russian Plain.

These warm episodes were separated by cold stages referred to as Dryas. An extremely cold spell, known as the Younger Dryas, marked the final episode of the Late Glacial. Over a few centuries, about 11,000 BP, the temperature dropped by 6–8°C. The climate again became as cold and as dry as during the glacial maximum, but this cold term was of short duration. Already at about 10,200 BP, a new warm wave announced the end of the Ice Age.

The Mousterian

The lower and middle sections of the Last glaciation in Europe and in the Near East coincided with the development of the Mousterian (or Middle

Stone Age) industries. Until recently, it was generally accepted that these industries were manufactured by Neanderthal man or *Homo sapiens neanderthalensis*. New studies show that these relationships were not so straightforward.

Recent discoveries evince that large-brained Neanderthals followed a long evolution from the range of the 'anteNeanderthals'. These included the hominids from the Pyrenees (Arago), Germany (Steinheim), Britain (Swanscombe), Greece (Petralona) and, probably, also the Caucasian 'Azykhanthropus'. The Neanderthals proper first appeared in Europe by the beginning of the last interglacial – Eemian-Mikulino (Bräuer 1989). Hence, a considerable part of Late Acheulean industries was produced by the groups of Neanderthals.

The Neanderthals were in existence in Europe until about 30,000 years ago. At least in one case, it was firmly attested that the remains of a typical Neanderthal at Saint-Césaire in western France are associated with the early Upper Palaeolithic ('Châtelperronian') industry and dated to 35,000–34,000 years ago (Zubrow 1989).

The number of Neanderthal finds on Russian territory is rather few. The most spectacular discovery was made in 1940 by A.P. Okladnikov at the Teshik-Tash cave site in southern Uzbekistan. A skeleton of a nine year-old child was found in the Upper Mousterian level of the cave. The skeleton was surrounded by the vertically set horns of a wild goat; a hearth was located nearby. These features are seen as an indication of a certain burial rite.

Two burials of the Neanderthals, one an adult and one a child, were discovered by G.A. Bonch-Osmolovsky at the cave site of Kiik-Koba in the Crimea. The adult woman was buried in a grave dug in the rock bottom of the cave. The child, 5–8 months old, was laid in an artificial enclosure made of large cobbles. The burials of five children, aged eight to twelve years, have been discovered in the Mousterian levels at the site of Zaskal'naya 5, in the eastern Crimea. At another site in the same area, Zaskal'naya 5, a fragment of human skull was found. V.P. Alexeyev (1978), the leading Russian anthropologist, regarded the Teshik-Tash child as belonging to the Near Eastern group of Neanderthals. The Kiik-Koba individuals were classified by the same scholar as the European Neanderthals. Many previously held hypotheses regarding the hominid evolution are now being revised, particularly after the introduction of molecular genetic studies. Yet the established fact that the evolution of Neanderthal man in the territory of the former USSR was following a pattern common for the entire Neanderthal world is hardly questionable.

Like the Lower Palaeolithic, the Mousterian sites concentrate predominantly in the southern areas of the former USSR. They are particularly numerous in the Caucasus. All Palaeolithic cave sites in the central Caucasian upland – Kudaro I–III and Tsona – contain Mousterian levels. A number of Mousterian occupations have been established in caves facing the Black Sea coast. Thick Mousterian deposits were found at the Azykh cave in Karabakh. Mousterian shelters were found beneath the Quaternary lava flows in the Armenian highland. Several cave sites are regarded as base camps of prolonged habitation; others were used only seasonally. The remains of cave bears made up the bulk of the faunal remains, while other mammals included wild goat, red deer and aurochs. The series of radiocarbon and TL dates suggest that Mousterian occupation in the Caucasus lasted from 96,000 to 44,000 BP.

Mousterian sites equally exist on the northern slopes of the Greater Caucasus. Bison dominated the faunal assemblage of the Barakayevskaya cave situated in the canyon of Gubs, 50 km south of Maikop. A large open-air site, Il'skaya, is located on the upper terrace of the River Il', a tributary of the Kuban. Bison made up sixty per cent of the faunal remains; other species included mammoth, wild horse, wild ass, gigantic deer, red deer, cave bear and other animals (Lyubin 1989).

Another area of major concentration of Mousterian sites is the Crimean peninsula. A large group of cave sites with Mousterian levels clusters in the Crimean mountains: they are Kiik-Koba, Kosh-Koba, Chagorak-Koba, Volchi Grot, Chokurcha, Shaitan-Koba, Bakhchisarai and several other sites. Animal remains found at these sites belonged to mammoth (a few individuals), woolly rhinoceros, wild horse, antelope-saiga, bison, wild ass, and other species.

An important group of Mousterian shelters was discovered by Yu.V. Kolosov (1979) at Zaskal'naya (Ak-Kaya) in the eastern Crimea. The fauna was essentially the same as in other Crimean sites; faunal assemblages included a few bones of mammoth, as well as wild horse, antelope-saiga, gigantic deer and red deer.

One of the Crimean cave sites deserves special attention. That is Starossel'e, situated in the valley of a small mountain river, near the town of Bakhchisarai. This site, which was found and excavated by A.A. Formozov in the 1950s, exhibits a typical Mousterian assemblage. In the middle part of the lower level, an extended skeleton of a child, 18–20-months-old was found. The most unusual thing is that, according to the opinion of several leading Russian anthropologists (Yakimov and Kharitonov 1979), this child belonged to the anatomically modern human, *Homo sapiens sapiens*. It is one of the rare cases when the Mousterian industry is clearly associated with modern humans. Other examples are the two cave sites in Israel – Qafzeh and Skhul. In these cases, the remains of *H.s. sapiens* were found in the levels with Late Mousterian industry.

Yet another cluster of Mousterian sites is located in the catchment of the River Dniestr. One of the best-studied stratified sites is Molodova I. This open-air site lies on the upper terrace of the Dniestr, not far from the town of Chernovcy. Mammoth dominated the faunal assemblage. Less numerous were the remains of wild horse, bison, reindeer and woolly rhinoceros. Several grinding stones found at the site were probably intended for the processing of plant food. Molodova I is one of the few Mousterian sites with the remains of an artificially constructed dwelling. A structure consisting of circular patterned mammoth bones eight to five metres in size was interpreted as a living space (Chernysh 1973). Another group of sites clusters at Stinka, near the town of Khotin, upstream (Anisyutkin 1978).

All the Mousterian sites dealt with above are found in the southern fringe of the Russian Plain. Yet there are at least two important sites situated far to the north. One of these sites, Sukhaja Mechetka, lies in the southern outskirts of the town of Volgograd (Stalingrad). The Mousterian deposits were found in a palaeosol, exposed in a ravine which cut into the higher terrace of the Volga. The palaeosol was overlain by loam and clay accumulated by the Khvaynian (Würm) transgression of the Caspian Sea. The probable age of the site is one of the mild intervals at the very beginning of the Last glaciation. The Mousterian deposits contained fragments of bones, among which were identified bison, wild horse, saiga and mammoth.

The northernmost Mousterian site, Khotylevo, is located in the Desna valley, 18 km northwest of Bryansk (Zavernyaev 1978). The chronological position of the site is uncertain. The Mousterian deposits were found in the alluvium of the high river terrace. In all probability, these deposits are roughly contemporary to those of Sukhaya Mechetka and correspond to one of the early Valdai mild intervals.

Based on the typological characteristics of the stone industries (the presence/absence of bifaces, the Levallois technique etc.), the prominent French prehistorian, François Bordes, distinguished several Mousterian types or 'facies' such as: Mousterian of the Acheulean tradition, Typical Mousterian, Denticulate and La Ferrassie (Bordes 1981). He argued that these 'facies' correspond to distinct cultural groupings of prehistoric population, which are identifiable in the entire Mousterian world. At the same time, Bordes admitted that certain industries in central and eastern Europe were 'highly original'. Based on a more detailed list of variables, Gladilin (1985) distinguished seven variants in the Ukrainian and Crimean Mousterian, each comprising several facies and types. This classification is questioned by Praslov (1984), who argued that such properties as the high rate of denticulates in that area may have resulted from the character of raw material and the specificity of their use (for example, for working timber).

One may suggest that the Mousterian 'facies' originally resulted from the peculiarities of their use, the availability of the raw material and other environmental factors. Later on, these technical peculiarities became established in cultural traditions, becoming a part of the cultural heritage of distinct social groups.

Summing up existing evidence regarding the Mousterian sites in Russia, one may propound that groups of hominids (presumably the Neanderthals) increasingly penetrated the Russian Plain in the course of the Early/Middle Valdai. These groups originated from the neighbouring areas of central and southeastern Europe. The Caucasus was settled by groups moving from the Near East. Mousterian groups, which were gradually adapting to the cold periglacial environment, exhibited a considerable social complexity.

The Upper Palaeolithic

The most abstruse change in the social complexity and biological adaptability of Palaeolithic mankind occurred during the course of the Middle Valdai, 40,000–30,000 years ago. On the one hand, this marked the emergence of anatomically modern humans and on the other, the appearance of Upper Palaeolithic technology. Both these processes were interrelated but not in a straightforward manner, as had been thought previously.

Recently collected evidence suggests with an increasing certainty that modern humans, *Homo sapiens sapiens*, emerged in Africa south of the Sahara more than 100,000 years ago (Bräuer 1989). The presence of modern humans (the so-called 'Proto-Cro-Magnons') is well attested at the Near Eastern sites of Skhul and Qafzeh and is dated to more than 90,000 BP. The earliest *H.s. sapiens* appeared in central Europe about 36,000–34,000 years ago and in western Europe less than 30,000 years ago. Hence, there was an overlap, suggesting the coexistence of Neanderthal and *sapiens-sapiens* groups in Europe for at least 2000 years (Zubrow 1989). The finds of the early *H.s. sapiens* in the Russian Plain came from only two areas – Kostenki and Sungir. As Alexeyev (1978) has stressed, morphologically all these finds fall within the variability range of similar finds in Europe.

The problem of occurrence of 'racial types' among the Upper Palaeolithic in Europe, based on classical craniological criteria, is being continually debated in physical anthropology. Opinions vary between the acknowledgement of taxonomic homogenity and the occurrence of main racial types in the Upper Palaeolithic (Gokhman 1966a). The main differences are noted between the dolichocephalic moderately broad- and long-headed (Solutrean) and brachiycephalic broad-faced and broad-nosed varieties. The skull from Markina Gora in Kostenki shows characteristics similar to the so-called 'Negroids' from the Grimaldi cave in southern France, while the skeletons from Sungir and Kostenki, two sites in central Russia, reveal broad-faced features typical of the archaic Cro-Magnon type (Gerasimova 1981).

The Upper Palaeolithic phenomenon as a whole may be seen as a package of economic, social and cultural innovations which has guaranteed the survival of prehistoric mankind in the harsh environment of the Last glaciation. In the first place, it was during the Upper Palaeolithic that the settlement of early humans in the Russian Plain reached the maximum extent, with groups of Palaeolithic hunters penetrating into the northernmost ice-free areas. A group of early Palaeolithic sites (Bear cave and Byzovaya open-air site) have been found in the upper stretches of the Pechora river, at 65°N (Kanivets 1976). Yet the greater concentration of Upper Palaeolithic sites is found in the so-called periglacial-forest-steppic zone, in the catchment of Middle Dniepr and Middle Don rivers. The sites are usually located on the upper river terraces, in areas of lake-like widening of the river floors. Olga Soffer (1985), basing her analysis on the detailed investigations of Ukrainian Upper Palaeolithic sites, noted a linealization of the settlements along the waterways. She also made a suggestion about a social and seasonal hierarchy of the sites, which included complex base camps (cold weather), simple base camps (both cold and warm weather), hunting base camps, hunting camps (warm weather), collecting camps (warm weather) and lithic workshops (warm weather).

The economy of Upper Palaeolithic groups in the Russian Plain was based on the highly efficient hunting of large herd animals (mammoth, woolly rhinoceros, wild horse, reindeer, bison) supported by the procurement of fur animals. The location of hunting camps near swampy flood-plains, suggests that a considerable number of large animals were not hunted but scavenged. A significant number of mortars and grinding stones suggests that the collecting and processing of edible plants played an important role in the subsistence of these Palaeolithic groups.

One of the most important features of the Upper Palaeolithic settlements in the Russian Plain was the occurrence of so-called dwellings made of mammoth bones (Fig. 9). These dwellings were typical of 'complex sites' (Mezhirich, Eliseevichi, Mezin, Dobranichevka, and several Kostenki sites, for example). The construction of these dwellings showed a sufficient complexity: a sorting of bones of particular size; 'retaining walls' made of mammoth skulls, a herringbone 'chin down' pattern, and other features. These structures contained decorative objects, including the 'exotic' amber and fossil marine shells imported from far-away areas. Numerous sites of this category included 'pithouses' filled with bones and artefacts; they were usually located on the periphery of the sites.

Another spectacular technological innovation of the Upper Palaeolithic was the emergence of the so-called prismatic blade technique. This technique involved a special preparation of a core which enabled the Palaeolithic craftsmen to produce a great amount of thin parallel-sided blades. They served as standard blanks and were easily transformable by retouching into a variety of different tools.

The earliest radiocarbon dates obtained for an Upper Palaeolithic level came from the cave of Bacho-Kiro in Bulgaria – more than 43,000 BP. Several dates from the early Upper Palaeolithic levels from the sites in central Europe (Austria and Hungary) cluster around 39,000–40,000 BP. Recently, dates of the same order were received from cave sites in northern Spain (Straus 1990). The earliest dates thus far for the Upper Palaeolithic in the Russian Plain were obtained from level 1a of Kostenki 13 site: 32,000±700 BP.

35

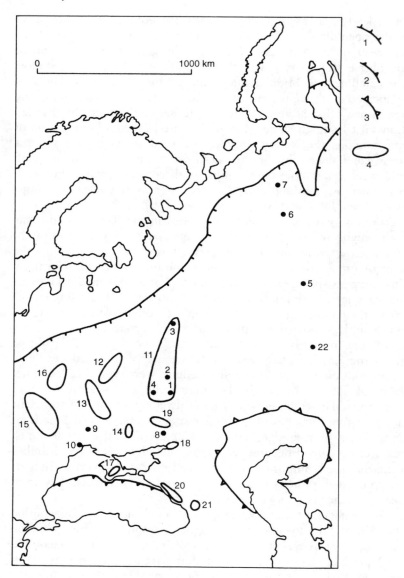

Fig. 8   The Upper Palaeolithic.
   Key. 1 – Limits of the Last glaciation; 2 – Limits of the Black Sea; 3 – Limits
of the Caspian Sea; 4 – Groups of sites.
Sites and groups of sites: 1 – Kostenki; 2 – Gagarino; 3 – Sungir; 4 – Avdeevo; 5 –
Talitsky; 6 – Bear cave; 7 – Byzovaya; 8 – Amvrosievka; 9 – Anetovka; 10 – Greater
Akkarzha; 11 – Kostenki-Avdeevo group; 12 – Desna group; 13 – Upper Dnieprian
group; 14 – Middle Dnieprian group; 15 – Dniestrian group; 16 – Lipian group;
17 – Crimean group; 18 – Avov Sea group; 19 – Seversky Dobets group; 20 – Black
Sea group; 21 – Western Georgian group; 22 – Kapova Cave.

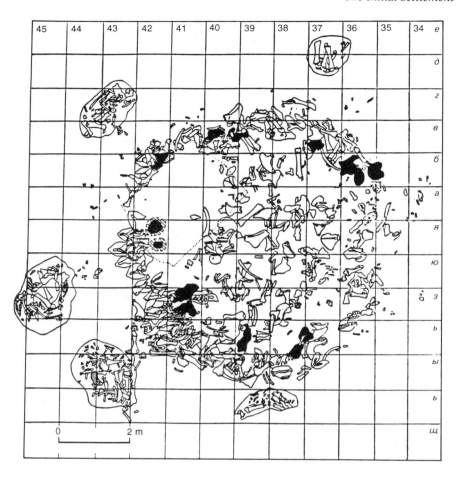

Fig. 9 Upper Palaeolithic 'dwelling'. Kostenki 11, stratum 1a.
Source. N. Praslov & A. Rogachev, *Paleolit Kostenkovsko-Borshevskogo raiona.*
Leningrad: Nauka, 1982.

This level was underlain by two more levels, which may be several millennia older. Hence one may expect that the age of the earliest Upper Palaeolithic sites in easternmost Europe may reach a value of *c.* 40,000 BP.

At least three stages are distinguishable in the evolution of the Upper Palaeolithic. The first stage lasted from *c.* 40,000 to 24,000 BP and corresponded to the final climatic fluctuations of the Middle Valdai interval. The most important feature of this stage was the parallel existence of two distinct traditions: one featured an archaic tradition with numerous Mousterian survivals; the other, a fully developed blade technique. This was a common phenomenon throughout Europe. Thus, the Châtelperronian in France contained numerous Mousterian elements, yet it coexisted with a fully developed Upper Palaeolithic–Aurignacian. Archaic elements are present in the Szeletian industries of central Europe; Aurignacian sites appeared in that particular area at the same time, or only slightly later (Allsworth-Jones 1986, 1989).

Archaic elements are attested in the assemblages of sites belonging to the Streletskian tradition, which include a number of sites in the Kostenki area (Kostenki 12/3; Srteletskaya 3; Kostenki 1/5; Kostenki 11/5; Kostenki 12/1a) and, possibly, the site of Sungir. The inventory of these sites contains archaic Mousterian implements: side-scrapers and triangular points, the blade technique being totally absent. The radiocarbon dates for these sites range between 32,000 and 24,000 BP. Russian scholars have made a very important observation: the closest analogies to these archaic tools are found either in the Moldova (Trinka 3 Cave) or in northern Caucasus (Il'skaya) (Rogachev and Anikovich 1984).

The number of sites markedly increased during the second stage, which roughly corresponded to the maximum of the Last glaciation. It is highly remarkable that at the time of maximum cold and dryness of the climate, in an extremely inhospitable environment, Upper Palaeolithic groups developed a complex socio-cultural network which enabled them not only to survive, but also to achieve an outstanding progress in all spheres of their activity.

Formerly, all cultural entities of the Upper Palaeolithic in central and eastern Europe were usually designated by an umbrella of 'Eastern Gravettian'. New studies have shown that a developed Upper Palaeolithic in the Russian Plain, similar to the rest of Europe, included several distinct cultural traditions or 'cultures' showing particular patterns of development. One such entity, referred to as the 'Kostenkian' or 'Kostenki-Avdeevo culture', was identified at several sites in central Russia. The inventories of the sites belonging to this 'culture' included several common elements, such as specific 'Kostenki' shouldered points, and leaf-shaped points. Similarities were also found in bone, antler and ivory tools. It is at this stage that the structure of dwellings became more complex. Grigor'ev (1993), basing his analysis on the similarity of certain classes of tools, distinguished a large 'cultural' unit which included several Upper Palaeolithic sites in central Europe (Willendorf in Austria and Pavlov in the Czech Lands) and in the Russian Plain (Kostenki 1/1, Avdeevo, Berdiyzh, Molodova 5/7). Both he and Soffer (1993) argued that this entity resulted from an eastbound 'demographic shift' which occurred between 28,000 and 24,000 BP.

Basing her analysis on several characteristics of living space and artefacts, Olga Soffer argued that during that period the Upper Palaeolithic groups in the Russian Plain reached a level of considerable social complexity (Soffer 1985). This implied a social hierarchization and the emergence of 'high-status' individuals, allegedly located at 'simple cold-weather base camps'.

The most transparent evidence supporting the occurrence of a social hierarchization comes from the site at Sungir, situated on the River Klyazma, east of Vladimir, in central Russia. Since 1964 several burials of anatomically modern humans have been found there. Several of these individuals apparently were of a high social rank. One of them was male, 55–65 years old, and interred in an extended posture on the back. The rich grave goods included twenty thin bracelets of mammoth tusk, a flint knife, a side-scraper and a flake on the bottom of the grave, a bone fragment with spiral incisions as well as 3,500 perforated beads of mammoth tusk. Another grave near by contained two skeletons of adolescents, a boy of 12–13 and a girl of 7–8 years of age, buried in an extended position with their heads pressed against one another. The grave goods included numerous bracelets of mammoth tusk; two rods of reindeer horn were laid at the girl's feet; two flint knives were found in the body of the boy and one of them was clasped in his hand. Yet the most unusual find consisted of two large spears (1.66 and 2.24 metres long) made of straightened mammoth tusk and deposited in the grave close to the bodies. Radiocarbon dates of this site suggest the age ranging between 26,000 and 20,000 BP (Bader 1978).

One of the particularly spectacular phenomena of the Upper Palaeolithic in the Russian Plain was the development of figurative art (Fig. 10). Female ivory figurines have been found in the entire area of eastern Gravettian. As Grigor'ev (1993) has stressed, figurines from the Willendorf-Kostenki cultural area had distinct stylistic characteristics. Other articles were ornamented in an abstract manner. S.N. Bibikov (1981) suggested that certain large bones of mammoth ornamented by abstract designs were used as musical percussion instruments.

In the same respect, the finds at the Upper Palaeolithic Kapova cave in the southern Urals are highly significant. This cave contained rock paintings concentrated in four separate galleries. These paintings, effected in red colours, represented animals (mammoth, horse, rhinoceros) as well as geometric signs and symbols. Archaeological deposits found beneath the paintings in the cave have been radiocarbon dated to 15,000–13,000 BP. Thus, both stylistically and chronologically, examples of cave art in the Urals are basically similar to the classical area of Franco-Cantabria in western Europe (Bader 1965; Shchelinsky 1989).

Hence, one may conclude, that during the second stage of the Upper Palaeolithic, which coincided with the maximum of the Last glaciation, the entire ice-free area of the Russian Plain was intensively settled by groups of hunters and food-collectors. The population density in the Russian Plain during that time was much higher than ever before; in contrast to the mountainous areas of the Caucasus and the Crimea where, at the same time, the density of the Upper Palaeolithic population markedly diminished. The highlands of the central Caucasus and Transcaucasia seem to have been totally abandoned. All Upper Palaeolithic sites in the Caucasus were clustered in a few mountain ridges facing the Colchis and the Black Sea

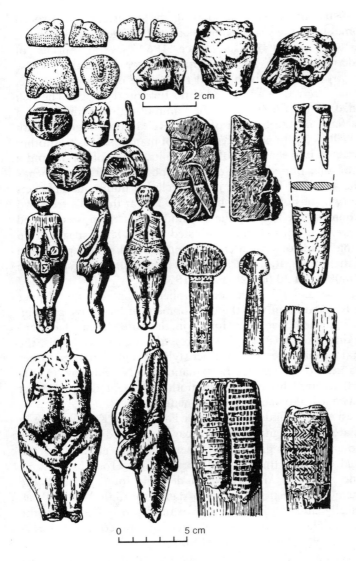

Fig. 10   Palaeolithic 'portable' art from Kostenki sites.
       Source. I. Gerasimov, *Arheologija i paleogeografija pozdnego paleolita Russkoi ravniny.* Moscow: Nauka, 1981.

coast. There are only a very few Upper Palaeolithic sites in the Crimea.

Seen as a whole, the development of the Upper Palaeolithic in the Russian Plain was generally following the pattern of central and western Europe with some differences obviously due to the peculiarities of the physical and cultural environment. There are numerous indications of repeated migratory shifts generally directed from the west to the east, from the areas of central Europe, deep into the Russian Plain. Yet, based on the peculiarities of economy, mode of life and certain manifestations of culture, one may distinguish two major provinces in Upper Palaeolithic Europe. The first province is located in central and eastern Europe and includes predominantly open-air sites. The inhabitants of this province lived in comparatively large settlements which were located along major waterways and often included permanent structures made of large mammoth bones. They hunted large herd animals adapted to the periglacial environment. On these grounds this province may be referred to as the 'Periglacial'. The second province includes the sites in Atlantic Europe and Mediterranean coastal areas. Its analogies may be found in the Levant and western Caucasus. This province (we call it the 'Mediterranean') consisted predominantly of cave sites. The livelihood of its inhabitants was based on the hunting of mountain-forest game.

The Late Glacial

The situation in the Russian Plain had drastically changed at about 15,000 BP, when the increase in temperature and precipitation triggered a massive recession of the ice-sheets. At that time, the entire network of the Upper Palaeolithic settlement in the catchment of the Don and Dniepr rivers started to disintegrate. A total collapse followed soon. This went together with the mass-scale extinctions of the mammoth and woolly rhinoceros. Herds of wild horse shifted to the south, while reindeer migrated to the north. The entire resource base of the Upper Palaeolithic economy rapidly disappeared.

Scholars still argue about the causes of these dramatic developments. According to the majority view (Martin and Klein 1984), this was essentially due to an increase in temperature and precipitation resulting in a deeper cover of snow being formed in the winter time, particularly in open interfluves. In these conditions, the animals could no longer reach the fodder buried beneath the snow. Weakened by winter famine, they became an easy target for Palaeolithic hunters. Whatever were the causes, the fact remains that by 14,000 BP there were practically no major Upper Palaeolithic sites left in central Russia.

At the same time, there occurred an intensive settlement of the North European Plain, recently freed from ice. An initial settlement of these plains by the communities of Late Glacial reindeer hunters occurred during the Older Dryas. The earliest identifiable groups are comparable to the Bromme-Lyngby, a cultural tradition whose core area was restricted mainly to the territory of Denmark and north-eastern Germany. The cultural assemblage of this group included particular types of club-like reindeer antler and the 'Bromme type' tanged points. The only available radiocarbon

41

date for the Bromme-Lyngby tradition came from the site of Trollesgave in Denmark – *c.* 11,000 BP (Fischer and Tauber 1986).

Similar assemblages are also known in Poland (Nowy Mlyn, Grzybowa Gora; Schild 1975) and in Lithuania, where Rimantiene (1971) identified the Lyngbian tradition in a group of sites near Vilnius. The Lyngby points were reported from several sites in the catchment of the Upper Dniepr and Sozh rivers in northern Ukraine and Belorussia (Kopytin 1979; Isaenko Mitrofanov and Shtykhov 1970). The site of Anosovo in the Upper Dniepr valley, where Lyngby points were found in a context of an archaic Palaeolithic assemblage that included one- and two-platform cores, end-scrapers and burins, is of particular significance (Gurina 1965).

A different tradition is referred to as Ahrensburgian. Ahrensburgian layers were first identified in a clear stratigraphic position at the sites in the 'tunnel valley' near Hamburg: Stellmoor, Meiendorf and Poggenwisch. Using the AMS technique, Fischer and Tauber determined the age of the Ahrensburgian sites in that area as 10,200 BP, close to the Younger Dryas/Preboreal transition (Fischer and Tauber 1986). Burdukiewicz (1979) identified typical Ahrensburgian assemblages at a number of sites in Lower Silesia (Siednica 17 and 6). Rimantiene (1971) distinguished several Ahrensburgian sites in the area of Vilnius (Vilnius, Ilgis, Mitriskes 6A and others). Kopytin (1979) and Zaliznyak (1979) reported Ahrensburg-type points from several sites in the catchment of the Upper Dniepr, Pripet and Desna rivers. In some cases, Ahrensburg and Lyngby points were found jointly within the same assemblages, as was the case of the archaic assemblage of Anosovka in the Upper Dniepr valley (Gurina 1965).

The most intensive settlement of the northeastern European Plain corresponded to the spread of so-called Swiderian assemblages, which occurred during the cold spell of Younger Dryas. Sites of this type were originally identified in southern Poland. In the light of recent research, the Polish sites located in the catchment of the Vistula and Oder (Schild 1975) make up but the western sector of the total Swiderian distribution area.

A large cluster of Swiderian sites has been found in the catchment of the Neman, in Lithuania and northwestern Belorussia (Rimantiene 1971; Charnyavski 1979). A large concentration of these sites lies in the Pripet valley (Zaliznyak 1979). Yet another cluster of Swiderian sites is situated in the catchment of the Upper Dniepr, including the Desna and Sozh valleys (Bud'ko 1970). Artefacts are usually associated with the sand dunes developed on the terraces of rivers and residual ice-dammed lakes. As recent studies show, the formation of similar sand sheets and dunes was actively under way in the course of the Younger Dryas in the entire area of northern Europe (Kozarski 1991).

The northwestern limits of the penetration of Swiderian groups are found in the catchment of the western Dvina. Assemblages containing the tanged points of the Swidry type were found within the depression of Lake Usvyaty in the southern part of Pskov district (Dolukhanov and Miklyayev

1986; Dolukhanov 1979). In that area several clusters of stone and bone artefacts were found on top of sand dunes developed on the shores of an ice-dammed lake allegedly of the Alleröd/Younger Dryas Age. These materials included both Swiderian points and two-sided harpoons. Assemblages with Swiderian points in similar geomorphic conditions were also found in the Upper Volga catchment (Kol'tsov 1989).

A large concentration of Late Palaeolithic sites is located in the area of Poless'e, in the terraced accumulative valley of the Pripet river, the border-area between Ukraine and Belorussia. During Late Glacial times it was one of the main channels of drainage of the Upper Neman ice-dammed lake in the Dniepr catchment (Kvasov 1975). Several sites of Late Glacial Age in the Pripet catchment feature the presence of Lyngby points: Opol 2, Veliky Midsk, Tur, Pribor. Ahrensburg points have been identified at several sites in the same area (Zaliznyak 1979). Yet the greater part of the Late Glacial sites in Poless'e is clearly attributable to the Swiderian tradition. Sites of this type have been found on the dunes developed on the sandy terraces of the Pripet and its tributaries. In one case (Pribor 13) five clusters of lithics, each *c.* 10 metres in diameter, allegedly corresponding to living areas, have been identified (Zaliznyak 1979).

Several hypotheses concerning the origins of the Swiderian tradition have been suggested. Based on the typological similarity of Swidry points with leaf-shaped Upper Palaeolithic implements, Schild (1975) envisaged the sources of the Swiderian in the central European Upper Palaeolithic. Using the same criteria Gurina (1965) has identified the origins of the Swiderian in the assemblage of Borshevo II on the River Don. The stratified site of Grensk on the River Sozh (Bud'ko 1970) seems to support a case for the local development of the Swiderian. The lower level of the site contained implements similar to those of the Upper Palaeolithic sites situated in the same basin (such as Yudinovo and Gontsy). Hence one may conclude that the Swiderian assemblages in the northern and northeastern European Plain resulted mostly from gradual movements of social groups from the main areas of Upper Palaeolithic settlement in the periglacial zone of central and eastern Europe, and particularly from the catchment of the Dniepr and Don (Fig. 11). The subsistence of these groups was mostly based on nomadic hunting of reindeer. Seasonal camps were restricted to the areas richest in biomass, that is the shores of residual ice-dammed lakes and the related hydrological network.

While retaining their cultural identity, the Swiderian groups were in constant contact with economically and socially similar groups of different origin within the greater area of the northeastern European Plain. These contacts are documented by the occurrence of different types of tanged point (Lyngby and Ahrensburg) in the Swiderian-dominated area. Thus the entire northeastern European Plain in the Late Glacial may be seen as a single socio-cultural exchange network, within which several distinct cultural traditions were in constant interaction.

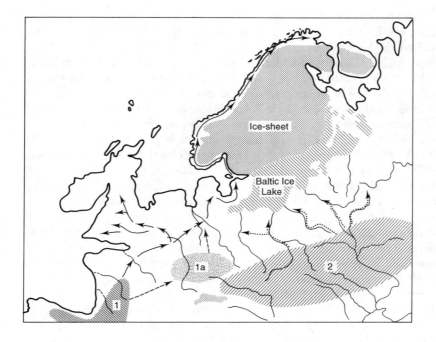

Fig. 11   Late Glacial migrations.
  Key. 1 – Atlantic zone; 1a – South German sub-zone; 2 – Periglacial zone.

Early languages

Now a very sensitive problem will be touched upon: what was the language of the Palaeolithic hunters of the Russian Plain? There are no reasons to doubt that even early hominids capable of manufacturing working tools were able to transmit and to perceive some kind of information; this implies the existence of some primitive means of vocal communication.

Based on the comparative study of the 'supralingual airway' recorded in the anatomy of fossil hominids, Lieberman (1984) has concluded that the austolopithecines (*Australopithecus africanus, A. robustus* and *A. boisei*) were unable to produce human-like sounds. The marked change is observable in the anatomy of *Homo erectus*, and particularly, *Homo sapiens neanderthalensis.* The latter, according to Lieberman, was able to utter sounds resembling the 'cries of a newborn human baby'. Yet the range of vocal signals that the early hominids were able to transmit was fairly limited. It consisted of a standard assortment of signals linked together by some sort of primitive grammar. One may reasonably suggest that the 'language' used by the Neanderthals was universally comprehensible.

The emergence of the real 'fully encoded' human speech became possible only with the rise of the anatomically modern human, *Homo sapiens sapiens*. Mastery of speech enormously enhanced the productive capacities of the human, enabling him to codify, to transmit and to perceive all kinds of information pertinent to social, economic and cultural behaviour. Intensive flows of information were transmitted horizontally – from one social group to another – and vertically – from one generation to the next. One may suggest that the acquisition of human speech was responsible for the extinction of the Neanderthals who could not resist their more vocalized relatives. At the same time, the advantage offered by speech was one of the important factors that enabled humans to survive the harsh conditions of Valdai glaciation.

Since the speech of early *H. s.* was basically similar to that of modern humans, one may try to find their modern analogies. These attempts are purely speculative: we can never hope to find any records of extinct speech among the Palaeolithic artefacts. Nonetheless such attempts are being made. I have recently made a suggestion that the 'Periglacial province' of the Upper Palaeolithic in central and eastern Europe, corresponded to the Proto-Uralic languages (Dolukhanov 1994).

There are several kinds of arguments that may support this suggestion. In the first instance, there are arguments based on archaeological evidence. As I will demonstrate in the following chapters, archaeological records show a considerable cultural continuity which may be traced from the Upper Palaeolithic to the ethnographically recognizable Finns. A different set of arguments is based on linguistics. Uralic languages are extremely archaic; there is hardly any doubt that they predate the spread of Indo-European speech. No less important is the semantic analysis of the vocabulary common to all modern Uralic languages (Hajdu 1975). This seems to reflect the mode of life of ancient Uralic speakers. These words are related to *fishery* (fish, net, river, bog, high river bank, etc.), *hunting* (bow, arrow, bow-string, reindeer, marten, squirrel, etc.), *plants* (forest, spruce, cedar, larch, pine, berry, bark, etc.), *nourishment* (fire, charcoal, fat, honey, salt, millet), *dwelling* (hut, pole), and *inventory* (flint, axe, awl, iron, tin, silver, gold). There are common words denoting *cold climate* (ice, frost, mist, ski, to thaw), but there are no common words relating to domestic animals, except 'dog'. Taken as a whole, this common vocabulary seems to show a predominantly periglacial environment, cold climate and the foraging economy typical of the Upper Palaeolithic. As for millet, it could originally have corresponded to some wild edible herb (collecting edible plants was an important element in the Upper Palaeolithic subsistence). The same logic may be applied to the metals; they may well have originally designated minerals, and only at a later stage were these minerals used as ores (these cases are common in other languages).

There are several hypotheses relating to the original location and the time of disintegration of the Proto-Uralic language. In the nineteenth century several linguists, basing their findings on the affinities between the Uralic and Altaic languages, suggested that their common ancestral language (the Ural-Altaic) was located in southern Siberia, in the Altai and Sayan mountains. Nowadays, the majority of scholars tend to locate the initial Proto-Uralic language in the area stretching from the Baltic Sea to the Urals. The period of existence of this proto-language is thought to be 10,000–7,000 BP (Hajdu 1975).

D. László (1961), the Hungarian linguist, argued that Proto-Uralic had existed much earlier – 12,000–10,000 BP. He related the Proto-Uralic language to the Late Glacial Swiderian industries. In his arguments, László used both archaeological and linguistic evidence: for example, several names of rivers and lakes in Poland are of Finno-Ugric origin. My own theory goes a step further in suggesting that the Proto-Uralic language (or rather its dialects) were spoken in the entire Upper Palaeolithic periglacial province (Dolukhanov 1994). In the same book I put forward yet another hypothesis, suggesting that the Mediterranean Upper Palaeolithic province corresponded to a hypothetical Basque-Caucasian linguistic entity. As I have said earlier, there is archaeological evidence for multiple contacts between the two Upper Palaeolithic provinces. Indirectly, these contacts are confirmed by other linguists: Hubschmied (1960), for example, noted significant structural similarities between the Basque and Uralic languages.

Postglacial Farmers and Hunters

The Holocene

A new epoch began *c.* 10,000 years ago, that of the Holocene. This term, coined from two Greek words (*holos* meaning 'whole' and *kainos* meaning 'time'), was in use from 1867, when it was officially endorsed by the International Geological Congress in Bologna, Italy. The shortest of all geological periods (we are still living in it), the Holocene is studied and understood better than any of the previous units of the geological history of our planet, at least partly because Holocene deposits are found in a much better state of preservation. What is no less important, particularly in the study of the most recent stages of the Holocene, is that the traditional palaeoenvironmental methods have been supplemented by the information taken from written records and even from instrumental observations during the last two centuries.

Of all the sources of information pertinent to the change of vegetation and climate during the Holocene, the study of peat-bogs proved to be the most significant. The consideration of plant remains in the sequences of peat-bogs at the turn of the century led two Scandinavian botanists, Axel Blytt and Rutger Sernander, to an important discovery. Having noted regular changes in the composition of plants, from the bottom to the top of peat deposits, they concluded that these changes were due to modifications of the climate and they distinguished several climatic 'zones' in postglacial Scandinavia. This division is still largely in use and bears the names of its founders. The original Blytt-Sernander scheme included five 'zones': Preboreal, Boreal, Atlantic, Sub-Boreal and Sub-Atlantic. Later, with the introduction of pollen analysis, this division became more detailed. Originally, climatic zones were dated approximately, by means of the correlation of bog deposits with annually laminated varves. Since the 1950s, radiocarbon dating has become available, as a result of which climatic zones are now precisely dated in absolute figures (Fig. 12).

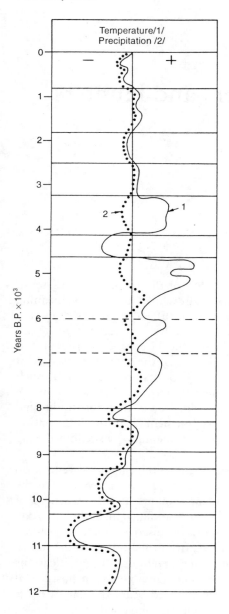

Fig. 12. Climatic oscillations of the Holocene.
  Source. N.A. Khotinsky, in *Izvesttija Akademii Nauk SSSR, ser. geograf.,* 1991/3. Moscow: Nauka.

Russian scholars such as K.K. Markov, M.I. Neishtadt, N.A. Khotinsky and many others have made important contributions to the study of the Holocene. N.A. Khotinsky and his associates (Khotinsky 1977; Khotinsky et al. 1991), based on the large number of analytically studied pollen profiles supported by the radiocarbon measurements, have worked out a detailed stratigraphy of the Holocene for the Russian Plain. The beginning of the Holocene was marked by the recession of the glaciers from the last 'line of defence', the morainic ridge stretching from southeastern Finland (Salpausselkä) to central Sweden across the Baltic Sea. Until that time, the ice-free area of the Baltic was taken up by a cold basin known as the 'Baltic Ice Lake'. Its level, which was subject to fluctuations related to the movement of the ice-sheet, remained much higher than the ocean of that time. The recession of the glaciers from the area of Mount Billingen in central Sweden led to Baltic water breaking through into the ocean, an event which occurred *c.* 10,200 years ago. As a result, the level of the Baltic fell rapidly. Geologists referred to the new basin that emerged as the 'Yoldia Sea'.

The Yoldia Sea was roughly contemporaneous with the Preboreal, the initial 'zone' of the Holocene. Khotinsky et al. (1991) distinguish at least two stages during its course: the short-lived warm 'Polovetsk' stage (10,200–10,000 BP), followed by a much longer and colder 'Pereyaslavl' stage (10,000–9,300 BP). During the former, the birch and pine forests massively spread on the Plain. During the latter, they retreated and treeless tundra again dominated the vegetation cover.

The subsequent period, the Boreal, featured a total supremacy of pine and birch forests. Here, too, Khotinsky et al. (1991) distinguish at least three stages: two warm – Boreal 1 (9300–8900 BP) and Boreal 3 (8300–8000 BP) – separated by a 'Thermal Optimum' – Boreal 2 (8900–8300 BP). According to computer simulation, during the Optimum the mean annual temperature was 1°C higher than today whereas precipitation was below the present value.

At that time, important changes occurred in the Baltic basin. Due to the 'glacial isostatic rebound', the area of central Fennoscandia, which had sustained the maximum loading of glaciers during the Ice Age, experienced a considerable uplift in the postglacial time. This upheaval ultimately led to the closure of the strait in central Sweden, which connected the Baltic with the ocean. The open sea turned into a land-locked basin which geologists call the 'Ancylus Lake'. This occurred *c.*9300–9200 BP.

The Atlantic (also known as 'Alti-thermal' or 'Climatic Optimum') was the most important time-span in the Holocene. As computer estimates based on recently obtained data have shown (Zubakov 1986), the solar radiation at that time exceeded present values by 7 per cent. The concentration of carbon dioxide in the atmosphere reached values of about 350–380 million^{-1}, resulting in a global increase of annual temperature by about 1°C (the winter temperature by 0.8°C and the summer temperature by 1.2°C).

Based on computerized estimates for the Russian Plain, Khotinsky et al. (1991) argue that the mean annual temperature rose by at least 2°C. These changes in the climate had serious consequences for the vegetation cover and the animal world. Mixed forests, with a considerable participation of warm-loving broad-leaved trees (oak, lime and alder) and an underwood of chestnut, spread over huge areas of the Russian Plain, reaching the Kola peninsula in the north. They penetrated deep into the south, along the river floors, into the Pontic lowland. The steppe, much reduced at that time, was enriched by mesophilous herbs. A much higher productivity of terrestrial and aquatic plants resulted in an overall increase of the biomass. According to recent observations, the live weight of animals in natural habitats was 1292 kg per sq.km for broad-leaved forests and 552 kg per sq. km for mixed coniferous/broad-leaved forests. Comparative figures for the taiga and tundra were 224 and 126 kg per sq. km respectively (Khodasheva 1966).

The total duration of the Atlantic is estimated as *c.* 8000–4500 BP. According to recent evidence (Khotinsky et al. 1991), at least two 'warm culminations' are distinguishable during that time: *c.* 7500 and *c.* 5000 BP. My own studies in northwestern Russia (Dolukhanov et al. 1989) have given me an opportunity to measure the duration of a short cool stage that separated the two climatic optima. This turned out to be *c.* 6200–6000 BP. As we shall see later, this cool stage, which was of a comparatively short duration, had very serious consequences for the life of prehistoric groups. Hence, we can distinguish at least three stages in the Atlantic: Atlantic-1 (warm) – 8000–6200 BP; Atlantic-2 (cool) – 6200–6000 BP; and Atlantic-3 (warm) – 6000–4500 BP. At the same time, a global rise of the ocean level took place. This was mostly due to eustasy, an accumulation of glacial meltwater: the melting of ice becomes more intense with the beginning of the Climatic Optimum. A combination of tectonics and eustasy led, yet again, to the connection of the Baltic with the ocean, this time via the Danish Straits. The newly emerged basin with a saline water has been named the 'Litorina Sea'; it came into being *c.* 7000 BP.

Studies of the Litorina Sea beaches were conducted in all Baltic countries, the ancient shore-lines being situated at various heights along the Baltic coast due to isostasy. These studies, combined with the analysis of deposits in coastal peat-bogs, have shown that the level of the Litorina Sea was unstable. At least four minor transgressions are distinguishable during the Atlantic and the following early Sub-Boreal: 7000–6900; 6300–5900; 5600–4600; 4300–4000 BP respectively. These rises of sea-level regularly alternated with recessions (Mörner 1969).

My studies in northwestern Russia and Latvia (Dolukhanov 1979) have led to yet another observation. Based on the multidisciplinary studies of wetland sites, I and my associates discovered that the levels of several lakes in that area experienced minor fluctuations. Precise dating of the rises and falls of lake levels have shown that in most cases they coincided with fluctuations of the Litorina Sea. My own studies were restricted mainly to the catchment of the Western Dvina. Independently, similar observations were made in various parts of the Russian Plain (Davydova 1992), as well as in Fennoscandia and the Alpine area. Recent studies show that fluctuations of the lakes in different parts of Europe were also roughly synchronous. It seems probable that these fluctuations were climatically controlled (Harrison et al. 1993).

No less spectacular events have occurred in the basin of the Black Sea. During the maximum of the Valdai glaciation, the level of the sea was at least 60 metres below its present position. During the Late Glacial, starting at *c.* 15,000 BP, the level of this sea began to rise. The transgression which followed was named a 'New Euxine' by Fedorov (1978). By 11,000 BP the level of the sea reached –20 metres. Molluscs collected in the corresponding deposits consisted mainly of fresh- and brackish-water species. It seems obvious that this transgression was mainly due to the massive influx of the glacial meltwater.

After a short regression during the Younger Dryas, the sea started to rise again at 10,000 BP. This rise intensified after 9000 BP when the connection between the Mediterranean and Black Seas was re-established. At that time, the levels of both seas reached the threshold of the Bosphorus. The following rise of the sea-level led to the emergence of a 'New Black Sea'. This rise was evidently of eustatic origin, roughly synchronous with the 'Flandrian' sea-level recognizable in the Mediterranean and along Atlantic Europe, as well as with the Litorina in the Baltic. The New Black Sea reached its maximum (2–2.5 metres) between 5300 and 3000 years ago.

The Mesolithic

The emergence of agriculture was the most important event in the social life of prehistoric mankind and coincided with the beginnings of the Holocene, certainly in one part of the world. There are at least three major landmarks in the course of the prehistory of mankind. The first was the beginning of tool-making and the emergence of man as a social being. The second was the emergence of the anatomically modern human, and the establishment of the Upper Palaeolithic (as we previously noted, these two phenomena are not directly linked). The third major landmark that has greatly shaped human destinies was the emergence of agriculture. One may say that modern civilization, with its colossal advances and no less spectacular losses, had its origins in the first farmlands in the Zagros mountains at the dawn of the Holocene.

The earliest evidence for initial 'food production' came from sites of the 'aceramic Neolithic' in the Near East. Radiocarbon date levels of these sites yield the age of 10,300–10,200 BP. This time-span corresponded to the Younger Dryas which featured a cool and dry climate in the area of Levant

(Arl. Leroi-Gourhan 1981: 127). The area of initial agriculture included the hilly piedmont and the intermontane valleys of the huge arch which consisted of the Zagros, Taurus and the hills of the Mediterranean façade. This area (the 'Fertile Crescent') covered the primary habitats of the wild progenitors of cereals (barley, wheat), legumes and pulses, as well as easily domesticated animals (sheep and goat). I have discussed various hypotheses relating to the origins of agriculture elsewhere (Dolukhanov 1994). Here it is sufficient to say that during the following millennia (10,000–8,000 BP), which saw a marked increase in temperature and humidity, a farming economy rapidly spread in the Near and Middle East. Settlements of early farmers appeared in Europe during the course of the early Atlantic, first in the intermontane depressions of the Balkans, and later, in the loessic plains of central Europe. As we shall see later, the emergence and spread of agriculture had a profound effect on the social and ethnic processes in eastern Europe, including the Russian Plain. Yet it took several millennia before the impulses triggered by the Neolithic revolution became conspicuous in the densely forested expanses of Russia.

The archaeological period which had started in the immediate aftermath of the Ice Age in Europe is referred to as Mesolithic. It is necessary to say a few words about the origin of this term. In the 1840s several Danish archaeologists introduced a so-called 'Three-Age system' which divided human prehistory into the periods of Stone, Bronze and Iron Age. A group of French archaeologists (Gabriel de Mortillet, Edmont Piette and others) took it a step further when they divided the Stone Age into Palaeolithic and Neolithic. Palaeolithic was viewed as the period with chipped or flaked tools, and Neolithic as a period with polished stone tools. The irony is that this archaic division of the Stone Age, based entirely on formal archaeological criteria, is still largely in use in the former Soviet Union, notwithstanding its proclaimed emphasis on social and economic principles. New discoveries, particularly the finds of *kjökkenmöddinger* (the middens of shell-fish) of postglacial age along the coasts of Denmark and other parts of Atlantic Europe, proved that the bipartite division of the Stone Age was insufficient. Consequently, in 1892, Allen Brown suggested a new term, Mesolithic, to denote an intermediate period between the Palaeolithic and Neolithic (Daniel 1975). For a long time, Mesolithic was seen as a period of cultural degradation and stagnation. Thus V. Gordon Childe (1958) characterized the Mesolithic as a period of 'surviving food-gatherers': 'Mesolithic groups appear in general isolated and poorly equipped in contrast to Magdalenians or Predmostians' (1958: 3). Only comparatively recently was Mesolithic recognized as a time of a considerable social, economic and cultural complexity.

What were the most typical features of the Mesolithic in eastern and northern Europe? First and foremost, its spatial extension: during the Mesolithic human groups penetrated and exploited practically every landscape suitable for human habitation. Another aspect of Mesolithic settlement and subsistence was an intensive use of resources in in-shore lagoons: for example those of the Yoldia Sea and Ancylus Sea. Let us look at a few examples. One of the earliest sites in the Baltic basin is Antrea (or Antrea-Korpilahti). The site now lies in Russia, about 20 km southeast of the Russo-Finnish border, 15 km east of the town of Vyborg. Finds were first reported by Pälsi in 1920 and included a fishing net comprising double-threaded cord made from the bast of willow bark with eighteen oblong pine-bark floats and sink stones. Stone implements also included adzes and a chisel with its working edge hollowed by polishing into a gouge-like form. Among the bone and antler implements was a knife handle made from a pointed piece of elk shin-bone, a hollow chisel made from a tubular bone, a short stout point, and a knife-like tool with traces of engraved lines. Based on the geomorphic situation of the finds, one might suggest that the site was originally located in a small bay of a strait which connected the Yoldia Sea with Lake Ladoga. Samples of the net and the bark floats presented uncalibrated dates of 9230±210 BP (Hel-269) and 9310±140 BP (Hel-1301). Mesolithic settlements are also known in the in-shore lagoons north of St Petersburg (Lakhta), in northern Estonia (Narva and Kunda), in western Estonia (Sindi) and elsewhere.

Another type of Mesolithic settlement is that found within the depressions of lakes. In all these cases the lakes are the remnants of huge ice-dammed basins which were in existence during the Late Glacial times. Mesolithic sites were constantly bound to the shores of these lakes; in some cases one could see how the Mesolithic settlers were changing the location of their sites following the transgression or recession of the lake. Such finds are known south of St Petersburg, in the catchment of the Western Dvina and in the Upper Volga, and in other areas affected by the Valdai glaciation.

The subsistence of Mesolithic groups relied on the exploitation of a wide spectrum of food resources. This included the hunting of land mammals – the elk was usually the most numerous, supplemented by red deer, wild pig and other animals. The hunting of seal was important in coastal areas. Alternative sources of food were provided by the hunting of waterfowl, fishing, and the collecting of edible plants (particularly the water chestnut). The latter gained in importance with the beginning of the Climatic Optimum.

In contrast to the earlier views which treated the Mesolithic as a basically stagnant and egalitarian society, new evidence increasingly shows it as a dynamic and socially complex period. An increased social complexity is particularly conspicuous in the Mesolithic cemeteries. Oleni (Reindeer) Island in Lake Onega, in Russian Karelia, is the largest of its kind in Europe. The site was excavated by V.I. Ravdonikas in 1936–38 and N.N. Gurina in the 1950s. It included more than 400 graves. The deceased were buried 0.60–1.20 metres below the ground surface, usually in a single burial; there were sixteen double burials and three triple burials. The bodies were usually placed on their backs in an extended posture, facing towards the east. After

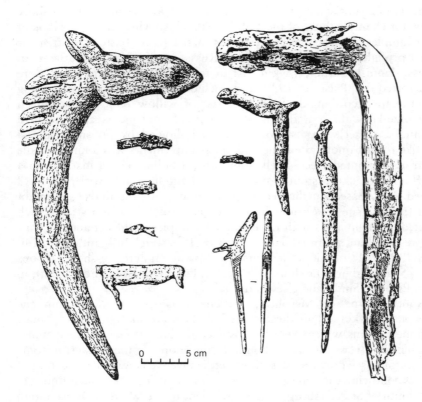

Fig. 13   Figurines from Oleneostrovski cemeteries (Karelia and Kola peninsula).
   Source. N.A. Gurina, *Materialy i issledovanija po arheologii SSSR,* v. 87.
Moscow: Nauka, 1961.

inhumation the body was sprinkled with red ochre. Four individuals in the northern part of the cemetery were interred in funnel-shaped shafts 1.3–1.8 metres deep, in a standing posture facing a westerly direction. Hunting equipment prevails in male graves. This includes bone and stone points, bone daggers, slate knives, harpoons, fishhooks and quivers. Female graves, which are in general poorer than the male examples, contained household artefacts, flint blades, awls, polishers, burins and scrapers, as well as perforated beaver incisors and snake effigy figures. One of the shaft graves contained six beaver mandibles. The grave goods included forty-two sculptured or ornamented objects. These were representations of elk, snakes and humans carved in stone, wood and bone (Fig. 13).

   After a multivariate analysis of the grave goods, O'Shea and Zvelebil (1984) made very important conclusions. They argued that the cemetery belonged to a large and stable population with a considerable internal status differentiation. The population was involved in an active regional exchange network, demonstrated by the wide variety of raw materials and exotic goods (for example, arrowheads and knives made of gray flint) and imported from far-away areas. A recently obtained series of radiocarbon dates placed the cemetery in a time-span ranging from 7700 to 7300 BP or 6500 to 6300 BC (Price and Jacobs 1990).

The anthropological analysis of skeletal remains published by Yakimov and Kharitonov (1979) still arouses considerable controversy. All researchers are in agreement that the major component of the assemblage should be classified as Europeoid. However, the assemblage also includes another element that is often viewed as showing Mongoloid affinities. Some see it as invoking the admixture of trans-Uralic mongoloids; others as a presence of a hyper-variable racially undifferentiated population morphologically midway between the classic Europeoid and Mongoloid types; and yet others view it as remnants of a so-called Cro-Magnoid type present in Russia from the times of the Upper Palaeolithic, and particularly well pronounced at such sites as Sungir and Kostenki 2.

Large Mesolithic cemeteries are also known in the southern part of the Russian Plain. A group of Mesolithic cemeteries, Voloshski-Vassil'evka, lies on the bank of the River Dniepr south of the town of Dnipropetrovsk (Ukraine). Voloshski cemetery, excavated by O.V. Bodyanski and V.N. Danilenko, contained nineteen burials, eighteen adult and one juvenile. In the western part (thirteen graves) the dead were buried in a contracted posture on their right sides, with their heads directed to the south. The eastern part (six graves) reveals no distinct pattern; the dead were buried in a contracted posture on their backs or stomachs, or in an extended posture on their backs. The burial inventory consisted of numerous flint implements, including backed bladlets, end-scrapers, burins, points and flakes. An arrowhead was found embedded in the cervical vertebra of one skeleton.

Vassil'evka 1 cemetery, excavated by A.D. Stolyar in 1953, contained twenty-four burials in an area of *c.* 20 sq. metres. Single burials prevail; only three pair burials were noted. All the dead were buried in a contracted posture on their sides with the head directed either to the west or to the east. In eleven graves, traces of red ochre were identified. Flint tools were found in three graves: backed bladlets, burins, fragments of points and microliths.

Vassil'evka 3 cemetery had already been disturbed when it was excavated by D.Ya. Telegin. Forty-five burials were identified in the excavated area; thirty-four graves contained burials in a contracted posture, either on the right (twenty-four cases) or on the left (nine cases) side, with the heads directed either to the south or to the west. A second group included three triple burials with the heads directed to the southwest, and one single burial. All the dead were interred in an extended posture (Fig. 14). The graves of the first group contained flint implements, which were mostly arrowheads. Two arrowheads were found inserted in the bones of the dead, one in a rib and another in a spine.

Based on the classical craniometric analysis at Voloshski-Vassil'evka

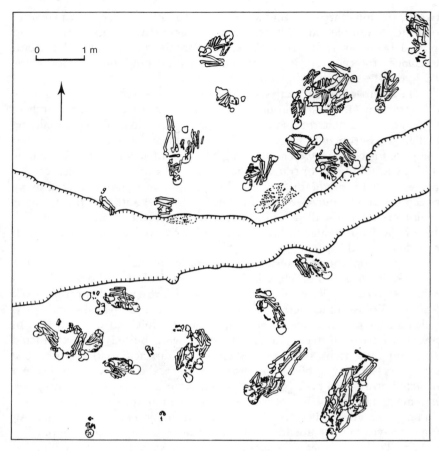

Fig. 14 Vassil'evka 3 cemetery.
   Source. D. Telegin, *Arheologija Ukrainskoi SSSR,* v. 1. Kiev: Naukova Dumka,
1985.

and other cemeteries, anthropologists (Gokhman 1966b; Konduktorova
1973) have been able to distinguish three anthropological types in the
Mesolithic population of Ukraine: (1) Mediterranean gracile narrow-faced
(Voloshski); (2) prognate narrow-faced (extended burials of Vassil'evka; and
(3) ortognate moderately broad-faced (Vassil'evka 1 and contracted burials
of Vassil'evka. Gokhman argued that the latter type was similar to one
established at Oleni Island, and viewed both as remains of the most ancient
population of the Russian Plain, containing substantial 'Cro-Magnoid'
elements. In contrast to that, Jacobs, based on his recent odontometric
studies, argued that Ukrainian Mesolithic teeth lack 'either typical western
(European) or eastern (Mongoloid) traits' (Jacobs 1993). He interpreted the

observed change in the chemical composition of the teeth, from Vassil'evka 3 to Vassil'evka 2, as resulting from a dietary shift – a significant reduction in the consumption of meat. Recently obtained radiocarbon dates for human bones from Vassil'evka 3 suggest an unexpectedly early age: three dates cluster around 10,000 BP (uncalibrated). The dates for another cemetery, Vassil'evka 2, show a younger age: 8020–7620 BP uncalibrated (Jacobs 1994). Hence, the Mesolithic cemeteries show not only the social complexity of Mesolithic groups, but also their immanent dynamism. Various Mesolithic groups were in constant movement; they were involved in unstable networks. The character and dimensions of these networks were subject to change, depending on the direction of the social and economic interaction and the availability of resources. On the other hand, it may be interesting that Jacobs, based mainly on the odontometric studies of Oleni Island, Mesolithic cemeteries in Ukraine and some Danish materials, concluded that the observed differences are due to the formation of comparatively closed mating networks or the so-called 'founder effect' (Jacobs 1992).

The fragmentation of Mesolithic space is manifested in archaeologically recognizable 'cultures'. One of these cultures, Kunda, is found in Estonia, Latvia and neighbouring regions of northwestern Russia. This culture takes its name from the Mesolithic site in northern Estonia, 110 km east of the city of Tallinn, in the coastal area of the Gulf of Finland. Mesolithic remains were found upon a hill (Lammasmägi) in the middle of the peat-bog and in the bog itself, in a layer of marl. The bones of elk formed 96 per cent of the faunal remains, the rest were formed by brown bear (1.5 per cent), wild pig (1 per cent), wild horse (0.5 per cent) and seal (1.5 per cent). The stone implements were made of flint and quartz, and included tanged arrowheads of Swiderian type, burins, scrapers, backed bladlets and microliths, while numerous bone and antler tools included a 'Lyngby'-type antler axe, fishhooks and picks. Radiocarbon dates obtained for the site suggest a calendar date of *c.* 7200–4900 BC.

The earliest site of the same culture, Pulli, is situated on the bank of the Pärnu river, in southwestern Estonia, in the stratified deposits of a lagoon of the Yoldia Sea. The fauna included elk, brown bear and beaver. A Kunda-type industry comprises tanged points and adzes. A specimen of wood from the cultural stratum was radiocarbon dated to 7659±120 BC uncalibrated (TA–245). The age of the overlaying peat deposits is 7370±75 BC uncalibrated (TA–175). Thus one may suggest a calendar date of *c.* 8000 BC.

The stratified site of Narva on the River Narova, on the border between Russia and Estonia, was originally located on the southern shore of an in-shore lagoon, 110 km east of Kunda. Faunal remains were dominated by elk (37–55 per cent) and also included red deer, wild pig, roe deer, brown bear and seal. Radiocarbon measurements of specimens of charcoal and wood suggest a calendar date of 6650–4900 BC. The Mesolithic site of Osa, in the depression of Lake Lubana in eastern Latvia, included the bones of wild pig (40.5 per cent) and elk (24.5 per cent). Radiocarbon dating of a specimen of wood from the cultural stratum suggests calendar dates of 6650–4900 BC. Sites attributed to the Kunda culture have also been found near the town of Luga (130 km south of St Petersburg) and near the town of Velizh in the upper stretches of the Western Dvina (Smolensk district, Russia).

Another cultural unit (the Neman) is located mainly in the area of present-day Lithuania and neighbouring regions of Belorussia. Yet another culture (the Upper Volga) is identifiable in central Russia. In all cases, these 'cultures' are distinguished based on the typology of several classes of stone and bone tools. Both the settlement pattern and their subsistence remain basically the same. It should be noted that Polish writers (notably, J. Kozłowski and S. Kozłowski 1979) argued that all Mesolithic cultures in the northern areas of the Russian Plain belonged to a large cultural entity, the 'Northern Technocomplex'. Its lithics included Swiderian and 'post-Swiderian' points, polished axes and retouched blades.

A slightly different picture emerges when one examines the Mesolithic sites in the southern areas of the Russian Plain. These sites, normally of a small size, are usually located on low terraces of rivers crossing the Pontic lowland. The character of the deposits suggest that they were short-lived, probably seasonal, camp sites. There are few exceptions. At least two large sites, Mirnoe and Beloless'ye, were found in the western part of the lowland, close to the Danube delta. One of the sites, Mirnoe (Stanko 1982) was particularly large. This site lies on the flood-plain of the small river Drakula, which at that time emptied directly into the Black Sea, the level of which was some 20 metres below its present position. Pollen analysis suggests that the river floor was forested; the forest consisted of pine, birch, hornbeam, oak and elm; feather-grass and forb steppe covered the watershed. Faunal remains were dominated by aurochs (nearly 50 per cent); other species included wild horse, wild ass, antelope-saiga and kulan (*Equus gmelini*). The latter species dominated the faunal assemblage of another Mesolithic site of the same area – Beloless'ye. The analysis of use-wears on several flint blades has led G.F. Korobkova, the Russian expert, to suggest that these tools were used for harvesting wild grasses. Although no distinct remains of houses were found, V.N. Stanko, the excavator of the site, noted several clusters of flints on the periphery of the living space. Several hearths and 'frying pits' were identified in the middle part. It was suggested that Mirnoe was a base camp, settled more or less permanently. A group of much smaller hunting camps was found in the surrounding area.

The lithic inventory of Mesolithic sites in this area often includes a considerable proportion of geometric microliths or 'geometrics' (Fig. 15a). These tools, which were worked into regular geometric shapes (triangles, rhombi, trapezes and crescents), were probably inserted into wooden or bone shafts forming composite projectile points. These started to appear in increasing numbers in the 'Epipalaeolithic' assemblages of the Near East at

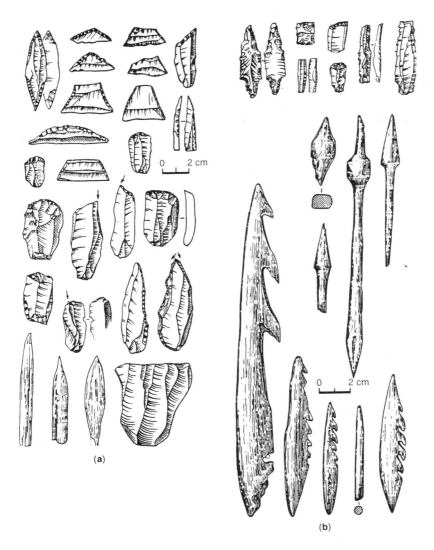

Fig. 15 Mesolithic tools. (**a**) – Southern Ukraine; (**b**) – Estonia (Kunda).
Source. L.V. Kol'tsov, *Mezolit SSSR*. Moscow: Nauka, 1989.

about 19,000 BP. The Mesolithic microlithic industries, often designated by the broad term 'Tardenoisian', were widely spread in some parts of western Europe and in the Mediterranean basin. A more detailed stylistic analysis shows that, in reality, a complicated mosaic of Mesolithic cultures is distinguishable there (Kozłowski and Kozłowski 1979). They include the 'Epi-Gravettian', 'Castelnovian' and some other traditions in a dynamic

59

interaction. Based mostly on the rate of geometrics, Ukrainian archaeologists have distinguished at least two major Mesolithic 'cultures' in the Pontic lowland and the Crimea: Grebenkian and Kukrekian (Telegin 1981). Geometrics, and notably trapezes, were prominent in the tool-kit of the former. In contrast, geometrics were almost absent in the inventories of the Kukrekian. This cultural tradition, identified in a number of cave sites in the Crimean mountains, as well as at the Pontic open-air sites, features the common occurrence of a particular type of instrument, the Kukrek point. Radiocarbon dates obtained for several Kukrekian sites (Kukrek, Igren' 8) show the uncalibrated age of 9000–8000 BP.

Summing up existing evidence, one might try to define the basic characteristics of the Mesolithic in the Russian Plain. First of all, the composition of the inventory clearly suggests a cultural continuity in relation to the preceding Late Palaeolithic groups, and the occurrence of numerous tanged points of Swiderian and 'post-Swiderian' types in the Mesolithic industries of the Baltic area and in central Russia is a clear indication of this. Mesolithic industries in the southern part of the Plain contain numerous tool-types inherited from the Late Palaeolithic traditions in the same area. Secondly, the Mesolithic featured a much fuller exploitation of a wider scope of food resources. The hunting strategies became much more diversified, including a broad range of terrestrial mammals. The exploitation of the estuarine and lacustrine resources is a characteristic innovation of the Mesolithic. Yet another feature was an increasing reliance on the harvesting of edible food, including molluscs from the in-shore lagoons and river floods and the gathering of water chestnuts that were rich in protein. There is evidence for data suggesting the collection of edible plants in the Mesolithic sites of the Pontic area. Recently, Jacobs, based on the chemical composition of bones and several characteristics of postcranial skeletons (an increased postcranial robustness) of the Ukrainian Mesolithic, suggested a significant reduction in the consumption of meat and, correspondingly, a rise in the consumption of plant food (Jacobs 1993: 321–2).

Thirdly, although our data indicate no major population displacements occurring during the course of the Mesolithic, there are some indirect indications, based primarily on anthropological records, for some influx from outside. If these movements really took place, they were of a minor scale, with new populations being comparatively rapidly absorbed in the old one, and, consequently, acquiring the mode of life and basic cultural characteristics of the majority group.

Finally, the Mesolithic space was split up into a number of regional groupings perceived as 'archaeological cultures' (Fig. 16). These groupings were of ephemeral character and probably consisted of several social groups forming mating networks with a large degree of closure, which included the regular exploitation of the resources of a distinct ecological area, as well as a cultural, economic and social interaction (Jacobs 1992). Seen as a whole, the Mesolithic in the Russian Plain does not show any major difference in

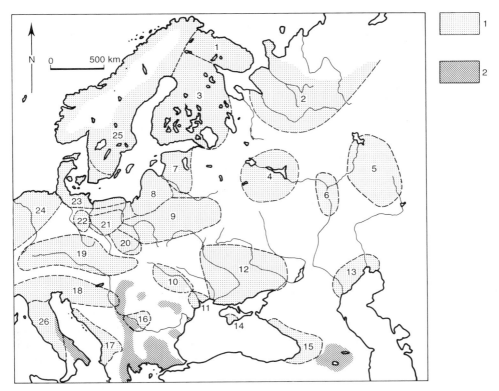

Fig. 16   Mesolithic cultural groupings in eastern and central Europe.
    Key. 1 – Hunter-gatherers; 2 – Early farmers
Cultural groups: 1 – Kola peninsular; 2 – North-eastern Russian; 3 – Suomusjärvi;
4 – Upper Volga; 5 – Cisuralian; 6 – Volga-Kama; 7 – Kunda; 8 – Neman; 9 – Upper
Dniepr/Janislawice; 10 – Dniestrian; 11 – Grebenikian; 12 – Central Ukrainian; 13 –
North Caspian; 14 – Crimean; 15 – West Georgian; 16 – Lepenski Vir;
17 – Castelnovian; 18 – Epigravettian/Sauveterrian; 19 – Beuronian; 20 – Pienki;
21 – Chojnice; 22 – Jünsdorf; 23 – Kongemose; 24 – North-western groups; 25 –
Scandinavian groups; 26 – Apennine groups.

regional affiliation in comparison to the epoch of Upper Palaeolithic. Hence,
if one accepts the previously advanced hypothesis, that Upper Palaeolithic
groups in the Russian Plain spoke dialects of the Proto-Uralic language, this
remains valid also for the Mesolithic.

   Notable changes in the overall economic, cultural and social situation
in the Russian Plain became apparent only with the beginning of the
Climatic Optimum. At that time, the implications of agricultural revolution,
which had heralded the beginning of the Holocene in the Fertile Crescent of
the Near East, reached the doorstep of Europe. Early agricultural settlements

61

appeared in the intermontane depressions of the Balkans, areas of open oak forests with sufficient rainfall and fertile soils. Agriculture in Europe appeared in a developed form with a wide range of domesticated cereals (emmer, einkorn wheats and six-row emmer) and animals (cattle, sheep, goat and pig). The radiocarbon measurements show the age of the early agricultural sites in the Balkans as being *c*. 8200–8000 BP uncalibrated.

Early Neolithic .

Large-scale agricultural 'neolithization' of southeast Europe occurred during the time-span 7000–5500 BC. At that time, agricultural settlements spread into the intermontane depressions of Bulgaria, the Lower and Middle Danubian lowlands and the Moldavian highlands. Permanent settlements, which formed 'tells' or settlement mounds, have emerged in some intermontane valleys (for example, the valley of Maritsa in Bulgaria) on light fertile soils. Archaeologically, this stage corresponded to the cultures of Starčevo-Körös-Criş which had several common elements.

In some areas farming communities lived side-by-side with groups of hunter-gatherers. Lepenski Vir and several related sites in the area of Iron Gates in the Danube valley provide an outstanding example of such coexistence. In that area a group of sedentary foragers coexisted over a considerable period of time with the Starčevo-type farmers, maintaining their economic strategies and cultural identity (Chapman 1993).

Yet another example of the farming-foraging interaction may be found in the sites of the so-called Bug-Dniestian culture on the Rivers Dniestr and Southern Bug in Moldavia and Ukraine, and principally investigated by V.N. Danilenko and V.I. Markevich. A full cultural sequence was established at a group of sites near the town of Soroca (Soroki) situated on the narrow flood-plain of the River Dniestr in Moldavia. The lower levels (3 and 2) of Soroki 1, which have yielded no pottery, have been radiocarbon dated to calendar dates of *c*. 6500 and *c*. 6400 BC respectively. These levels contained the remains of two oval-shaped semi-subterranean dwellings. The stone inventory of Mesolithic character included end-scrapers, trapezes, triangles and retouched blades. The identified bones belonged very largely (80–90 per cent) to wild animals: roe deer and red deer were the most common. A few bones of domesticated animals were found, including pig and cattle. Fragments of fish bones were numerous, and included roach, pike, sturgeon and catfish. The deposits contained several hundred shells of molluscs, among which *Unio crassus* was the most common species. Pottery-bearing levels at the sites of Soroki 2 and Soroki 5 have been radiocarbon dated, suggesting calendar dates of 5800–5500 BC. The ratio of domesticates among the faunal remains increased, reaching in several cases 50 per cent (pig, cattle); wild animals were still largely roe deer and red deer.

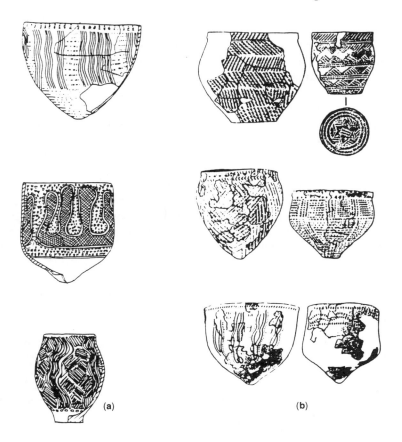

Fig. 17 Bug-Dniestian (**a**) and Dniepr-Donetsian (**b**) ceramics.
Source. P. Dolukhanov & V. Timofeyev, *Études et recherches archéologiques de l'Université de Liège,* Liège, 1993.

The number of wild animals represented in the faunal analysis was much greater (over 90 per cent) at the sites on the Southern Bug. Impressions of three varieties of wheat – emmer, einkorn and spelt – were identified on the potsherds. Oval semi-subterranean dwellings were constructed at several sites. The lithic industry retained a Mesolithic character. Coarse pottery, made with an admixture of sand, crushed shells or organic matter, was dominated by spherical and biconical bowls decorated by rows of wavy lines, shell impressions and finger-nail impressions (Fig. 17a). These ceramics reveal similarities with the 'barbotine' type pottery of the Balkan Early Neolithic. At the sites of Soroki 5 and Baz'kov Island (the Southern Bug) fragments of imported Linear Pottery have been found.

V.N. Danilenko (1969) and V.I. Markevich (1974) view the

Bug-Dniestrian sites as reflecting a gradual transition from foraging to agriculture. The main arguments for this assumption are based on the rare impressions of cereals on the potsherds, the occurrence of blades with sickle-gloss, hoe-like implements made of red-deer antler, and querns, and a gradual increase of the rate of domesticates in the faunal remains from the earlier to the later phase.

I have argued that the topographic situation of Soroki and other Bug-Dniestrian sites makes effective agriculture very unlikely (Dolukhanov 1979). These sites were located on a narrow stony flood-plain, covered with meadow soils poor in humus. The nearest arable land lies 5 km away, separated from the settlement by steep and almost impassable slopes. Thin archaeological deposits and the lack of permanent dwelling structures suggest that the sites were occupied seasonally by small groups of foragers; the occurrence of domesticates may be explained by intensive cultural and economic contacts with nearby communities of farmers. It seems likely that the grain, pigs and cattle (which, in number, never exceeded eight individuals) were procured in exchange for the products of hunting and food-gathering. The blades with sickle-gloss, the querns and the hoe-like implements could all have been used for harvesting and processing wild plants. The occurrence of cultural contacts with farmers is further substantiated by the resemblance between the pottery, as well as by the direct import of Linear Pottery ceramics in the later stages. The Bug-Dniestrian sites may thus be viewed as belonging to the 'availability phase' of the proto-Neolithic, as described by Zvelebil and Dolukhanov (1991).

At a slightly later date, a similar cultural entity, the Dniepr-Donetsian, spread in an area further to the north. Dwelling sites and cemeteries belonging to this tradition are found mainly in the basins of the Rivers Dniepr and Severski Donets (in Ukraine and northern Belorussia. According to the available radiocarbon dates, the Dniepr-Donetsian culture existed between *c.* 5000 and 3000 BC. The culture, first identified in 1927–33, was intensely studied in the 1950s and 1960s by D. Ya. Telegin (1968).

Dniepr-Donetsian sites are usually located on flood-plains. Only in rare cases could the remains of small oval-shaped, semi-subterranean dwellings be identified within a living space. The economy was based predominantly on hunting (aurochs, red deer, wild boar, elk), fishing and food-collecting. Quite rarely, and only at the later sites, were bones of domesticated animals (cattle, pig, sheep, goat) found. An impression of barley (*Hordeum sativum*) was identified in a single case: on a potsherd at the site of Vita Litovskaya near Kiev. The stone inventory included geometric microliths of Mesolithic type, bifacially retouched arrowheads and spearheads, and large polished axes.

The earliest stage of this culture (often viewed as an independent cultural unit) is represented at the Strumel-Gastyatin group of sites near Kiev. These sites contained the fragments of large conical vessels ornamented by rows of comb impressions. The following types of ceramic are typical of the Dniepr-Donetsian culture: (1) egg-shaped wide-mouthed pots with pointed base and a straight or slightly flaring rim; (2) wide-mouthed pots with a pointed base and a straight rim; (3) spherical bowls with a pointed bottom, a short cylindrical neck and a straight or out-bent rim; (4) hemispherical bowls with a flat bottom and a straight rim (Fig. 17b). The ornamental patterns consist of rows of comb impressions, incised lines, geometric patterns (triangles, rhombi, rectangles) formed using closely set strokes. These patterns are generally similar to those of the Bug-Dniestr ceramics, while the practice of using strokes to make geometric patterns is similar to the stroke-ornamented ware of the Funnel Beaker tradition in central Europe.

The Dniepr-Donetsian tradition includes several large cemeteries which feature at least two types of burial rite. Burials belonging to an earlier stage were made in deep oval ditches. Later burials were made in rectangular graves filled in with earth mixed with red ochre. The richer graves of the latter type contained prestigious ornaments in copper, and gold and stone mace-heads. The cemeteries of Yasinovatski, Osipovski and Nikol'ski have been radiocarbon dated, and in calendar years date to between 5200 and 4500 calibrated BC.

The sites of the Dniepr-Donetsian culture largely coexisted with settlements belonging to yet another cultural entity – the Cucuteni-Tripolye. The spread of these settlements marked the most dramatic change in the subsistence of prehistoric groups of the south of the Russian Plain: the spread of the first agricultural economy.

The culture was named after the type sites of Cucuteni (Department of Jaşi, Romania) and Tripolye (Ukraine), investigated by Romanian and Russian scholars respectively. Although both Cucuteni and Tripolye make up a single cultural entity, two separate chronologies, based upon pottery styles and other elements of culture, have been developed independently (these are correlated in Table 1). At its developed stage (Tripolye B) the cultural assemblage included painted pottery (vessels painted red, black and white) with the spiral and its derivative being the main decorative motifs. Several sites have yielded evidence for the use of up-draught kilns and specialized manufactories – large ground-floor workshops with drying lofts above. Anthropomorphic and zoomorphic clay figurines form yet another important element of the culture, female figurines being particularly common.

The culture was first recognized by V.V. Chvoika (Khvoika), the Ukrainian archaeologist of Czech origin, in the 1890s, after the excavation of sites in the Middle Dniepr area, including the site of Tripolye (Tripil'ye), now within Greater Kiev. At about the same time the first excavations of Cucuteni sites were conducted in Romania by N. Belduceanu, Gr. Butureanu, D. Butculescu and H. Schmidt. A large number of important Tripolye sites were excavated by T.S. Passek and by S.N. Bibikov between the 1930s and the 1960s. Passek was the first to suggest the conventional chronological division of Tripolye which comprises three stages: early (A), middle (B) and late (C) with subdivisions. An independent chronological division was suggested for the Cucuteni sites by the Romanian archaeologists (Vl. Dumitrescu, M. Petrescu-Dîmboviţa and others). A unified chronological scheme may be suggested on the basis of available radiocarbon measurements (see Table 1).

Table 1 Chronologies for the Cucuteni-Tripolye culture

Age C-14 BP uncalibrated	Age C-14 BP calibrated	Ukraine, Moldavia	Romania
6000	5250		Precucuteni I
6000	4750	Tripolye A1	Precucuteni II
5700	4500	Tripolye AII	Precucuteni III
5000	4370	Tripolye BI	Cucuteni A 1–3
5200	4250	Tripolye BII	Cucuteni A–B 1–2
5000	3750	Tripolye CI	Cucuteni B 1–3
4500	3250	Tripolye CII	Horodiştia
4200	2750	Tr.CII–ũII	Floreşti I

Early Tripolye sites tend to be located on low terraces of the rivers Prut, Dniestr and Southern Bug (and their tributaries). The settlements, rather small in size, included large plaster platforms (*ploshchadka*) which are now recognized as foundations of rectangular houses. Each house was flanked by a storage pit. At the site of Luka-Vrublevetskaya, the dwellings were of a semi-subterranean type and formed a row (over 200 metres long) along the bank of the Dniestr. A child burial was found under the hearth of one of the dwellings of this site; another dwelling included a bull's skull. Ceramics included bowls, beakers, biconical and other vessels with covers; anthropomorphic vessels also occurred, as did female figurines made of clay paste to which grains of wheat were added (Fig. 18). The lithic inventory maintained a Mesolithic character, and wild animals made up 50 per cent of the total faunal remains.

Towards the end of the Early Tripolye stage, evidence for metallurgy and metal-working begins to emerge. Particularly impressive metal tools were found in a hoard near Karbuna, in Moldavia. This hoard was secreted in an anthropomorphic vessel, placed in a storage pit amidst the dwellings. The vessel contained 852 artefacts of which 444 were manufactured in copper. These were: spiral bracelets, cylindrical beads, plates of various form and shape (including anthropomorphic examples), as well as copper celts of various styles. As the spectral analysis shows (Chernykh 1992), the early Tripolian metal implements, by their chemical composition, were remarkably similar to those from the northern Balkans. In most cases they were manufactured from a 'pure' copper. As for the objects from the Karbuna hoard, they were hammered from copper with significant levels of

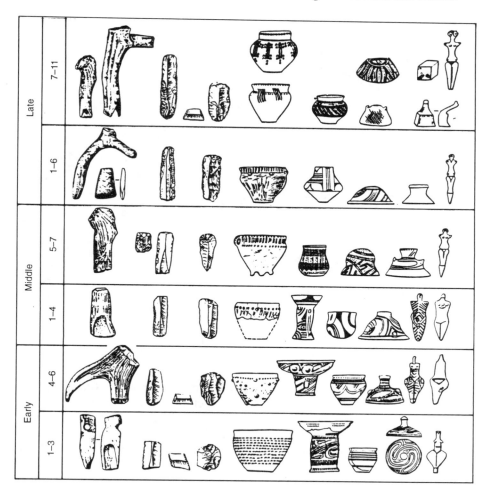

Fig. 18 Tripolian antler and stone implements, ceramics and figurines.
Source. V.M. Masson & N.Ya. Merpert, *Eneolit SSSR*. Moscow: Nauka, 1989.

'impurities', such as lead, bismuth and arsenic. Based on them, Chernykh suggests that these implements were smelted from the ore produced at the Ali Bunar copper mine in northern Bulgaria (Chernykh 1992: 39)

In the Middle Tripolye stage, the culture expanded east of the Dniestr, penetrating to the Southern Bug catchment and reaching the Dniepr. Copper-working became more developed, the implements included various ornaments and at least two types of celt. The settlements located either on flood-plains or on the promontories of higher terraces increased in size, in several cases reaching an area of 10–40 hectares. In the Middle Dniepr area,

Fig. 19 Kolomiishchina settlement (reconstruction).
Source. V.M. Masson & N.Ya. Merpert, *Eneolit SSSR*. Moscow: Nauka, 1989.

the houses tended to form circles, and often numbered 30–40; the largest rectangular houses excavated at Kolomiishchina reached the size of 30 by 6–7 metres (Fig. 19). West of the Dniestr, two-storied dwellings appeared.

Furnaces were regularly used for firing pottery. The technique of painting the pottery before firing also became more common. Two large hoards containing metal implements (axes and ornaments) have been found in western Ukraine (Gorodnicy II near Ivano-Frankovsk and Ryngach near Chernovtsy). The chemical composition of metal has changed: copper-silver alloys came into use by the end of the Middle Tripolye. Female figurines were still the dominant form of sculpture, but the number of male representations increased.

The Middle Tripolye economy developed a predominantly agricultural character. Hulled wheats (emmer, einkorn and spelt) and hulled barley were the dominant crops. Garden pea and vetch were the most common pulses. The bones of domesticates – cattle, sheep/goat and pig, in that order of importance – constituted more than 80 per cent of the total faunal remains.

Scholars still argue about the mechanism of the spread of a farming economy. Two major schools of thought are distinguishable. The first theory which clearly stems from a concept put forward by Gustav Kossina, the German archaeologist, at the turn of the century links the dispersal of agriculture with a large-scale migration of a new 'folk'. Strangely enough,

Kossina's views, which had a conspicuous nationalistic bias, were largely shared by V. Gordon Childe, the prominent British-Australian, Marxist-oriented prehistorian. Childe argued that the 'light always came from the East' (*Ex Orientum Lux*) (1952). Agriculture originated in the Near East and was automatically adopted by food-collectors, provided they were 'culturally' ready and 'archaeological circumstances were appropriate'. More recently, the concepts of Kossina and Childe were revived in the form of a 'wave of advance' theory. According to this, the spread of a farming economy resulted from migrations which were triggered by an 'intrinsic' increase of population following the adoption of food-production (Ammerman and Cavalli-Sforza 1973). Support for the migration hypothesis has also come from a different corner. Based on the sampling of 'genetic systems', which included red cell antigens, plasma protein, enzymes, etc., of modern populations from different areas of the Near East and Europe, the conclusion was drawn that these systems show a significant agreement with the hypothesis of 'demic expansion' following the adoption of agriculture (Sokal, Oden and Wilson 1991). I find it hard to agree that the distribution of genetic systems among the modern ethnic groups can be of any relevance for the process of 'demic expansion' which occurred 10,000–5000 years ago. Historically, identifiable large displacements of population, particularly in the first millennia BC/AD, would have completely deformed the genetic map of Europe.

In contrast to the migratory hypotheses, another school of thought tends to attach a much greater weight to the impact of local Mesolithic groups in the process of transition to a farming economy. The 'autochtonous' model does not completely rule out migrations, they being the only way by which domestic plants and animals, as well as technological knowledge, could reach people in new territories. Yet a much greater importance is attached to the establishment of a new cultural and economic network which increasingly incorporated the groups of foragers into a new pattern.

This controversy is particularly obvious in debates revolving around the origins of the Tripolye. Comşa (1987) and Zbenovich (1989) argued that this cultural phenomenon resulted mainly from the eastbound displacement of the groups of 'Boian,' the Neolithic 'culture' which originally spread in southern Romania, and later extended into Transylvania and Moldavia after their fusion with groups producing Linear Pottery. Other scholars (notably Passek, Danilenko and Markevich) repeatedly stressed the local origin of Tripolye; the Bugo-Dniestrian culture, in particular, was often mentioned as its source because of the similarities in the geographical location (often in the same river valleys) and the likeness of stone inventories. The fact remains that the Tripolye appeared in the southwestern part of the Russian Plain as a 'cultural package' in a ready-made form. Its various cultural manifestations, particularly obvious in the types of settlement and in the art (for example, 'portable' figurines and several ornamental patterns on pottery), show close similarities with the agricultural settlements of southeast Europe and the Middle East.

It is highly significant that the Tripolye was not the only food-producing culture in that area. Another culture, the Gumelniţa, was in existence at about the same time in the Low Danube lowland, Dobruja (the region on the western Black Sea coast, south of the Danube delta), and penetrated into the Danube-Dniestr interfluve. The economy of the Gumelniţa sites was based on productive agriculture and stock-breeding and on independently developing metallurgy.

Yet another cultural tradition, Sredni Stog, was in existence at the same time in the areas east of the main Tripolye regions. The sites belonging to this tradition are found mostly in the forest-steppic interfluve between the Dniepr and the Don rivers. Unfortified settlements were located on the low terraces of rivers which were intensely forested at that time. The most outstanding feature of the Sredni Stog settlements was that their economy included horse-breeding as an important component. In some cases (Dereivka, Molyukov Bogor, Alexandria) horse bones made up over 50 per cent of the total faunal assemblage.

The situation at Dereivka is typical (Telegin 1986). This site, with a total area of *c.* 3000 sq. metres, is situated on a low terrace of the River Omelnik, a tributary of the Dniepr. The single cultural layer included at least three subterranean dwelling structures and a ritual emplacement comprising a horse skull, a foot and foreparts of two dogs. The faunal assemblage of the site included the remains of at least fifty-two horses. The site was classified by Telegin to the middle stage of the Sredni Stog sequence. Four radiocarbon measurements date it to a time-span between 3380 and 4570 BC (calibrated). Several cemeteries were found at Dereivka and at other Sredni Stog sites; the ochre-covered dead were placed on their backs in a contracted posture in oval-shaped flat graves. In several cases (Yama near Donetsk and Koisug on the Lower Don) burial mounds were erected on top of Sredni Stog burials.

Both Ukrainian and western scholars (Telegin 1973, 1986; Anthony 1986), repeatedly argued that the Sredni Stog sites yielded the earliest evidence for the domestication of the horse, yet there are data suggesting that the horse was initially domesticated in areas further to the east, in the semi-deserts of Central Asia. One of the most apparent examples of this kind is the site of Batai in northern Kazakhstan, recently excavated by V.F. Zaibert (1993). This site provides indisputable evidence for a prolonged sedentism: no less than 200 circular dwellings were uncovered in a living area of 7000 sq metres. Horse bones made up 99.9 per cent of the total faunal remains. The earliest radiocarbon dates obtained from samples of horse bone show an age of 4340±160 BP (uncalibrated).

If one examines the available evidence, one may suggest the following scenario for the spread of an agricultural economy in the southern areas of the Russian Plain. Starting with the beginning of the Climatic Optimum, which considerably modified the ecological and the social environment of the entire area, local groups of foragers were increasingly involved in a socio-economic network of early farmers that had surfaced by that time in the entire area of southeastern Europe and the Near East. This included a limited displacement of population and, what was much more important, the influx of cultural information. The acceptance of agriculture by local groups was facilitated by a long tradition of experiments with the gathering and processing of edible plants, attestable at a number of Mesolithic sites.

The establishment of the first farming settlements and the inclusion of the area into the socio-economic network of early farming opened this area to a powerful influx of information and energy from the entire early agricultural world. It is in these conditions that the cultural packages of Tripolye and Sredni Stog became instituted. Another important observation is that the network of early farming became firmly established only in the geographical areas sufficiently rich in agricultural resources, water resources being particularly important. The steppic areas in the east, where water was scarce, saw the endowment of a different social and economic pattern, primarily based on stock-breeding. In several cases horse-breeding became prominent. Hence, the dry areas in the southeast of the Russian Plain became increasingly open to the impulses emanating from the semi-deserts of Central Asia.

Now let us have a look at the areas situated to the north. As we remember, in the conditions of the Climatic Optimum, mixed broad-leaved forests, sufficiently rich in biomass, became established there. Archaeologists, based on the analysis of the styles of various classes of artefact, have identified several cultural units in these densely forested areas of the Russian Plain.

One of these units is known as 'Narva'. Its name derives from that of the three sites, Narva-Riigiküla 1, 2 and 3, situated in the lower stretches of the Narova river, on the border between Estonia and Russia. Discovered and excavated by N.N. Gurina between the 1950s and the 1980s, the sites lay on a ridge of sand dunes and included the remains of oval-shaped semi-subterranean dwellings (6–7 metres in diameter). The faunal remains – practically identical at all three sites – included elk (which predominates), wild boar, aurochs, red deer, brown bear, seals, as well as waterfowl (mainly ducks and swans). The bones of a medium-sized whale were found at one of the sites. Among the numerous fish remains, pike, perch, salmon and catfish were the most common. The lithic inventory consisted of numerous arrow- and spearheads, large end-scrapers, axes and adzes. The prolific bone and antler industry included arrow- and spearheads, harpoons, axes, adzes, 'hoe-like' tools and fishhooks. The so-called Narva-type pottery included pots with either rounded or pointed bases, with rims either straight or slightly cut inside. Pots were decorated with comb impressions, notches, strokes, and small pits which formed horizontal rows and zigzag patterns.

Later, a group of Narva-related sites was discovered around Lake

Lubana in eastern Latvia. The Neolithic site of Osa was located in the vicinity of a Mesolithic site of the same name, on a lower terrace of the lake. This site contained typical Narva pottery and tools, and the faunal remains included wild boar, elk, marten, brown bear, aurochs, red deer, wild horse, beaver, badger, otter and dog. The site has been radiocarbon dated to *c.* 5500–4500 BC in calendar years.

A later variety of the Narva culture was found at a number of sites in Lithuania. An important group of sites has been discovered in the coastal peat-bog of Pajuris near the village of Šventoji in western Lithuania. The cultural assemblage, belonging to the later Narva tradition, has been identified at the earlier group sites, radiocarbon dated to the calendar years 3500–2600 BC.

Among other early pottery 'cultures' one should especially mention that of the Upper Volga. The sites belonging to this culture are located in the Upper Volga catchment of central Russia (Yaroslavl, Ivanovo and Tver districts). This culture was identified and studied by D.A. Krainov and N.A. Khotinsky in the 1970s. The main feature of the Upper Volga culture is the particular style of its ceramics: wide-mouthed vessels with straight walls and pointed or rounded bottom. The ornamentation consists of strokes, stamp impressions and incised lines which form horizontal and diagonal lines, as well as simple geometric motifs (triangles, rhombi and intersecting lines). The stone inventory is of Mesolithic character: burins, end-scrapers, arrowheads of post-Swiderian type, and knives made from blades. Furthermore, all faunal remains found at Upper Volga sites belonged to wild animals.

Many of these sites were discovered in peat-bogs. For instance, a large peat-bog of Ivanovskoye, northeast of Moscow, contained the remains of eight campsites, one of the stratified sites, Ivanovskoye 3, being located on an island in the western part of a huge peat-bog. An impressive series of radiocarbon dates suggests that the Upper Volga stratum was deposited between 5500 and 4800 BC (calendar years).

Four sites were discovered in another peat-bog in the same area, Yazykovo. Deposits of the Upper Volga culture at the site of Yazykovo 1 were found in a clear stratigraphic setting below the stratum containing a different kind of pottery, decorated by pit-and-comb ornament. The radiocarbon dating of the Upper Volga layer at this site suggests an age of *c.* 5200 BC in calendar years.

Another cultural unit almost exactly matches into the historical area of Finland. This culture, which is usually referred to as 'Sperrings', was first identified by Finnish archaeologists in the coastal area of the Gulf of Finland (Europaeus-Äyräpää 1930). Later, intensive studies by the Russian archaeologists (Gurina 1961; Pankrushev 1978) have sufficiently enlarged its area, which now covers the entire territory of Finland, the archipelago of Åland, and large areas of the St Petersburg district and Russian Karelia. The sites are usually located on raised beaches of the sea and inner lakes. It was reasonably suggested that these sites were originally located in the immediate vicinity of a beach. Based on this assumption, Finnish scholars have suggested a detailed chronology of Stone Age sites using a so-called gradient/time curve, where the isostatic uplifting and tilting of the shorelines are seen as function of time (Siiriäinen 1973, 1982). Based on this system of dating, the age of Sperrings sites was estimated as 6200–5200 BP uncalibrated.

As in all other similar cases, the Sperrings sites featured a particular style of pottery. These were conic vessels; the ornamentation was restricted to the upper part and consisted of impressions of particular types of stamp combined with incised lines. There were also several peculiar types of stone and bone tool, consistent with this culture, for example, a so-called 'Karelian-type hoe'. The economy of the Sperrings groups was entirely based on hunting, fishing and food-collecting. Siiriäinen (1980) noted a particular role of seal hunting in the economy of the sites along the Gulf of Finland.

Yet another cultural group, the Volga-Kama, was identified in the Middle Volga catchment, including the rivers Volga, Kama and their tributaries (Khalikov 1969). The pottery assemblage consisted of conic or round-bottomed vessels decorated by the impressions of stamps and incised lines, often forming simple geometric patterns. The stone implements were of Mesolithic character. The economy was also of a foraging type, elk being dominant in animal remains. Large numbers of fish bones (pike, carp, sterlet, sturgeon) indicated the importance of fishing. No reliable radiocarbon dates are available. Yet, relying on the typological evidence, one may reasonably suggest that all four cultural units discussed above (Narva, Upper Volga, Sperrings and Volga-Kama) were *grosso motto* contemporaneous (Fig. 20).

Now let us try to define the common elements of all these 'pottery-bearing' cultures. First of all, based on the available evidence, one may note that all of them have emerged at about the same time: 6200–6000 BP. As we remember, this time-span corresponded to a relative cooling in the course of the Climatic Optimum, denoted as Atlantic-2. For the present time, I would not suggest any plausible explanation for that; all I would say is that this was hardly coincidental. The economies of all four cultures were solidly based on foraging strategies. There is no indication of any kind of food production. The number of sites has increased by comparison with 'aceramic' Mesolithic. This may be seen as a clear indication of population growth resulting from an increased effectiveness of foraging strategies. This, in its turn, may be due to a general increase of the forest biomass which is clearly identifiable during the Climatic Optimum.

Now let us turn to the analysis of archaeological materials. The most important observation, which is particularly obvious in the character of lithic and bone implements, is the cultural continuity in relation to the preceding Mesolithic. One may hardly doubt that all ceramic cultures in the forested area developed locally, without any major influx of population from outside. On the other hand, the analysis of the ceramic materials

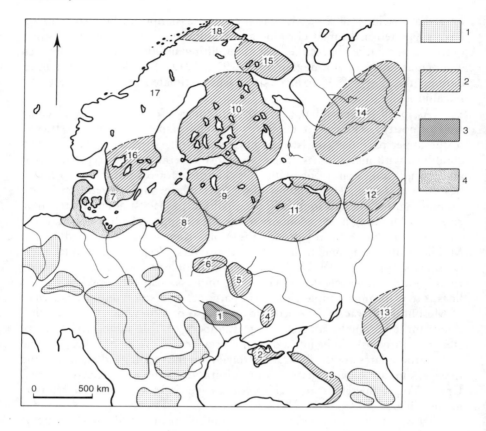

Fig. 20 Eastern Europe in the Early Neolithic.
   Key. 1 – Agricultural groups; 2 – Hunter-gatherers; 3 – Hunter-gatherers
with elements of agriculture; 4 – 'Intensive' hunter-gatherers.
Cultural groupings: 1 – Bug-Dniestrian; 2 – Crimean; 3 – West Caucasian; 4 – Sura-
Dnieprian; 5 – Early Dniepr-Donetsian; 6 – Polessian; 7 – Ertebølle; 8 – Nemanian;
9 – Narvian; 10 – Sperrings; 11 – Upper Volga; 12 – Volga-Kama; 13 – North
Caspian; 14 – Northeastern Russian; 15 – Kola peninsular; 16 – Linhult; 17 – Fosna;
18 – Komsa.

suggests much more intense contacts with the outside world. Earlier, when
discussing the predominantly foraging ceramic cultures in the south
(Bugo-Dniestrian and Dniepr-Donetsian), we could notice clear indications
of their contacts with farming communities. These contacts were particularly
identifiable in the ornamentation of pottery: the stamps and incised lines
being imitation imprints of shell-rims on the 'impressed' pottery. If we
scrutinize the pottery assemblage of the Narva sites, we may easily find a
similar ornamental pattern. Hence I make an important conclusion: the
Bugo-Dniestrian, Dniepr-Donetsian and Narva 'cultures' correspond to

groups of foragers who were involved in some kind of cultural exchange with early farming communities of southeast and central Europe.

Now, once again, we may touch upon a crucial problem – namely, what language did these peoples speak? To do so, it is necessary to take several steps back and to return to the initial farmers of the Fertile Crescent. Quite recently, several scholars independently advanced a highly promising hypothesis suggesting that the first farmers of the Near East spoke an early form of the Indo-European language. This suggestion was made by Colin Renfrew (1987) and was largely based on archaeological evidence. Independently, two scholars from the former Soviet Union, Gamkrelidze and Ivanov (1984) came up with a similar suggestion using linguistic arguments. These arguments included a new system of phonological correspondence. They identified the oldest group which included Anatolian languages (Hittite, Luwian, Palaic and other extinct languages of Asia Minor) together with Armenian and Germanic. They also observed similarities between the proto-Indo-European, Proto-Semitic and Caucasian languages. No less important was a semantic analysis of the common proto-Indo-European vocabulary, which suggests that the proto-Indo-European language was spoken by a social group (or groups) at an early stage of the agricultural revolution; the group (or groups) lived in mountainous country with access to the sea. This picture is essentially consistent with the landscape and the subsistence of early farming groups in the area of the Fertile Crescent.

Both Renfrew and Gamkrelidze and Ivanov argued that the dispersal of the Indo-European languages into both Europe and Asia resulted from the spread of agriculture by way of migrations. Accepting the bulk of their arguments, I suggest that the proto-Indo-European was a kind of a *lingua franca* of several social groups involved in the agricultural revolution (Dolukhanov 1994). The spread of both agriculture and the Indo-European language resulted from the establishment of a new social and cultural network which included the transfer of matter and information. If one accepts this theory, a natural conclusion is that the establishment of an agricultural network in southeast Europe automatically meant the penetration of the proto-Indo-European language into that area. Since the communities responsible for both the Bugo-Dniestrian and Dniepr-Donetsian cultures were actively involved in this network, together with early Balkan farmers, one may equally suggest that all these communities became familiar with Indo-European speech. If one moves further north, one encounters the Narva foragers whose material culture is equally indicative of contacts with the groups in the south. Hence, yet another suggestion arises: the spread of Narva pottery is the earliest evidence for the penetration of proto-Indo-European speech into the forested areas of the northern Russian Plain. I repeat that this has mainly resulted from the acculturation, that is the entanglement, of local groups into an expanding socio-cultural exchange network and involved only a limited displacement of population.

If one examines material remains of the other three early pottery 'cultures' of the forested Russian Plain, one can easily find numerous common elements. P.N. Tretyakov (1966) was the first to note some affinities between the Sperrings and Upper Volga pottery (the latter term was not in use at that time). V.P. Tretyakov, on the other hand, noted similarities between the Sperrings and Volga-Kama pottery. In all three cases the stone and bone inventory retains the Mesolithic character, clearly speaking for their local origin. Based on this evidence, I made a suggestion that both Late Palaeolithic and Mesolithic groups in that area spoke dialects of the Proto-Uralic language. As we shall see later on, the Sperrings assemblages, through several later intermediaries, may be directly linked to ethnographically identifiable Finnish antiquities. One may add that the area of Sperrings more or less exactly corresponds to the area comparatively recently occupied by Finnish-speaking peoples. There are also several arguments in the field of physical anthropology which seem to support this suggestion. I will discuss these later. All this makes valid a suggestion that the block of cultures, consisting of the Sperrings, Upper Volga and Volga-Kama, correspond to Finnish-speaking groups.

Middle Neolithic

At a later time there occurred a massive spread of Finnish-speaking groups across the Russian Plain. This is archaeologically attested to by the proliferation of a so-called 'pit-and-comb' pottery. This style of pottery, particularly characteristic of 'Middle Neolithic' sites in the East European Plain, consisted of conic-bottomed vessels of various sizes decorated with

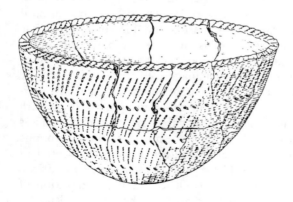

Fig. 21 Pit-and-comb pottery.
   Source. P. Dolukhanov & V. Timofeyev, *Etudes et recherches archéologiques de l'Université de Liège,* Liège, 1993.

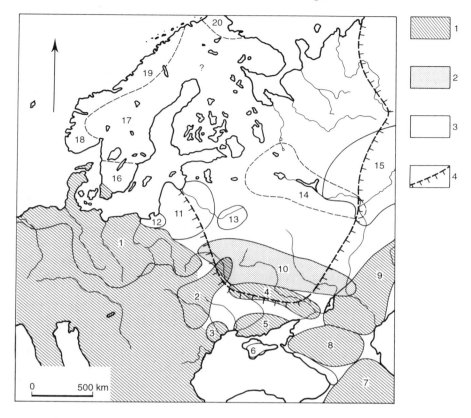

Fig. 22 Eastern Europe in the Middle Neolithic.
    Key. 1 – Agricultural and stock-breeding groups; 2 – Hunter-gatherers with elements of agriculture; 3 – 'Intensive' hunter-gatherers; 4 – Maximum expansion of pit-and-comb pottery.
Cultural groupings: 1 – Funnel Beakers; 2 – Tripolye-Cucuteni; 3 – Gumelniţa; 4 – Sredni Stog; 5 – Mikhailovka; 6 – Crimean; 7 – Kura-Araxes; 8 – Maikop; 9 – Early Pit-graves; 10 – Dniepr-Donetsian; 11 – Late Nemanian/Narvian; 12 – Zedmar; 13 – Usvyaty; 14 - Volosovo; 15 – Volga-Kama; 16 - Siekery; 17 – Lihult; 18 – Nostret; 19 – Fosna; 20 – Komsa.

comb impressions and small pits that form horizontal bands (Fig. 21). These patterns became more complicated at later stages; in several cases, stylized waterfowl (usually duck) may be recognized on the surface of pots.

    Pit-and-comb is also used to denote a distinct Middle Neolithic cultural tradition in the same area. The earliest pit-and-comb sites are located in the catchment of the Upper Volga and Oka (central Russia), where they are often considered as an independent cultural entity (the 'L'yalovo culture'). Sites such as Sakhtysh, Yazykovo 1 and Ivanovskoye in the Upper Volga catchment (see above p. 72) have been radiocarbon dated to around 4000–3500 BC. In all these cases, the pit-and-comb levels lie above those of the Upper Volga. At a later stage the pit-and-comb tradition expanded over a wide area of the East European Plain: up to the White Sea and Kola peninsula in the north, Latvia and Belorussia in the west, the Urals in the east, northern Ukraine and the middle stretches of the River Don in the south. Several local variants are recognizable: Balkhnian, Ryazanian, Belevian, Karelian, the White Sea, etc.

Pit-and-comb sites are usually situated on the flood-plains of small rivers and on the shores of lakes. In central Russia, pit-and-comb sites are often found in large peat-bogs (as in the Upper Volga catchment). The economy of these sites was based entirely on hunting and gathering. The following species were identified at the Ust'-Rybezhna site south of Lake Ladoga (east of St Petersburg): elk, aurochs, wild boar, brown bear, reindeer, seal, numerous birds. Catfish, pike-perch, perch and whitefish were the most common species of fish. In numerous cases the remains of oval-shaped semi-subterranean dwellings were identified. In one such case, at the site of Sakhtysh, a rectangular dwelling with a total area of 200 sq. metres was found.

The occurrence of rock carvings (petroglyphs), found on granite outcrops, and, particularly often, along the shores of Lake Onega, is one of the most outstanding features of the Karelian pit-and-comb culture. One of the most impressive assemblages, Besov Nos (Devil's Cap), comprises 116 compositions. They include figures of birds, fish, elk, red deer, seals, beaver, human figures, and three boats with oarsmen (Fig. 23). Another group of petroglyphs was discovered in the mouth of the River Vyg, in the coastal area of the White Sea: boats and hunting scenes are the most common motifs. The age of the rock carvings is estimated as 2800–1800 BC, a calculation based on their height above the water-level.

Yet there were considerable areas, particularly in the west of the Russian Plain, which were completely exempt from the expansion of the pit-and-comb tradition; one such area is located in the upper stretches of the Western Dvina catchment. Here, mostly due to the efforts of A.M Miklyayev and his followers, a group of sites, outstanding by its richness and complexity, was found. Over a number of field seasons, I was privileged to participate in the excavations of these sites (Miklyayev 1977; Dolukhanov and Miklayev 1986).

A group of early pottery sites was found in depressions of glacial lakes near the village of Rudnya. The earliest stratum at the site of Rudnya-Serteya contained blades and axe-like tools, and fragments of coarse conical vessels decorated with a combination of horizontal, vertical and diagonal rows of triangular impressions. The stratum corresponded to the palynological zone Atlantic-2 and was overlain by another layer of a younger age that has been dated by radiocarbon analysis to a calendar date of about 5100 BC (6200 BP uncalibrated).

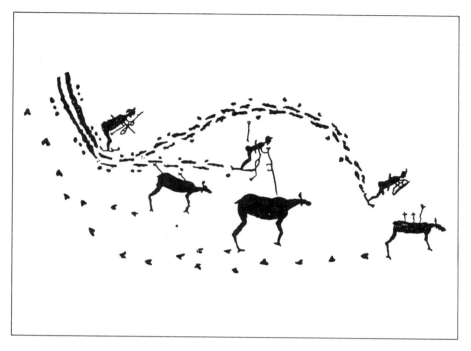

Fig. 23 Neolithic petroglyphs in Karelia.
   Source. N.N. Gurina, *Materialy i issledovanija po archeologii SSSR,* vol. 87.
Moscow: Nauka, 1961.

Cultural deposits of the upper stratum of the same site corresponded to the Narva tradition. They contained large and small S-shaped vessels decorated with comb and triangular impressions which formed horizontal and diagonal rows. The stone inventory included end-scrapers, axes and arrowheads, while an antler industry comprised needle-like points, tanged points and knives. A series of thirty radiocarbon dates suggests a span in calendar years of 5100–4900 BC.

When the lake level rose again during the early Sub-Boreal, about 3300–3100 BC (calibrated), a completely new cultural tradition appeared: pile-dwellings emerged in the coastal areas of the Usvyaty and Sennitsa lakes. A third village of pile-dwellings, Naumovo, emerged around 2500 BC in the off-shore area of Lake Zhizhitsa. All three settlements belonged to the same cultural tradition, Usvyaty, which existed between 3300 and 2500 BC.

It has been noted that all these sites were located in a similar environmental setting – their catchment area included the fringes of morainic hills bordering sandy fluvio-glacial plains and coastal areas of shallow lakes. The subsistence of these sites was based on the exploitation of all three landscape units including hunting land mammals (elk, brown bear, roe deer, wild boar, and aurochs) and water-fowl, and fishing. Among the fish-bones were identified pike, pike-perch, bream and carp. Cultural deposits contained numerous acorns, chestnuts and water chestnuts – a clear indication of a great importance attached to the gathering of edible plants. This strategy, based on the complex and effective exploitation of wildlife resources, proved to be highly efficient: in some areas, pile-dwellings remained in existence for more than 2000 years.

Chapter 5 ....

The Beaker Folks

The Post-optimum

Momentous environmental changes, marking the end of the Climatic Optimum, became perceptible by 5000 BP. In the 1920s and 1930s it was generally thought that these changes took the form of a dramatic aridity of climate ('xerothermic phase'). It was believed that during this phase forests disappeared and lakes dried up in the greater part of the Russian Plain. New studies have shown that this was not the case. Yet the transformation in the environment was significant.

In the original Blytt-Sernander scheme, the zone which had followed the Atlantic is referred to as Sub-Boreal. Khotinsky and his associates (Khotinsky et al. 1991), based on the pollen analysis of numerous peat-bogs in central Russia, now distinguish three stages in its course. The first stage (Sub-Boreal 1) lasted from 5000 to 4500 BP (uncalibrated); during its course the climate became remarkably cold and dry. The next stage, Sub-Boreal 2, was in progress from 4500 to 3200 BP (uncalibrated) and was marked by the substantial increase of temperature and humidity. The final stage, Sub-Boreal 3, featured a new fall in temperature and humidity.

These data are in accordance with the evidence obtained in other parts of the Russian Plain. Kremenetsky (1991) who gathered his pollen data in southern Ukraine and Moldova, argues that in the early Sub-Boreal (4200–2700 BP) the climate in that area became cool and dry; pollen spectra showed the disappearance of *Ulmaceae* from the forests in the Moldavian highlands; warm-loving trees such as oak and lime withdrew from the forests of Volhynia. The areas taken by treeless vegetation gained in size in the forest-steppic interfluve. Notable changes were also marked in the vegetation of steppic areas where a forb-bunchgrass variety was increasingly replaced by dry-resistant bunchgrass steppe.

The pollen evidence was confirmed by signals from different sources. Analysis of soils buried beneath burial mounds in the Pontic and Caspian lowlands showed that a southern variety of chernozem, formed under an arid and continental climate, started to build up around 4500 BP (Ivanov 1989). Similar types of soils also appeared at that time in northern Caucasus and the lower Don valley. The same kind of analysis showed that saline soils stretched out in the southern Caspian lowland between 4500 and 3500 BP (Demkin et al. 1984).

The transition to a dryer climate is apparent in the stratigraphy of laminated lake deposits in the Crimea, notably Lake Saka, near Eupatoria, as well as in similar deposits in various parts of the Russian Plain (Rauner et al. 1983). Palaeohydrological studies (Shvets 1978) have demonstrated that the overall discharge of the Dniepr river significantly diminished at that time. All these data point in the same direction: the climate grew significantly dryer and cooler. This was accompanied by glacial advances, established by geologists both in the Alps and in Scandinavia. Strong glacial advances in the Alps were recorded between 3000 and 2400 BC and between 150 BC and 100 AD (Lamb 1977). The advances of the Scandinavian glaciers occurred 1900–1300 BC and 1300–50 BC (Karlén 1982).

Post-optimum climatic alterations formed a natural background against which the social life of human groups in Europe developed. The changes were particularly apparent in settlement patterns: sites which might have been regarded as central places gradually disappeared, and smaller and undifferentiated settlements increased in number. Another basic feature was a growing socio-economic inequality which was particularly obvious in burial rites (Champion et al. 1984).

Andrew Sherratt (1981) has suggested a new term for the process which took place at that time in Neolithic Europe: 'secondary product revolution'. He wrote:

> Some time around the middle of the fifth millennium BC . . . the tight regional groupings disappeared; settlements dispersed or became less continuously occupied; burials received greater emphasis; . . . the bulk of regionally traded products was replaced by smaller quantities of exotic items, . . . objects symbolizing individual status appeared, . . . the figurines became more schematic and less overtly female; there are greater contrasts in the new forms of wealth both within regions and in individual cemeteries. The use of ritual within established and long-lived communities was thus replaced by an apparently more fluid system in which more explicit statements about rank were necessary, and a wider range of competition was possible . . . (Sherratt 1981: 127).

The Corded Ware

In archaeological terms, this period featured the appearance of two major cultural phenomena: Bell Beakers in Atlantic Europe and Corded Ware in

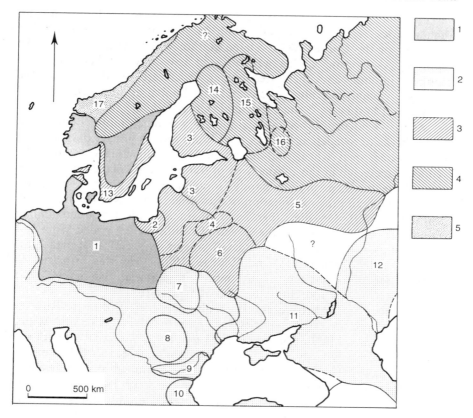

Fig. 24 Eastern Europe in the late Neolithic/early Bronze Age.

Key. 1 – 'Secondary product' groups; 2 – Agricultural and stock-breeding groups; 3 – 'Intensive' hunter-gatherers with elements of stock-breeding; 4 – Hunter-gatherers; 5 – Coastal hunter-gatherers.

Cultural groupings. Corded Ware groups 1–7 (1 – Central European; 2 – Złota; 3 – Eastern Baltic; 4 – North Belorussian; 5 – Fatyanovo; 6 – Middle Dnieprian; 7 – Carpathian); 8 – Cotofeni; 9 – Cernavoda; 10 – Ezero; 11 – Catacomb Graves; 12 – Poltavka; 13 – Pitted Ware; 14 – Finland's final Neolithic; 15 – Karelian; 16 – Kargopolian; 17 – North-Scandinavian.

the northern and northeastern parts of the continent. In its 'classical' form, a Corded Ware assemblage includes corded, decorated beakers, amphorae and a battle-axe in a 'single grave'. It was judged that this assemblage was initially fairly homogenous, being referred to as a 'pan-European horizon' (*Einheitshorizont*), and only later was it split up into a number of 'cultures', including the Single Grave culture of Jutland, northwest Germany and Holland, the Swedish Boat-axe culture, and the Saxo-Thuringian or 'classical' Corded Ware culture. For a long time, it was generally accepted that the economy of Corded Ware groups was based predominantly on nomadic stock-breeding (Wiślański 1980: 443). Hence the supposition that the spread of the Corded Ware-related culture was a result of a pastoral migration. As Gordon Childe wrote: '. . . a new wave of herdsmen had colonized Jutland, and their free-grazing stock ate up the young tree seedlings'[1]. Archaeologically these grazers are known by little cemeteries of barrows, and so they are termed the Single Grave folk' (1958: 159).

As new evidence shows the real picture was much more complicated. In some areas of Sweden at least Corded Ware groups practised agriculture and cultivated spelt wheat and naked barley (Malmer 1962: 280). The so-called Rzucwewo in the coastal area of northeastern Poland and western Lithuania featured a predominantly foraging-type economy based on hunting, fishing and the exploitation of estuarine resources (Machnik 1979; Rimentiane 1980). On the other hand, there is a distinct trend among western archaeologists to view the spread of Bell Beakers, Corded Ware and similar 'cultures' as resulting from developments in social and ideological spheres. Thus Shennan (1982) and Whittle (1985) view this primarily as reflecting the introduction of a 'more inegalitarian ideology' and, particularly, a new form of the expression of male status.

A number of Corded Ware-related cultures is identified in the Russian Plain. They include such entities as Eastern Baltic Corded Ware, North-Belorussian, Middle-Dnieprian and Fatyanovo. The situation with the Belorussian culture is fairly typical: levels containing materials belonging to this culture have been identified by Miklyayev at a number of pile-dwelling sites in the Upper Western Dvina catchment, in the south Pskov district and in northeastern Belorussia (Krivina, Osovets and several others). Radiocarbon measurements of these sites show an age of 2500–2100 BC calibrated. Faunal assemblages of these sites contain bones of domesticates – sheep, goat, pig and cattle – yet their total number never exceeded 14 per cent. The size of pile settlements markedly increased at this stage; the coring shows that living areas of several sites (such as Naumovo, upper level) exceeded one hectare (Dolukhanov and Miklyayev 1986).

Ornamental patterns of the entire pottery corpus of the stratified site of Naumovo were processed by techniques of multivariate analysis (Dolukhanov and Fonyakov 1984). The principle analysis plot for the lower and middle levels of this site produced two clearly distinguishable clusters of signals which tended to merge at the uppermost level. One obtained an obvious impression of an intrusion of an alien tradition which was gradually absorbed by an old one.

A number of 'Late Neolithic' sites in the eastern Baltic area contains

---

[1] This statement is based on the interpretation of the decline of elm, noticeable in the pollen diagrams, as resulting from the use of this plant as fodder by the invading pastoral groups. The pollen data obtained by the Russian palynologists (Khotinsky 1977: 155) show the decline of warmth-loving species occurring at that time in northern Siberia, where no anthropogenic impact was possible.

elements of the Corded Ware culture. In several cases these sites (Nainiekste, Kreiči, Leimaniški, Eini and Lagaža) contained typical Corded Wares, yet they never formed a dominant feature in the assemblage of pottery. The greater part of the ceramics belong to a 'porous' variety: vessels were made of a porous mass with an admixture of crushed shells. Both flat-bottomed and base-pointed vessels were decorated by impressions of combs and incised lines, often forming simple geometric patterns: zigzags, nets, triangles and rhombi. Radiocarbon dates obtained for these sites suggest a calibrated age of 2800–2300 BC. As in the case of the Upper Western Dvina catchment, the absolute majority of the animal remains belong to the wild species. Among the domesticates cattle, sheep, goat and pig were identified, their rate being less than 10 per cent.

As in the case of Western Dvina catchment, the settlements at this stage in Lubana were of a considerable size, the living area at the site of Lagaža exceeding one hectare. At the same site, remains of a rectangular dwelling structure were recovered. Remains of the furnace suggest the existence of the copper metallurgy (Loze 1979).

Several sites with Corded Ware are known also in Estonia: Tamula, Villa and others. Radiocarbon measurements of charcoal samples from these sites show an age of 4000–3500 BP (Ilves et al. 1974). The number of domesticates at these sites is even less than in Latvia, only two bones of the cattle (0.2 per cent of the total assemblage) being identified at the site of Tamula (Paaver 1965).

Further north, in Finland, Corded Ware assemblages were identified in the local culture of Kiukainen. Based on a sporadic occurrence of the cereal pollen in corresponding spectra of peat-bogs, Siiriäinen (1982) suggested the occurrence of agriculture at the Kiukainen sites. This conclusion was questioned by Donner (1984) on palynological grounds. As Edgren (1970) has stated earlier, there is no evidence whatsoever suggesting any kind of agriculture or stock-breeding in Finland at that time.

If one turns to the south, the most conspicuous Corded Ware assemblages are found in sites belonging to the Middle Dnieprian culture. These include both settlements and burials. More than 200 settlements are known to this day: they are usually located on sandy hills inside river floors of the Middle Dnieprian catchment. Dwellings, identified at a number of sites, were mostly surface-type of a rectangular shape, often two-chambered, 4–5 by 5–6 metres, with remains of posts supporting the walls and stone hearths usually found inside the room. Cemeteries were usually located in the vicinity of settlements, often on the fringe of the upper terraces. They included both 'flat' graves and burial mounds, the burial rite including both inhumations and cremations. Burial mounds were generally small, rarely reaching 2–3 metres in height, their number varying from one or two to twenty-four. 'Flat' cemeteries were more numerous, the largest one (Syabrovichi, near Gomel) consisting of 132 graves.

Ceramics were the most common product found both in dwelling sites

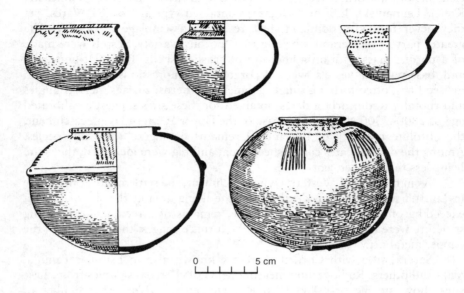

Fig. 25 Fatyanovo Ware.
   Source. O.N. Bader, D.A. Krainov & M.F. Kosarev, *Epoha bronzy lesnoi polosy SSSR*. Moscow: Nauka, 1987.

and graves. They include rough, flat-bottomed kitchen ware made of sand-tempered paste and decorated with impressions of cord and other stamps forming simple geometric patterns. A different group of ceramics consisted of thin-walled vessels made of a paste tempered with sand and crushed pottery; it included deep bowls with a rounded base, ovoid beakers with rounded base and funnel-shaped neck, and flat-bottomed biconic amphorae. Ornaments consisted of cord impressions, incised lines, impressions of linear stamps and strokes forming horizontal bands, chevrons and triangles. Stone inventory included battle-axes, arrowheads, knives. Grave goods included personal ornaments: amber beads, necklaces made of wolf and red deer teeth, hammer-headed pins. One of the graves of Strelitsa cemetery contained two copper diadems and a faiance bead. Copper implements were rare; they included awls, knives, shaft-hole axes as well as personal ornaments: rings, temple spirals, and bracelets. All these implements were made of arsenic copper, allegedly of the Balkan-Carpathian origin. So far only a single radiocarbon date is available, 2400–50 BP uncalibrated, for a sample from barrow No. 5 of Belynets cemetery. This date is consistent with the supposed age of this culture.

   Another important cultural unit, Fatyanovo, which is generally viewed as an eastern variant of Corded Ware culture (Fig. 25), was first identified by A.S. Uvarov, A.A. Spitsyn and V.A. Gorodtsov in the late nineteenth and early twentieth centuries, after excavations of a cemetery of that name situated near Yaroslavl, north of Moscow, and was intensely investigated by D.A. Krainov from the 1940s onwards. Fatyanovo sites, almost exclusively cemeteries, are spread over vast areas of northern and northeastern Russia, from Lake Ilmen in the west to the Middle Volga in the east. Based on the typology of battle-axes and pottery, Krainov (1972) distinguished several local variants: Dvina-Ilmen; Moskva-Klyazma; Upper Volga; Oka-Desna; and Sura-Sviyaga (or Balanovo group, often regarded as an independent cultural tradition). Cemeteries are usually located on elevations, close to river valleys or lakes. The number of flat graves in cemeteries varied from two to ten at an early stage, to 125 at later stages. The dead were usually interred in a contracted posture.

Structures of graves and the composition of grave goods are indicative of a social inequality and, especially, of a particular male status. Males were usually found laid on their right side, the head directed to the west, while females lay on their left side, the head to the east. Burial goods included stone, bone and metal implements, ceramics and animal bones. Shaft-hole axes were usually found near the head in male graves; in children's graves they were put at the feet. Copper battle-axes, usually in bark cases, were found exclusively in rich graves, and apparently belonged to the élite. Female graves contained numerous ornaments made of animal bones and teeth, and in rare cases, metal ornaments (bracelets, rings, pendants). As spectrographic analysis shows, metal objects were manufactured predominantly from local ore, mainly copper-bearing sandstone outcropping in the Vyatka-Kama catchment, west of the Urals (Chernykh 1992). In rare cases, ornaments made of Baltic amber were found. Pottery consisted mainly of beakers and amphorae, ornamented with rows of cord impressions and incised lines forming geometric patterns.

Animal bones found in graves belonged largely to domesticates (pig, sheep, goat), bones of wild animals (brown bear, reindeer, elk, wild boar, roe deer, fox, beaver and others) being much less numerous. Fish bones and shells of riverine molluscs were also found. Radiocarbon dates obtained from Turginivi cemetery (Moskva-Klyazma) and Volosovo-Danilovo cemetery (Upper Volga) suggest a calendar date range of 2300–2000 BC.

One of the important aspects of settlement in central Russia at that time was the fact that Fatyanovo sites coexisted, over a significant period of time, with a distinct cultural unit referred to as 'Volosovo'. Volosovo sites were first discovered at the turn of the century (Gorodtsov 1901) and have been explored ever since, yet several problems relating to this controversial culture remain unsolved. Scholars are still in disagreement about its area, chronology and cultural attributes, as well as its origins and possible ethnic affiliations. A dense concentration of Volosovo sites has been found in central Russia, in the catchment area of the Middle and Lower Oka, Lower Kama and Middle Volga. Dwelling sites are usually located in river-floors

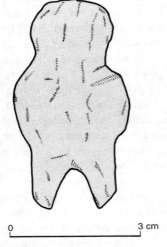

0   3 cm

Fig. 26   Volosovo flint figurine.

and in the vicinity of lakes. Settlements were large; they consisted of up to 15–20 dwellings of semi-subterranean type with roofs supported by posts, and hearths usually located in the middle of the living space. The economy was of a foraging character with a high reliance on fishing and food-gathering. There were indications of metal-working at the latest sites. The Volosovo culture is usually roughly dated to 4000–2000 BP. In the 1970s Krainov (1978) has distinguished a separate proto-Volosovo stage which starts at about 4700 BP.

Ceramics of the Volosovo sites were quite distinct from both pit-and comb and Fatyanovo styles: pots were manufactured from local clay combined with crushed shells or organic matter. Conic thin-walled vessels were ornamented by impressions of toothed or combed stamps, whipped cords, or by pots of various shape and size forming geometric patterns. The flint industry was traditional 'forest Neolithic': various types of end-scraper were the most numerous and included arrow and spearheads, chisels, axes and daggers. The occurrence of both zoomorphic and anthropomorphic figurines made of chipped flint was a specific Volosovian feature (Fig. 26). Ornaments made of Baltic amber were common both in dwellings and burials. Both collective and individual burials were found within settlements, either within or in the immediate vicinity of the dwellings. Skeletons were found in a supine posture, variably directed. Grave goods were rare; in some cases they included flint tools. Both skeletons and grave goods were covered with red ochre.

Relationships of Volosovo and Fatyanovo cultures deserve a special interest. As both stratigraphic and typological evidence show, in most cases Volosovo sites antedate Fatyanovo ones. According to one hypothesis (V.

Tretyakov 1990), Volosovo culture came from the east, originating from a Kama-Volga variety of the pit-and-comb pottery, and later transgressing to the west. Later Volosovo sites (Sakhtysh in the Upper Volga and many others) show the occurrence of Fatyanovo ceramics. On the other hand, the presence of Volosovo pottery is attested in a number of Fatyanovo graves. It seems to be highly significant that at some sites (Sakhtysh 1 and 2) the Volosovo dead are anthropologically similar to the Fatyanovo individuals.

As I had mentioned earlier, problems of Volosovo cultures are far from being solved. Yet, as a preliminary hypothesis, one may visualize the Volosovo/Fatyanovo relations as a coexistence of two major arenas of power: the domestic arena of a foraging type (Volosovo) and the mortuary arena with a strong pastoral symbolism (Fatyanovo).

Now we may view the problem of the origins of Corded Ware cultures in the East European Plain and their possible ethnic affiliations from a different angle. As I have already mentioned, the migratory hypothesis of its origin was a leading paradigm until quite recently. Gustav Kossina (1911) suggested that a 'Battle-axe culture' developed initially in Jutland through the acculturation of local Mesolithic dwellers, whence bearers of the resultant 'Single Grave culture' spread across central and eastern Europe, ultimately reaching the Aegean and Caucasus. Sulimirski (1970) discussing the origins of the Fatyanovo culture, stressed a particular similarity between the Moscow group and the 'Thuringian' group. He wrote:

> the Fatyanovo culture had no roots in the country. Its burial ritual . . . and grave goods reveal close connections with the groups of the Corded Ware/Battle-axe assemblages of the forest zone further to the west . . . Battle-axes and other weapons found in graves imply that the Fatyanovians were a warlike people. In invading the country they met the native population, hunters and fishermen . . . They probably displaced (!) some of them, but the bulk of the local population did not leave its homeland and lived side by side with the newcomers (Sulimirski 1970: 196–8).

For a long time, anthropological data were quoted as one of the main arguments in favour of the migratory hypothesis. Krainov (1972, 1978) who argued that the Fatyanovo resulted from an eastbound migration from the Vistula-Neman area, wrote that the Fatyanovians were 'dolicocephalic Europeoids' essentially similar to the Corded Ware population further to the west. Yet new evidence increasingly shows that the Corded Ware population was heterogeneous in an anthropological sense. Thus Denisova (1985), based on the analysis of vast amounts of craniological materials, asserted that Corded Ware groups in the eastern Baltic area were essentially similar to preceding Narva groups. It should be noted that in the 1930s Russian scholars (V.I. Ravdonikas, P.N. Tretyakov, B.S. Zhukov and others) generally shared the view that the Fatyanovo was a result of local development; a convergent evolution of local societies in an environment of transition to stock-breeding. Seen in the perspective of a secondary product

89

revolution in Europe, one may suggest the following scenario. The general decline of agricultural productivity in central Europe, in an environment of Climatic Post-optimum, triggered significant structural changes in local societies. It took the form of an economic restructuring with an increased reliance on dairy husbandry and the appearance (in some areas) of a plough agriculture. In its turn, it led to a considerable social change: the social differentiation and the rise of an élite comprising male warriors. Yet another important element of social change was the intensification of inter-regional links and the establishment of large-scale social networks which increasingly included areas in the east. Hence, Corded Ware cultures in the Russian Plain may be primarily viewed as resulting from an eastbound expansion of a central European socio-cultural network. This may have included the displacement of limited numbers of people, yet the transfer of ideas and knowledge was much more important. As our experiments with ceramics of Upper Western Dvina sites show, these took the form of an introduction of a new cultural tradition rapidly absorbed by the old one.

The spread of Corded Ware pottery coincided with the appearance of elements of food production, mostly stock-breeding, in the forested areas of the Russian Plain. It is highly significant that the role of food production strategies was clearly dependent on the local ecological and socio-cultural environment. One may clearly affirm that the importance of stock-breeding was negligible in the northwestern and northern regions of the Plain, the economy in those regions retaining its essentially foraging character. In contrast, the role of stock-breeding seemed to be much higher in the areas of the Fatyanovo and, particularly, in the Middle Dniepr where elements of agriculture are firmly attested. Yet the relative importance of stock-breeding versus foraging may be exactly estimated only when sufficient numbers of Fatyanovo dwelling sites are found and properly explored.

There exists yet another, ethnolinguistic, approach to the Corded Ware problem. The intensification of inter-regional links and the establishment of large-scale socio-cultural networks implies, in the first place, an intensive cultural exchange. This, in its turn, implies the necessity of a common communication medium, that is a mutually comprehensible language. Hence, one may argue that the spread of a Corded Ware network corresponded to a more vehement proliferation of the Indo-European speech into that part of Europe. Since the Corded Ware network was of a comparatively limited extent, one may suggest that it corresponded to a dialect or, rather, to a dialectal group of the Indo-European language. In this respect, it is highly significant that A. Ya. Bryusov (1961) has suggested that the Corded Ware/Battle-axe culture corresponded to a 'Proto-Baltic-Slavic-Germanic linguistic unity'. The existence of this unity was asserted by Georgiev (1959) on the ground of several linguistic similarities. Based on their own phonological system, Gamkrelidze and Ivanov (1984) equally suggest the existence of such unity.

As we can see, the spread of a Corded Ware network into the forested areas of the Russian Plain included close interaction with local groups, some of which were allegedly Finno-Ugrian speakers. These contacts were particularly intense in the area of present-day Finland and Karelia as well as in the entire area of Fatyanovo and Volosovo. There are numerous words and constructions of Baltic origin in East Finnic languages. It is highly probable that the penetration of these words into Finnic languages corresponded to the spread of a Corded Ware network (Serebrennikov 1957). It is also significant that, as Nieminen (1957) argued, Finnish borrowings corresponded in time to the existence of an undifferentiated Slavonic language, which coincides with the suggested period of their initial contacts.

The steppe groups

As far as the southern part of the Russian Plain is concerned, the most outstanding process that occurred there was a gradual disintegration of the Tripolye culture. The gradual fragmentation and a wider dispersal of Tripolye space are particularly obvious in its later stages. One of the local groups (Vykhvatintsy) gradually spread from the Middle Dniestr to the south, to the steppic areas of the northwestern Pontic lowland. Later, it developed into the Usatovo variant of Late Tripolye. Subsequently, Usatovo sites spread over a vast area of the Prut-Dniestr-Southern Bug interfluve and further west into the Lower Danube valley and into Romanian Moldova.

Simultaneously, another Tripolye group, Brynzeny, spread to the north, to eastern Volhynia, where the Troyan variant emerged. A subsequent movement led to the establishment of the Sofievka variant in the Middle Dniepr area. The economy of Usatovo was largely dependent on stock-breeding, especially of horse and sheep and goat. Cattle-breeding was dominant among the groups settled in the Middle Prut and Dniestr area (for example Brynzeny). This type of mixed agriculture was equally typical of the Volhynia and Middle Dniepr region.

Late Tripolye sites bear witness to the further development of metal-working which at that time acquired a status of independent craft. Based on the spectrographic and stylistic analysis of bronze tools, Chernykh (1992) argues that they show close links with the Carpatho-Balkan area, as well as the Aegean and Asia Minor. By their chemical composition – predominantly arsenical bronze and pure copper – these tools are very similar to the bronzes from the northeastern Balkans, especially Ezero. Ryndina (1971) using the metallographic analysis, was able to establish that such tools as daggers, knives, adzes and chisels were cast in two-part moulds, and subsequently, the working edges of these tools were forged and hardened

In contrast to rich Usatovo metal assemblages, the tools of Sofievka are much more limited in number and variety. These tools were mostly manufactured of pure copper, presumably from the Carpathian ore (Chernykh 1992).

Settlements and cemeteries of Usatovo are usually located on high terraces, on the edges of watershed plateaux high above the Black Sea. The most important sites, Usatovo and Majaki, lie on the edge of a high cliff of the Dniestr *liman* (estuary), west of Odessa. Two groups of burial mounds (kurgans) and two cemeteries with flat graves, were located near the settlement of Usatovo. The graves under kurgan barrows often contained rich inventories: central graves in kurgan cemetery No. 1 contained ornaments made of Baltic amber and Near Eastern antimony, numerous rings and beads of silver and copper, arsenic copper daggers, copper flat-axes and chisels (Zbenovich 1974). Burials of Usatovo bear evidence for a marked social stratification in Late Tripolian society. It seems clear that common people buried their dead in simple flat graves, while the social élite were interred in impressive tombs with exotic prestige goods.

The further development lead to a total collapse of Late Tripolian agricultural society. A new cultural unit, known as the Pit-Grave or Yámnaya made its appearance in the South Russian steppe. This cultural tradition, which is generally classified as Early Bronze Age, spread over a vast area from the Urals in the east to the Lower Danube in the west in the course of the late third and early second millennia BC, and was first identified by V.A. Gorodtsov in 1901–03. The most characteristic feature of the Pit-Grave culture were burials in pits ('*yama*' in Russian, hence the name) of rectangular (rarely of oval) shape, located beneath kurgans. The kurgans were of various size, and in some cases several stages in their construction could be distinguished. Pits were often covered with wooden slabs; reed, grass and/or red ochre often lined their bottom; red ochre, which covered the body, was an essential element of the mortuary rite. In some cases, wheels or even remains of complete wheeled carts were found inside the pits (for example, Storozhevaya Mogila, near Dnepropetrovsk on the Dniepr). The position of skeletons – mostly on the back or on the side with legs contracted – finds an obvious antecedent in the Sredni Stog and, particularly, Usatovo traditions. Other Sredni Stog features may be found in stone cairns, cromlechs and anthropomorphic stelae incorporated in kurgan constructions.

The economy of the Pit-Grave culture was based on stock-breeding. Faunal evidence from the upper layer at Mikhailovka (Shaposhnikova 1985) makes this particularly clear: nearly 90 per cent of the determined faunal remains belonged to domesticates, among which cattle was the most common (38 per cent), sheep and goat came next (32.5 per cent), followed by horse (17.6 per cent). It is assumed that the ox was used as a draft animal. At the same time, there is evidence that crops were grown at least at some sites; this is true of the middle layer at Mikhailovka where the impressions of emmer wheat, hulled barley and millet have been identified (Pashkevich 1991). At its final stage, this settlement grew to a size of 1.5

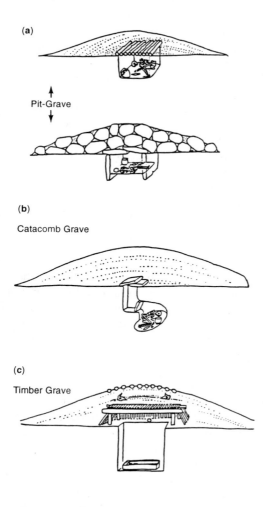

Fig. 27 Pit Graves (**a**) Catacomb Grave (**b**) and Timber Grave (**c**).
After. T. Sulumirski, *Prehistoric Russia.* John Barker: Humanities Press, 1970.

hectares, and was surrounded by fortifications which included stone ramparts and ditches.

The western outpost of the Pit-Grave culture stretched to northern Bulgaria, Hungary and Romania, where so called 'ochre graves' are found (for example, Hamangia-Baia tumuli in Dobruja, the area between the Lower Danube and the Black Sea). Mortuary rites included kurgans with stone cairns and cromlechs and all the usual elements of Pit-Grave mortuary practice. According to N.Ya. Merpert (1968), Pit-Grave sites formed a distinct 'cultural-historic entity' based on a common subsistence economy (predominantly nomadic stock-breeding) and common ideology (the kurgan mortuary rite, primarily). According to Merpert, this entity came about from the integration of numerous local traditions over a vast area: from the Urals in the east to the Lower Danube in the west.

Basing her analysis on some formal elements of the burial ritual and the cord ornamentation of the pottery, M. Gimbutas (1971) expands the 'Kurgan culture' to a still wider area: to the Balkans, central and northern Europe, the Caucasus and even to the Near East. According to Gimbutas, between 4000 and 2500 BP three consecutive waves of 'Kurgan people', identified with Indo-European speakers, pushed to the west, to the north, and later expanded southwards through the Caucasus to occupy Asia Minor. M. Gimbutas argued that several groups moved on towards India, while the others remained in the steppe and pressed into the Iranian Plateau and Central Asia. Variations of this hypothesis have been shared by many scholars, including N. Ya. Merpert (1968) and J.P. Mallory (1989).

The main deficiency of this hypothesis resides in the direct identification of archaeological entities (in this case, Pit-Grave or Kurgan 'culture') with linguistic and/or ethnic groups. It seems more likely that the emergence of Pit-Grave assemblages was related to the social development of various local Bronze Age communities. It represents an expression of social stratification and the emergence of chiefdom-type nomadic social structures. The development of nomadic chiefdoms was accompanied by the intensification of inter-group information exchange between essentially heterogeneous social groups.

It would seem that a better understanding of what actually happened in the South Russian steppe during the Early Bronze Age may be attained in the frameworks of the ethnoarchaeological and contextual approach. Both the collapse of the Tripolye and the subsequent spread of a Pit-Grave network may be viewed as different aspects of adaptations to the Sub-Boreal environment. The basic feature of this environment was a decrease in temperature and rainfall resulting in the shrinking of food resources. It was noted (Hodder 1982; Whittle 1985) that heightened competition for scarce resources may have led to a sharpened sense of group identity and the maintenance of group boundaries. Hence the social hierarchization and the emergence of group-oriented chiefdoms with the increased role of male individuals exercising more stringent control over the territory and its resources, and the kurgans as territorial markers and symbols of regional power. It is interesting to note also that there are other symbols of power to be found in the Yámnaya graves, for example, polished maceheads.

The emergence of high-status chiefdoms was particularly apparent in northern Caucasus where impressive kurgans belonging to 'Maikop culture' emerged. A group of mounds situated in the town of Maikop was discovered and excavated in 1897 by N.I. Veselovsky. The largest of these mounds was 11 metres high: its burial chambers contained pottery, metal tools and ornaments, two golden and fourteen silver vessels. The most remarkable finds included gold figurines of bulls and lions, which were sewn on to garments; gold and silver bull-figurines adorning canopies; gold beads and rings; gold, silver, turquoise and carnelian beads, copper axes, tanged axes and spearheads. Some of these prestige items were of Middle Eastern origin.

By comparing Maikop finds to similar assemblages from a number of sites, Russian archaeologists (Iessen 1950; Munchaev 1970) have identified a Maikopian culture concentrated mainly in northwestern Caucasus but with influences spreading to northeastern Caucasus and Transcaucasia. A.A. Iessen (1963) has distinguished two stages in its development: the Maikop proper and the Novosvobodnaya. The former is characterized by the occurrence of large rectangular burial chambers beneath kurgans. Novosvobodnaya-type kurgans contained dolmens and cromlechs. Based on the typological analogies, Iessen (1950) dates Maikopian culture to 2500–2000 BC. A series of radiocarbon measurements for the Ust'-Jegutinsky cemetery near the town of Cherkessk suggests calendar dates of *c.* 2500–2400 BC.

The intensification of inter-tribal contacts was much facilitated by the development of transport: remains of presumably ox-drawn wheeled vehicles were found in several Pit-Graves. Yet another means of transport, namely riding horses, is attestable in the steppe since at least early Eneolithic (Sredni Stog, Batai). Hence, since the early Sub-Boreal, one may witness the establishment of a 'steppic corridor' in the South Russian Plain. This was a powerful channel through which groups of people, as well as goods and ideas, were freely circulating between the heart of Central Asia and Europe.

The development of metallurgy and metal-working as well as the trade in metalwork was yet another important factor which greatly contributed towards the establishment of inter-group links. The Maikopian sites, particularly the 'royal' tombs are extremely rich in metal implements. They were manufactured exclusively of arsenical bronze with the content of arsenic varying between 1 and 5 per cent (Chernykh 1992: 74). Based on this evidence Chernykh suggests the Transcaucasian and, partly, the east Anatolian ore as a probable source of Maikopian bronzes.

The Caucasian, and particularly the Maikopian influence was strongly felt throughout the Pontic area, particularly in the steppe. This influence is particularly obvious in all the types of bronze implements; very often they are direct copies of the Maikopian prototypes. Eventually this led to the establishment of a 'Circum-Pontic network' or a 'Circum-Pontic metal-lurgical province' as Chernykh (1970, 1992) prefers to call it.

There are various archaeological indices for multifaceted trade contacts along the shores of the Black and Aegean Seas. Zbenovich (1974) notes the similarity of Usatovo daggers with those of Troy II and Early Cycladic II–III. Equally strong contacts are attested with the Maikopian culture in north Caucasus. They included imported pottery and several types of copper tools (for example, hafted axes).

These processes do not imply large-scale migrations, nor are they related to the initial spread of the Indo-European language. Yet, as in the case of the Corded Ware network further north, one may suggest that the Circum-Pontic network implied the establishment of a common communication medium in the form of an Indo-European dialect. In this respect, it seems tempting to suggest that the communication medium in use in the Circum-Pontic network was nothing other than a dialect of the Anatolian languages. These extinct languages include Hittite, an official language of the Hittite state, which is attested historically to the second millennium BC, and several related languages: Luwian, Palaic, Lydian and Lycian. There is an increasing amount of data suggesting that there was an Indo-European presence in Anatolia long before the rise of the first powerful Hittite state *c*. 1650 BC. Recognizably Indo-European names were identified among cuneiform documents of an Assyrian trade colony at Kultepe in central Anatolia. This colony was in existence *c*. 2000–1900 BC. Based on this and other indirect evidence, a suggestion was made that Indo-European speaking groups were present in the area of Anatolia since the establishment of the first agricultural settlements (Gamkrelidze and Ivanov 1984; Dolukhanov 1994).

Based on linguistic arguments, Gamkrelidze and Ivanov (1984) date the separation of Anatolian languages from the proto-Indo-European, to 6000–3000 BC. Further development, according to the same writers, led to the separation of a Greco-Armenian-Aryan entity, which at a later stage split up into separate Indo-Iranian, Greek and Armenian groups. If one accepts these arguments, one may envisage the occurrence of a Circum-Pontic network consisting of a great number of closely interrelated chiefdoms, which spoke mutually comprehensible dialects of an Indo-European language. These languages included the Anatolian, Indo-Iranian, Greek and Armenian groups[2]. The contacts between Corded Ware and Pontic networks are well attested archaeologically. In this sense, similarities of Praslavonic and Hittite languages, which include not only the syntax but also folklore (Ivanov 1965), are highly significant.

The Bronze Age

The subsequent stages of Sub-Boreal, which corresponded to Middle and Late Bronze Age, in the Russian Plain saw the gradual development of later Corded Ware traditions. The situation in the eastern Baltic area was fairly typical in that sense. In the sphere of economics, two major trends are

---

[2] It is very probable that the common Indo-European denominations for horse /*ek(h)uos/, wheel–wheeled chariot /*k(h)el-/, copper /*haie-os/ and many others spread at that period.

identifiable: first, a gradual rise in the importance of food production, mainly stock-breeding; secondly, a gradual rise of metallurgy and metal-working. There are notable changes also in settlement patterns. With the increasing importance of stock-breeding, settlements lost their close attachment to wetlands, being increasingly relocated on upper geomorphic levels. This was particularly obvious in the Upper Western Dvina catchment, where, during the Middle Bronze Age, the tradition of pile-dwellings, which was nearly 2000 years old, came to an end; settlements were moved to the higher areas, further from the lakes.

Middle and Late Bronze Age settlements in Latvia and Lithuania were located predominantly on the morainic hills, dominating the low-lying flood-plains. The settlements grew in size. Fortified settlements started to appear. Initially, fortifications consisted of one or, later, two rows of timber fence: turf ramparts and ditches emerged at a later stage. Dwellings inside protected areas were oval-shaped or rectangular wooden structures on poles 2.5–4 by 4–5 metres in size (Fig. 28) (Graudonis 1967; Urtans 1994).

Judging from faunal records, stock-breeding became the main strategy of the food-quest: cattle were the most important, pig came next. Numerous finds of horse bones indicate a considerable importance of horse-breeding. Finds of sickles show a gradual increase in the importance of agriculture allegedly of a swidden type. At the same time there is abundant evidence that foraging strategies – hunting, fishing and gathering edible plants – remained important sources of food.

Numerous finds of fragments of crucibles and moulds are seen as a clear indication of the existence of local metallurgy and metal-working. Several types of bronze axes, spearheads and ornaments were unquestionably of local, east Baltic origin. Ceramics remain the most common category in archaeological assemblages. Corded ornamentation gradually disappeared and flat-bottomed vessels were either smooth or decorated with simple hatched patterns.

Numerous cemeteries with flat graves are known for the early stages of the Middle Bronze Age. The first burial mounds appear at a later stage. A large mound excavated at Reznes near Riga (Graudonis 1967) included three stratigraphic levels of burials, indicating visible changes in the funerary rite. The oldest one included graves with inhumed dead, this being overlain by a level with cremations. The uppermost level included stone cists with both inhumations and cremations. Barrows with stone cists were particularly common in Estonia. One should note that at that time cremation became the dominant funeral rite, rather than inhumation, in the whole of central and northern Europe (Coles and Harding 1979).

If one looks further south, one may find a number of localized cultural entities. One of the best known, the Sosnitsian,[3] is situated in the catchment

---

[3] Berezanskaya (1985) views Sosnitsian as an eastern variant of the Trzciniec culture spread in eastern Poland.

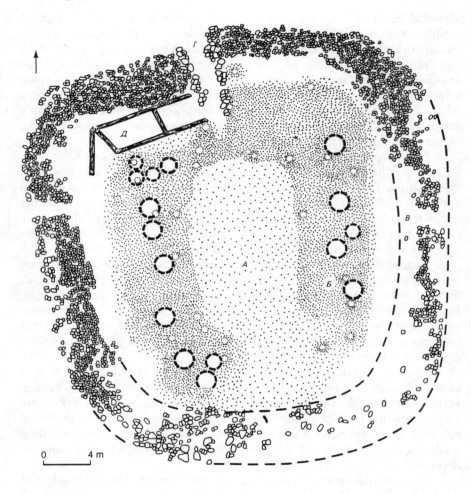

Fig. 28   Bronze Age fortified settlement at Kivukalns, Latvia
  Source. O.N. Bader, D.A. Krainov & M.F. Kosarev, *Epoha bronzy lesnoi polosy SSSR*. Moscow: Nauka, 1987.

of Upper and Middle Dniepr and practically overlaps the area of the preceding Middle Dnieprian culture. Settlements are usually situated on sandy hills within river floors, often on promontories of higher terraces. The size of the settlements was considerable; they varied between 10,000 and 40,000 sq. metres. In some cases settlements included 15–20 dwellings forming one or two rows along the waterway. Both surface and semi-subterranean dwellings are identified. They are usually large: 24–40 to 72–120 sq. metres. The most common, large houses constructed on posts, comprised two chambers: a living room and a kitchen with hearths, open ovens and storage pits. Stores of agricultural products with multiple post-holes were identified at two sites: Pustynka and Pochep. Ceramics included pots and beaker-like jars, decorated by pits, impressions of stamps and incised lines forming geometric patterns (Fig. 29). Bronze implements were not numerous but included arrowheads, knives, axes (celts), daggers, awls, pins, brooches, spiral-folded finger-rings and other personal ornaments. It has been suggested that the greater part of the bronze objects were imported from the Carpathian basins (Berezanskaya 1985). Yet there is evidence for local metallurgy: moulds for celts were found at the site of Zazim'ye.

Burial sites included both flat graves and burial mounds, with both inhumation and cremation funeral rites in use. Material remains as well as burial rites clearly indicate, on the one hand, the local origin of Sosnitsian, rooted in Corded Ware, and, on the other, its connections with Middle Bronze Age cultures in central Europe. Links with cultures further south and southeast are also visible.

The economy was solidly based on stock-breeding: faunal remains were dominated by cattle. Finds of numerous sickles suggest the occurrence of agriculture. Based on archaeological similarities, Sosnitsian is dated to 1500–1000 BC (Artëmenko 1987a). This was confirmed by a sample from the site of Pustynka that was radiocarbon dated to 3140±100 BP.

Western connections are yet more apparent at Komarovian sites which concentrate in the Upper and Middle Dniestr as well as Prut catchment. As in the previous case, this culture obviously developed from a preceding Corded Ware group. Settlements are usually located on upper terraces of rivers and on high lake shores. Remains of rectangular surface buildings, 4–5 metres in size, were identified at two sites: Komarovo and Nezvisko.

A cemetery with inhumation graves under barrows was found at Ivanovka near Lvov. Barrows with cremations were much more common; they have been studied at Komarov, Bukvina, Tenetniki and other sites. The largest cemetery, Komarovo, included sixty-five barrows. These barrows were usually small (0.5–3.0 metres tall, 10–30 metres in diameter), often encircled by stone slabs. It is significant that grave goods in both types of burial were similar. They usually included several ceramic vessels, flint axes, sickles, scrapers and arrowheads, bone awls and splinters, as well as bronze ornaments: bracelets, temple ornaments and beads. Pottery included reddish-brown slipped ware. One notes also tulip-shaped pots, small beakers, deep bowls, handled cups and other vessels. The decoration consisted of cised lines and rows of shaded triangles. One-handled cups with pedestal bases have direct analogies in Poland (Trzciniec) and the Slovak-Hungarian area. One notes also simple kitchenware made of paste tempered with crushed flint, sand or pottery.

Komarovian metal-work indicates direct links with Hungary, which is particularly apparent in antithetic spiral-terminal rings, bracelets, turtli and long pins. The economy of Komarovian settlements was based on stock-breeding and agriculture. On archaeological grounds, Komarovian is

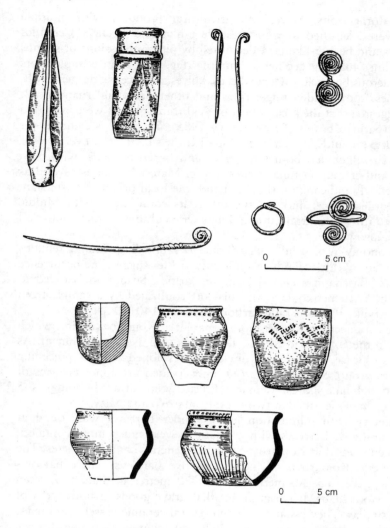

Fig. 29 Sosnitsian inventory.
   Source. O.N. Bader, D.A. Krainov & M.F. Kosarev, *Epoha bronzy lesnoi polosy SSSR.* Moscow: Nauka, 1987.

usually dated to 1600–1200 BC. There are two radiocarbon dates available: for the barrow at Ivan'ya, 3235±35 BC and for the settlement at Magala, 3260±100 BP (Artëmenko 1987b).

Yet another, rather loosely defined cultural entity, the Abashevian, occupied a large area of Russian steppic-forest, stretching from the east Dniepr catchment in the west to the Tobol catchment in Siberia in the east (Pryakhin and Khalikov 1987). This large area was unequally studied in the archaeological sense. Dwelling sites are better known on the River Don and in the southern Urals. Shilovskoe settlement, near the town of Voronezh, was located on an elongated promontory of the left bank of the Voronezh river, a tributary of the Don. The settlement, with the total size of *c.* 7500 sq. metres, was protected by a system of ramparts and comprised eight standard single-room post-framed houses, 14–20 by 10–14 metres with supposedly plank walls. One house probably served as a smith's shop: it contained numerous fragments of crucibles, copper slag and stone molds. Another house is seen as a sanctuary: it included fragments of a vessel with an engraved figure of a skier and a pit with remains of ostensibly sacrificial animals.

Abashevian cemeteries are better known in the Middle Volga area. These cemeteries usually consisted of groups of small barrows with flattened surface. Graves, often encircled by stone rings, contained the inhumed dead, buried in an extended posture with the head directed to the east or southeast. Several cenotaphs were also reported. The subsistence of Abashevian groups was largely based on sedentary stock-breeding with the predominance of cattle but also sheep, goats, pigs and horses. There are indications that cattle were at least partly used as draft animals. Remains of wheeled carts were found in several graves.

Abashevian sites bear abundant evidence for the development of locally-based metallurgy and metal-working. A social significance of metal-working in Abashevian communities is highlighted by the occurrence of high status burials of bronze smiths. These burials, which included moulds for shaft-hole axes, crucibles and other smithing artefacts, were identified in two cases: at Pepkino in the Middle Volga and at Kondrashovka in the Don basin (Chernykh 1992). Scholars have distinguished several types of bronze implement of Abashevian origin. They include several types of axe and adze, cast spearheads and personal adornments, notably rosette-shaped plaques and buttons, and several types of bracelet. One of the particular features of the Abashevian culture was the occurrence of 'hoards', which tend to cluster in the vicinity of sources of ore. One of the largest hoards, Galich, situated at the lake of the same name near the town of Kostroma, was discovered in 1836 (Tallgren 1911). This hoard contained a large number of metal objects hidden in a clay vessel. They included small silver buttons, a bronze shaft-hole axe, bronze knives with decorated handles, daggers with viper-shaped hilts, bronze arrowheads, bracelets, plaques, wire pendants, and bronze and silver beads. Small animal figurines and five 'idols' are of particular interest; they show naked males with their heads decorated with axes, birds or streams of fire. Abashevian ceramics were fairly characteristic; they included bell-shaped vessels and small ribbed pots decorated by incised lines and triangles made by the impressions of toothed stamps. There are no radiocarbon dates available for the Abashevian sites. On typological grounds this culture is dated to *c.* 1500–1600 BC.

Based on the archaeological and chemical data, Chernykh (1992) identifies two important Abashevian metallurgic centres. The first, located mostly in the southern Urals, was supplied by ore from the copper-bearing sandstone in the Belaya river catchment. The second centre, located predominantly in the southeastern Urals, had as a source of metal two important ore deposits east of the Urals: the copper-arsenic one at Tash-Kazgan and copper-silver at Nikol'skoe, both located in close proximity. The ore extraction from the Tash-Kazgan mines was in progress over a prolonged period of time. The finds of implements of an identical composition and even lumps of ore, suggest that this ore was transported through the mountains over a distance of at least 250–300 km.

Yet another culture which belongs to the Middle–Late Bronze Age, the Pozdnyakovian, had a much more limited extension (Bader 1987). Its sites, which include both settlements and cemeteries, are restricted to the catchment of the Upper Volga and Oka rivers. Settlements usually lie on the fringes of river terraces, above the flood-plain, or are located on watersheds. Rectangular post-framed houses of semi-subterranean type varied in size between 9–6 and 18–12 metres; each house included several hearths. Cemeteries tended to be located in the immediate vicinity of settlements. They included both barrows and flat graves. Inhumation burials were more common than cremations. Barrows were usually up to one metre tall and were encircled by a ditch. The largest barrow (in Borisoglebsk cemetery) was 4 metres in height and 35 metres in diameter. A rectangular grave under the barrow contained skeletons in a contracted posture, the head oriented to the northeast or northwest. Grave goods consisted of both intact and fragmented pottery, as well as flint arrowheads, knife-scrapers, bronze spearheads, daggers and ornaments. Cremations were more often found in the later sites.

Stylistically varied hand-made pottery included flat-bottomed pots with either straight or rimmed walls, bellied and open-mouthed jars and large vessels with straight walls and long neck. Ornaments usually consisted of complicated patterns made by the impressions of a toothed stamp. Combinations of zigzags, meander, swastika, rhombi and triangles were the most common. Several vessels were decorated with 'pictograms' which consisted of styled designs of moon, stars, and animals (hare).

As spectrographic analysis shows (Chernykh 1970), metal objects were manufactured from ore imported from the Ural and Volga-Kama sources. Metal tools included axe-celts, knives and sickles. Spearheads were the most common weapons; at least three varieties of them are distinguishable. Ornamental items included temple-rings, plaques, bracelets and beads. One of the temple-rings found at Borisoglebsk cemetery was made of a gold plate cast on a bronze base.

It is generally accepted that the subsistence of Pozdnyakovian groups was solidly based on stock-breeding, with a possible participation in agriculture, and supplemented by foraging strategies. As in the previous case, no radiocarbon dates are available. Based on typological analogies, this culture is usually dated to 1500–1000 BC.

A particular line of development during the Middle–Late Bronze Age may be traced in the densely forested northern part of the Russian Plain. The progress in metallurgy and stock-breeding was slowly proceeding there, while foraging remained the dominant strategy of food quest.

In large areas of northern Russia and Finland, the ceramics of this Age were often manufactured from clay tempered with asbestos and decorated by incised lines forming a closely set network. For this reason, these styles are usually referred to as either 'asbestos' or 'network' pottery. At the same time, several cultural groupings in that area show clear evidence of continuity. The percentage of network pottery at sites of Late Kargopolian culture, which developed east of Lake Onega, is less than 15 (Oshibkina 1987). The bulk of the pottery, as well as the lithic and bone industry, shows a direct continuity from the preceeding Fatyanovo and pit-and-comb related entities.

Sites tend to be located at a slightly higher geomorphic level and at a greater distance from waterways than earlier. Faunal remains belong only to wild species: elk, reindeer, beaver, squirrel, marten and badger. At the same time, one notes the presence of a limited number of domesticates: cattle, sheep, goat and horse. Local metallurgy is evident at a number of sites.

Network pottery has been identified at a number of sites in the St Petersburg district and southern Karelia. As in other northern Bronze Age sites, stone inventory, manufactured of schist, quartz and rarely flint, is basically traditional. One notes the appearance of polished tools in much greater quantity and there is evidence for metallurgy based on local outcrops of copper. Schematic motifs of water fowl, usually ducks, are noted on pottery.

Sites with asbestos pottery were found predominantly in eastern Finland, central and northern Karelia, spreading to the shores of the Barents Sea. The economy of these sites was based on foraging strategies. The remains of a large bronze smith's shop were discovered near Petrozavodsk.

A large number of Bronze Age sites has been discovered by Gurina (1987) along the northern shore of Kola peninsula. The economy of all these sites was largely dependent upon the exploitation of marine resources. This included the hunting of sea mammals, predominantly Greenland seal, but also walrus, seal, sea hare, polar bear and whale (the latter probably was washed up by the sea), supplemented by fishing (cod was most common) and collecting of molluscs. The hunting of water fowl and land mammals (elk, reindeer and fur animals – fox, glutton, beaver) was also important in the food quest.

The construction of 'labyrinths', circles or spirals of stones is a particular cultural feature of northern Bronze Age communities. A vertebra of a young whale was found beneath the central stone of one of the large labyrinths.

A characteristic feature of the Middle–Late Bronze Age in forested northern Eurasia was the emergence of large-scale cross-cultural networks

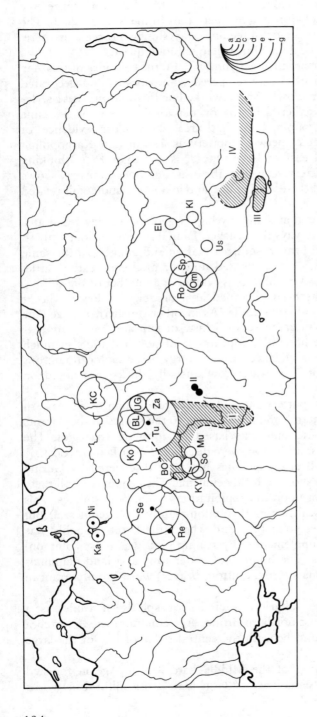

Fig. 30 Seima-Turbino sites.

Key. Sites: Se – Seima; Tu – Turbino; Ro – Rostovka; KC – Kanin Cave; Re – Reshnoe; Ka – Kagulino; Ko – Korshunovo; Ni – Nikol'skoe; KY – Krasnyi Yar; SO – Sokolovka; BO – Berezovka-Omary; Mu – Murzikha; BL – Bor-Lenva; Za – Zaosinova; UG – Ust'-Gaiva; Om – Om³ (hoard); Sp – Sopka 2; El – Yelunino; Kl – Klepikovo; Us – Ust'yanka. Mining areas: I – Copper sandstone of the Southern Urals; II – Tash-Kazgan and Nikol'skoe copper mines; III – Cassiterite ores of the Kalba and Narym Ridges (Eastern Kazakhstan); IV – Copper and polymetallic ores in the Altai Mountains (Southern Siberia).

Note. Diameter sizes (a = smallest, g = largest): a corresponds to 1–2 finds; b – 2–5 finds; c – 5–10 finds; d – 10–20 finds; e – 20–50 finds; f – 50–100 finds; g – >100 finds.

Source. O.N. Bader, D.A. Krainov & M.F. Kosarev, *Epoha bronzy lesnoi polosy SSSR.* Moscow: Nauka, 1987.

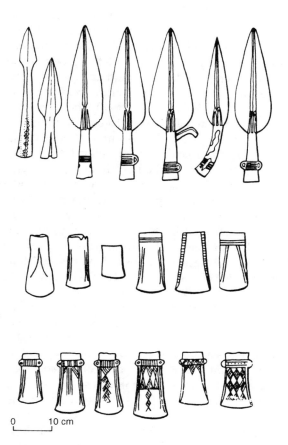

Fig. 31　Seima-Turbino spearheads (upper row) and axes.
　　　Source. O.N. Bader, D.A. Krainov & M.F. Kosarev, *Epoha bronzy lesnoi polosy SSSR.* Moscow: Nauka, 1987.

which extended over thousands of miles. Seima-Turbino complex is one of the most outstanding examples of this kind. This complex, which manifested itself in a particular metal-working tradition, was identified at various sites in European Russia and Siberia (Fig. 30). The dating of this complex is based largely on the typology of artefacts and a single radiocarbon date – from the Yelupino cemetery in the Altai mountains – suggesting the age of 1700–1600 BC.

　　The tradition was first recognized before the First World War by A.M. Tallgren and V.A. Gorodtsov, who noticed similarities between certain types of bronze implements. It was later studied by O.N. Bader (1970) among others. Much of the information regarding the Seima-Turbino culture comes from several cemeteries excavated over a prolonged period of time and with varying degrees of professionalism. Seima (Sejma) cemetery is situated on a sand-dune ridge on the left bank of the River Oka, at its confluence with the Volga. The site was excavated in 1912–1914 by a local military detachment, and judging from the incomplete records, no less than fifty graves were discovered. Out of the 112 metal objects found, no more than seventy have survived. Turbino-1 cemetery lies within the town of Perm. Excavated by A.V. Schmidt in 1924–27 and by O.N. Bader in 1958–60, the cemetery contained about 200 graves; no skeletal remains were found. Among the 3128 metal implements that were found were: forty-four socketed celts, forty daggers or knives, thirteen spearheads, three shaft-hole axes, twenty-three temple rings, and nine bracelets. At the neighbouring cemetery of Turbino-2, a knife with a terminal cast as a bull's head was found. Reshnoe cemetery is located in the Nizhni-Novgorod district, on a dune ridge on the right bank of the River Oka. It was excavated by Bader in 1974–75. He found eighteen graves arranged in three rows, but no human remains. The metal objects included socketed celts, spearheads, knives or daggers, adzes and awls. The grave inventory comprised numerous flint implements, two nephrite rings and nine ceramic vessels. Rostovka cemetery lies on the River Om, in the southern suburb of the city of Omsk. In 1966–69 V.I. Matyushchenko excavated thirty-eight shallow rectangular graves. The dominant burial rite was inhumation, but some cases combined with partial cremation. The remaining bodies were generally oriented to the west. Some bodies were beheaded. There were also separate burials of skulls.

Seima-Turbino metal tools fall into three main categories: socketed axes, socketed spearheads and daggers–knives with numerous sub-types (Fig. 31). Tin and tin-arsenic bronze alloys account for 41.4 per cent of the analyzed objects. Tools made of these materials were spread over a wide area, from Finland to the Altai. E.N. Chernykh (1970) suggested that these tools were manufactured from ores originating in the Altai mines. Copper sandstone east of the Urals probably formed the source of 'pure' copper. Metal artefacts showing Seima-Turbino characteristics were known from numerous sites over a very wide area: from Finland in the west to Western Mongolia in the east. Chernykh (1992) argues that this 'transcultural phenomenon' resulted from the gradual expansion of groups of metal-workers and warrior-horsemen from east to west along the Eurasian forest-steppe.

If one turns again to the 'steppic corridor' in the south, one may see the development of a different Bronze Age culture, that of the Catacomb Graves. This culture, corresponding to *c.* 2000 BC, is represented primarily by kurgan burial mounds in steppic regions of Ukraine and southern Russia. It was first identified by V.A. Gorodtsov in 1901–03 in the Severski Donets river area. The main feature of this culture was Catacomb Graves situated beneath mounds and consisting of a rectangular or an oval shaft leading to a burial chamber (see Fig. 27b on p. 93). The burial chamber contained one, and occasionally, two or three skeletons, laid in a contracted posture on their sides, and always included red ochre. Grave goods consisted of ceramics, stone mace heads and flint spear- and arrowheads. Bronze implements were common; they included shaft-hole axes, adzes, chisels and various ornaments (temple rings, spiral-rings, beads and pendants). The typology of metal implements reflects the influence of northern Caucasus (particularly the Maikopian). Tools were manufactured from arsenic-rich copper ores, presumably originated from the Donets basin. Several burials (for example, Malaya Ternovka in the Lower Dniepr area) contain copper slag, ingots, sets of tools for foundry and casting, and what is thought to be the founders' graves. Silver rings and amber pendants have been found in several Catacomb Graves near the town of Donetsk. In another grave, near the village of Bolotnoe in the Crimea, remains of a woven bag with wheat-ears have been found; the same grave contained four wheels and an axis of a cart. Settlements belonging to the same culture have been found in the catchment of the River Ingul and along the lower stretches of the Southern Bug; they are situated on promontories of upper terraces and include dwellings on stone foundations. Faunal remains mainly consisted of bones of cattle, sheep and goat.

If one tries to summarize the existing evidence for the Bronze Age in the discussed areas, the following picture emerges. The entire Russian Plain was engulfed in the process of transition to a food-producing economy (primarily stock-breeding), which affected various parts of this huge area in different ways. The southernmost steppic area was taken up by groups of nomadic stock-breeders. The area immediately to the north, comprising forest-steppe and mixed broad-leaved forests, was occupied by settled stock-breeders with elements of agriculture and a strong presence of foraging strategies. Groups in the entire coniferous north retained their basically foraging-type economy inherited from the previous time, although elements of stock-breeding have been found there in a number of cases.

The spread of metallurgy and metal-working was the second major element of change in Bronze Age economies. Several major exchange networks, primarily based on the trade of ore and metal products, crystallized in the Russian Plain. The steppic area, where a number of local chiefdoms have evolved, was part of a Circum-Pontic network which also included the Balkans, the Aegean, and Asia Minor. It is suggested that Anatolian languages were in use there as a communication medium.

Areas of forest-steppe and mixed broad-leaved forests to the north, which included later derivatives of Corded Ware cultures (East Baltic, Sosnitsian, Komarovian, and possibly Pozdniakovian), formed a different network. These groups supposedly used proto-Baltic-Slavic dialects. There are serious linguistic arguments supporting the existence of an undifferentiated Baltic-Slavic language in that area (see Chapter 7).

Areas in the north included groups with asbestos and 'network' ceramics. In all probability, they spoke Finnish dialects. Of course, this linguistic division was not as straightforward as presented here. There occurred numerous contact zones where several languages were in use. Such large networks as Abashevian or Seima-Turbino were not linguistically related at all, and included various ethnic and/or language groups.

Chapter 6   ....

The Age of Change

The Iron Age

The events which will be discussed in this chapter have occurred mainly during the course of the first millennium BC. This was a time of unstable climate. In palaeoclimatic terms it corresponded to the boundary between the Sub-Boreal and Sub-Atlantic periods. According to the pollen evidence from the central regions of the Russian Plain (Khotinsky et al. 1991), the final Sub-Boreal stage featured a cool and wet climate. The early Sub-Atlantic was marked by a general increase in temperature. A prolonged cool oscillation, from 880 to 320 BC, has been identified in the Swiss Alps (Beug 1982).

In the traditional archaeological chronology, this time-span is usually referred to as the Iron Age. The emergence of iron metallurgy was generally regarded as its principal technological innovation. Since it became apparent that iron was in use in the Near East much earlier than it was in Europe, it has been suggested that the technological knowledge penetrated Europe from there, via Asia Minor and Greece. However, recent studies show a much more complicated picture; it becomes increasingly obvious that iron metallurgy in Europe developed more or less independently, although this does not rule out the existence of multifaceted links between various parts of Europe and the Mediterranean world involved in the production and exchange of iron implements.

No less important was the discovery that iron was occasionally used in Europe before the 'official' commencement of the Iron Age. Iron occurred as inlay in bronze objects such as swords, rings, pins, and in composite tools, for example, bronze handles and iron blades, especially in swords and knives (Wells 1981). It took at least two centuries for iron technology to replace bronze as the principal metal for manufacturing tools and weapons.

Iron ore is usually found in two common minerals – hematite and limonite. The deposits of these minerals occur in many parts of Europe, particularly in the Alpine area. They are often found in the form of surface outcrops; in such cases ore may be procured without underground mining. In many parts of European Russia rich iron deposits are found in the form of 'marsh ore', in the bottom layers of peat-bogs and lakes.

Since its beginnings, iron metallurgy was a complicated full-time craft that necessitated a substantial investment of labour and professional management. A number of iron smelting and forging sites has been found in various parts of Europe. One of the most remarkable sites is the cave of Býcî Skála in Moravia which has been dated to the sixth century BC. The blacksmith's site included ash and charcoal from the furnace, lumps of smelted but not forged iron, and iron tools: hammers, anvils and tongues (Pleiner 1980).

Sophisticated and diversified techniques of iron technology were available in the early Iron Age. Some of the iron objects were made of plain wrought iron; others had been previously heat treated to improve the hardness. In several cases packet welding has been identified (Wells 1981).

The Bronze industry retained its importance at least in several parts of Europe. The principal regions of Iron Age copper mining in the Alpine area were in Upper Austria and in Tyrol. A well-documented bronze-working centre was found at Velem Szentvid, in western Hungary (Foltiny 1958). This site contained unworked copper metal and stone moulds. The bronze objects included bracelets, belt attachments and fibulae. A new technique had developed by the early Iron Age: large objects were manufactured from sheet bronze.

There is also evidence for other crafts. The kiln, located at a distance from the main settlement at Hascherkeller in Upper Austria, produced the bulk of the pottery used at the site and possibly also exported it elsewhere. Similar kilns were found at other sites in central and western Europe (Wells 1981). Textile production is attested by the finds of ceramic loom weights and spindle-whorls. Gold-working is evident at several Iron Age sites in Slovenia. 'Diadems' were the most common golden objects: sheer gold cut into a variety of geometrical forms and decorated with impressed circular or linear patterns. Other gold implements, usually found in the graves, included belt plates, earrings and armbands of sheet gold (Wells 1981). Glass-working appeared in the Alpine region in the Middle Bronze Age and continued into the Early Iron Age. At least one-third of the graves in the tumuli of Stiéina in Slovenia contained glass beads of various forms. The extraction of salt also played an extremely important role in the economy of Iron Age communities, particularly in the Alpine area. The site of Halstatt in Upper Austria was a blatant example of a large community which specialized in the extraction of salt for export trade.

Judging from the faunal remains, the rural economy of the Early Iron Age sites in the Alpine area comprised a large spectrum of domesticated animals: cattle, pigs, sheep, goats and dogs were identified both on the settlements and in the graves. Sheep were raised mainly for wool; goats and cattle provided dairy products, as well as meat and leather. Cattle were also used as draft animals. Wooden ards were well documented at a number of bog-sites in Denmark. They are also shown in rock carvings in Sweden, northern Italy and southwestern France. In these carvings the ards are pulled by two oxen. Limited numbers of wild animals included red deer, roe deer, wild boar and beaver.

The existing evidence suggests a sufficiently developed agriculture. Among grains were identified: einkorn wheat (*Triticum monococcum*), club wheat (*T. aestivum,* ssp. *compactum*), emmer (*T. dicoccum*), spelt (*T. spelta*), rye (*Secale cereale*), broomcorn millet (*Panicum miliaceum*), Italian millet (*Setaria italica*), barnyard millet (*Echinochloa crusgalli*), oats (*Avena sativa*), and naked six-row barley (*Hordeum vulgare*). Horse bean (*Vica faba*), pea (*Pisum sativum*) and bitter vetch (*Vica ervilia*) were identified among the legumes. Gold of pleasure (*Camelia sativa*) and opium poppy (*Poypaversomiferum*) were grown for natural oil. The botanical records included the seeds of fruits: grape, plum, cherry, apple. Bouzek et al. (1966) argued that a sophisticated system of land-use had developed in central Europe by 1000 BC. This included fallowing, manuring and initial rotating of crops. Agriculture was supplemented by the collecting of wild plants (hazelnuts, beechnuts, water chestnut and berries).

Yet the most spectacular development occurred in the social sphere. An advanced stage of social stratification and the crystallization of a social élite, increasingly associated with warfare from horseback, were the most important aspects of this development, the evidence of which can be found in 'princely' graves: inhumations in tumulus burials with a special 'status kit'. The emergence of fortified settlements or 'hill-forts', located on dominant landscape features, was no less important evidence for status differentiation: these hill-forts were usually princely residences.

There is yet another important feature of the Iron Age in Europe. During its course, several societies, particularly in the eastern Mediterranean world, reached the level of literacy. At this stage, archaeological records are no longer silent, but can be increasingly interfaced with, and controlled by, the testimony of ancient writers. One of the important consequences of this is that in certain cases scholars can identify archaeological entities with distinct ethnicities mentioned by the ancient historians and geographers.

The development of long-distance trade was yet another aspect of social development in the Early Iron Age. As special analysis has shown (Wells 1981), the Early Iron Age trade in the Alpine area included raw materials (iron, tin, copper and, particularly, salt) as well as various products. The latter included luxurious ornaments, ostensibly intended for the local élite. These prestige goods originated from Italy and other centres of the Mediterranean world and included such items as the bronze 'comb' helmets, glass bowls and cups, ornamented lids and situlae, as well as containers (ceramic craters and amphorae, and bronze vessels), bronze figurines and other objects. Numerous graves in Upper Austria and Slovenia contained amber beads of Baltic origin.

Hence, it is sufficiently apparent that by the Early Iron Age a network of trade links covered the greater part of Europe. This was a highly organized trade system, comparable to that of traditional societies, that has been documented historically and ethnographically (Wells 1983). The organization of trade was closely connected to the social structure. As in traditional societies, trade was controlled by the principal personage in each community, the senior man or headman. This individual acted as a regulator of the community's interaction with the outer world. He supervised production, chose the materials intended for export, and appropriated wealth in the form of imported goods.

Within this expanding network of trade links one may easily identify the areas of more intense interaction, perceived as archaeological 'cultures'. Two major archaeological cultures are traditionally distinguished in the European Iron Age: Halstatt (750–500/400 BC) and La-Tène (500/400–120/100 BC, preceding the Roman conquest). The Halstatt core area includes the northern and eastern Alps, the Upper Danube and the neighbouring areas of Slovenia, Czech Lands and Hungary. Its western sphere extends to Switzerland, southern Germany and Burgundy. Archaeologically, the Halstatt culture is recognized by the shared styles of iron tools, particularly swords and some types of ornament. In social terms, the Halstatt may be viewed as an arena of intense socio-political interaction, largely resulting from the power of local chieftains, effectively controlling the extraction and trade in metal (including ore) and salt. The La-Tène culture, that spread in Europe since the fifth century BC, is the first European archaeological entity which may be more or less distinctly associated with an ethnicity: it is usually allied with the Celts. Archaeologically, the La-Tène is identified by special types of weapon (swords and knives), yet more spectacular are the ornaments: bracelets, armbands and, particularly, fibulae. In the opinion of Bintliff (1984), it was ' . . . an indigenous amalgamation of Mediterranean East European and steppe Halstatt artistic influences with an original creative transformation of these components which resulted in the quite unique – Celtic art'. These works of art are usually found in the princely burials. The La-Tène élite burials, as in the preceding Halstatt period, contain exotic luxury pieces, often originating from Etruscan centres. The La-Tène sites are represented mostly by the cemeteries, although the fortified settlements (*oppidia*) are sufficiently numerous. Bintliff views the Halstatt/La-Tène transition as a 'gradual process of piecemeal abandonment of central places' (1984: 167).

The core area of the La-Tène culture centres on the Rhine and Champagne; its influence is attested in the greater part of western and central Europe. The spread of the La-Tène is usually associated with the Celtic migrations. The most apparent examples are the historically attested sack of Rome by the Celts ('Gauls') in 387–6 and their capture of the Italian north. The massive spread of the La-Tène to the east is equally associated with Celtic expansion, which was particularly active in the third century BC. Bintliff (1984) argued that the local élite of these regions were highly receptive to, and readily adopted, the La-Tène forms and ideas.

The Lausitz culture of present-day Poland and eastern Germany is an example of local development in the Early Iron Age. The emergence of large hill-forts, located on the prominent forms of landscape, was the most outstanding feature of the settlement pattern of the Lausitz culture. The setting of Biskupin hill-fort, 75 km north of Poznan, is fairly typical (Niewiarowski et al. 1992). The site was located in the area of young morainic landscape, on top of a hillock dominating the lake and the neighbouring fluvio-glacial plain. The hillock was surrounded by a breakwater made of oak and pine stakes. The ramparts were built of rectangular-placed oak logs interlocked at the corners. The inner structure of the hill-fort consisted of uniformly built rectangular houses, 9 by 8 metres, arranged along streets. The streets were made of oak and pine logs and covered with clay. The total settled area was *c.* 25 sq. km, and the population has been estimated as *c.* 800 persons.

The economy of the Lausitz culture was based on the developed agriculture of a plough type. Wooden ploughs, antler hoes and bronze sickles were in use. Ards, basically similar to those of Jutland, were also utilized. The macrofossil plant remains showed the cultivation of four species of wheat, two species of barley, millet, as well as peas, lentils, poppy, turnip and flax. The faunal remains were dominated by cattle, followed by sheep, goat and pig. The crafts included pottery-making and metallurgy. Gold-working, bone-carving and textile production were evident in a number of cases. Archaeologically, the Lausitz culture is recognized by certain types of weapon and ornament. The swords were of Halstatt and, later, of La-Tène types. The ornaments, identified mainly in the graves, included different types of pins and fibula, the latter having direct analogies in the Halstatt and La-Tène prototypes.

Scholars, both in the west and the east, are nearly unanimous in admitting the local origins of the Lausitz culture. Harding and Ostoja-Zagórski (1993) link it up with the Urnfield culture of central Europe and ascribe its extraction to the process of interaction and transformation that affected the entire area between *c.* 1500–500 BC. Grakov (1977), as well as many Russian and Polish scholars, traces its origin to the Corded Ware and Trzciniec cultures. However, the presence of multiple Halstatt and La-Tène imports and the general uniform character of its socio-economic development leaves one in no doubt that the Lausitz cultural phenomenon was a result of the inclusion of the local communities in the major socio-political network of the European Iron Age.

The northern hill-forts

During the first millennium BC, dramatic changes occurred among the communities of the Russian Plain. In the northwestern area of the Russian

Plain, for the first time since the beginning of the Holocene, settlements started to appear on top of the morainic hills. The hill-fort type settlements (*gorodishche* in Russian), were located on the predominant features of landscape overlooking the surrounding low-lying areas. The hill-forts also appeared on the promontories of higher terraces, extending into the river floors. Artificial fortifications, ramparts and ditches, appeared at a later stage. In some cases, these fortifications were complex, that is with two or more rows of ramparts. The hill-forts included both semi-subterranean and surface dwellings. The latter were more common. They were square or rectangular in shape, 10 by 16 metres in size, and built of wooden logs supported by posts.

Yet another fundamental innovation, which is associated with the advent of the Iron Age in the Russian Plain, is that for the first time the subsistence of local groups relied heavily on agriculture. Judging from the available palaeobotanic evidence (Krasnov 1971), the cultivated plants included wheats (mainly spelt), barley (*Hordeum vulgare* and *H. distichum*), both naked and hulled, and millet. In all probability, swidden cultivation was the dominant system of agriculture in the greater part of Iron Age communities, at least in the western and central parts of the Russian Plain.

The swidden type of agriculture (also known as slash-and-burn and shifting) is comparatively well studied ethnographically. Considerable parts of Fennoscandia and northern Russia were swidden agriculture areas *par excellence* as late as the seventeenth to early nineteenth centuries AD, and some areas of northern Russia (such as Arkhangelsk, Vologda and Novgorod districts), still practiced swidden cultivation in the 1920s. Swidden cultivation was ideally adapted to the densely forested morainic terrain of northeastern Europe. Clearances were usually located on hill slopes where there was no need for ditches to lead away the rain water. The earliest swidden areas were located in the proximity of rivers and lakes. The plots chosen for clearances in the deciduous forests were usually felled in the early summer and burned over the next spring. Prior to burning or felling, the conifer trees were often dried by the removal of bark. The clearances were cultivated for several years. The seeds were sown straight into the ashes; the plot was not cleared of unburned timber. Under normal conditions, a plot would give three to four crops, rarely more. Rye or barley were sown first, followed by turnip and sometimes flax and, since the late 18th century, oats. After that, the clearance was abandoned. The regeneration of forests on the abandoned plot took normally 15–30 years.

Sarmela (1987) quotes the following basic socio-economic properties of the swidden cultivation. 1) Swidden agriculture is sufficiently productive without major input of labour and investment. 2) It does not create wealth; in the swidden agriculture the private ownership of land is not known in the same sense as in the field cultivation. 3) Swidden cultivation requires large reserves of land to remain in balance with the environment. 4) Extended family (which may include up to 100 persons) was the natural family structure. 5) Swidden cultivation required rather a primitive set of implements, such as a wooden hoe and a special type of forked plough.

As in other regions of central and northern Europe, several cultures can be distinguished in the forest zone of the Russian Plain: (mostly, by the styles and types of artefacts). One of these cultures is referred to as that of 'stroked' pottery (Mitrofanov 1978; Isaenko et al. 1970). The sites belonging to this culture were spread mainly in central and northern Belorussia and in southeastern Lithuania and dated from the seventh to the first centuries BC. The unfortified and fortified (at the later stage) hill-forts were the main types of settlement. They were usually located on top of the morainic hills or on the high river terraces. The fortifications (turf walls and timber fences) started to appear in the fourth and third centuries BC. Still later, in the third, second and first centuries BC, the fortifications became more complicated: they included an outer rampart and one or several inner walls. Long houses comprised several square rooms (20–25 sq. metres); their construction included wooden posts supporting the roof and walls. The houses were built on flattened surfaces adjoining the walls from the inside. The central area was reserved for corrals and workshops. Numerous storage pits contained pottery, slag, animal bones and charred grains. The ceramics consisted mainly of flat-bottomed pots covered by the strokes (hence the name). The rate of domesticates in the faunal remains was 55–56 per cent; cattle were the most common, followed by (in the order of importance) pig, horse, sheep and goat. Among the wild animals identified were boar, elk, red deer, brown bear, otter and others. The crops included Italian millet, wheats, pulses and lentils.

Iron implements were numerous; they included sickles, axes, arrow- and spearheads, daggers, awls, needles and fishhooks. Rubber-stones, stone querns and plummets were commonly found. The ornaments included iron pins, bronze brooches, plaques, rings and bracelets. Some of these (plaques and brooches) were of Scandinavian origin. At later stages the imported goods denoted contacts with the La-Tène sites in central Europe and with the Greek colonies on the Black Sea. The finds of loom weights indicated the occurrence of weaving (wool and flax). Blacksmith's shops have been established at a number of sites; they included furnaces, lumps of smelted iron and the blacksmith's instruments: hammers, anvils and tongues. Local bog-ores were the main source of iron.

Another culture, Dniepr-Dvinian, occurred in the catchment of the Upper Western Dvina and Dniepr rivers, in northwestern Russia, northeastern Belorussia and northern Ukraine during the first millennium BC (Stankevich 1960; Isaenko et al. 1970). Settlements of the hill-fort type were usually located on top of the morainic hills, close to lakes or river valleys. At the early stage (seventh–second centuries BC) there were no artificial fortifications. Turf walls and ditches appeared at later stages during the second and first centuries BC. The size of hill-forts varied from 400 to 3000 sq. metres (usually 800–1500 sq. metres).

Two types of houses were distinguishable: small (3–3.2 metres) and long (3–10/14 metres). Both had hearths in the middle of the living space and wooden posts supporting the roof and walls. The material remains included numerous ceramics mostly flat-bottomed red-grey pots. Diverse iron implements included sickles, daggers, axes, spear- and arrowheads, and ornaments – brooches, rings and bracelets. Bronze implements were manufactured from ingots imported from the area west of the Urals. A find of a mould for a Scandinavian-type celt at the site near Nakvasino (the Upper Dniepr) was remarkable. The bone tools were similar to those of central Russia. Several specialized smelting and forging sites have been found (for example, Chernaya Gora near the town of Sebezh on the Russian-Latvian border). The rate of domesticates in the faunal remains varied between 40 and 80 per cent: pigs made up about one-third of the assemblage; cattle, 24 per cent; sheep and goats, 20–23 per cent, and horse 15 per cent (Sedov 1970a). Crops included bread and spelt wheats, and naked and hulled barley (Krasnov 1971).

Yet another culture, the Milogradian, was spread in the Upper Dniepr catchment (in northern and central Belorussia and the neighbouring area of western Russia and northern Ukraine) between the seventh and third centuries BC (Tretyakov 1966; Isaenko et al. 1970). The hill-fort-type settlements were usually located on the upper river terraces and on the elevated hills in the wetland areas. The settlements were of a considerable size (15,000–20,000 sq. metres). They often included two rows of fortifications (turf walls and ditches). The inner part was densely built up with rectangular (4 by 4 metre) houses with wooden posts along the walls and hearths in the corner niches. The outer protected area had few houses and was supposedly intended for corrals.

The ceramics consisted of hand-made round-bottomed vessels with straight or S-shaped necks. Numerous iron implements included two types of axe, sickles, knives with curved blades, spear- and arrowheads. Bracelets were the most common ornaments. Several types of spearhead, iron belt and bronze bracelet have direct analogies in the La-Tène assemblages of central Europe. A hoard near the village of Gorshkovo (near Mozyr, southern Belorussia) contained eleven bronze and silver bracelets of La-Tène type dated to the fifth–third centuries BC. Contacts with Scythian groups further south were demonstrated by numerous finds of Scythian-style arrowheads, ear-rings and hammer-headed pins.

All the sites include slag, fragments of crucibles and blacksmith's instruments, denoting the local smelting and forging of iron. The rate of domesticates in the faunal remains varied between 70 and 90 per cent, with cattle making up 40 per cent, followed by horse (30 per cent), sheep and goat (17 per cent) and pig (14 per cent). Numerous finds of sickles, querns, as well as the impressions of grains (wheats, barley, millet), proved the occurrence of agriculture.

Both surface graves and kurgan barrows were found; the burial rite included cremation and inhumation. No less than ten cemeteries with surface graves have been located. One of the largest cemeteries, Gorshkovo, included seventy graves. Shallow oval-shaped graves contained cremated human remains, fragments of ceramics and iron implements (arrowheads, rings and pins). Cemeteries with kurgan barrows were also reported, for example, Duboi, near Brest. One of the barrows contained a grave with the remains of two adults and one child, apparently belonging to the social élite; the grave goods included a golden ear-ring, an iron arrowhead and fragments of a hand-made vessel.

The Cimmerians, Scythians, Greeks and . . .

Now, we have to move further south, into the forest-steppic and steppic zones. In doing so, it is necessary to make several steps backwards which will bring us to the Late Bronze Age. At that time a new cultural phenomenon was spreading there: the culture of Timber Graves (or *Srubnaya* in Russian). This culture was first identified by V.A. Gorodtsov in 1901–03 in the Seveski Donets area and has been intensively studied by Russian and Ukrainian scholars, including N.Ya. Merpert, O.A. Krivtsova-Grakova, A.I. Terenozhkin and others. The sites were identified in a vast area, stretching from the Middle and Lower Volga in the east to the Lower Danube in the west and have been dated to *c*.1600–1200 BC (Berezanskaya and Cherdnichenko 1985; Haüsler 1974). The main feature of the culture is a rectangular burial chamber made in the form of a wooden framework ('*srub*' in Russian), 1.8–2.2 metres long, 1.2–1.4 metres wide and 0.4–0.6 metres high, beneath the kurgan mound (see Fig. 27 on p. 93). Stone cists are also common. The dead were usually laid in a contracted posture on their left side, with their heads directed to the east. The grave goods were usually restricted to one, rarely two, ceramic vessels. A few rich graves have been found, containing bronze knives and ornaments: spirals, rings and wooden vessels with bronze inlays. Animal bones were often found in the graves (for example, six bull skulls in kurgan No. 5 at Kamushevakha, near the town of Bakhmut on the Severski Donets). The barrows formed small groups (numbering 5–10) usually along the edges of the plateaux. More than 100 settlements belonging to the Timber Grave culture are known in the Severski Donets catchment alone; they are usually situated on the dunes or small hills in the river floor. The remains of fortifications have been found in a few cases. The semi-subterranean houses of square or rectangular shape (7 by 7 or 6 by 8 metres) were arranged in one or two rows.

It is widely accepted by scholars that the Timber Grave culture population consisted of predominantly sedentary groups, their economy based on the developed stock-breeding, agriculture and metallurgy. The faunal remains consisted of the bones of cattle, sheep and goat, pig and horse. Flint and bronze sickles, pestles and quern stones were indicative of agriculture. At the site of Usovo Ozero (near Donetsk), G.A. Pashkevich (1991) has identified the grains of einkorn and club wheats, six-row barley, rye, oats and Italian millet. Metallurgy was particularly developed in the area close to the copper mines in the Donets basin, near the villages of Klonovoe, Pilipchatino, Kalinovka and Pokrovskoe. These sites contained the remains of workshops which included furnaces, slag, ingots, fragments of crucibles and clay molds. Another metallurgical centre was located in the western Urals, and, like the preceeding cultural entities, especially Poltavka, was based on the local copper-bearing sandstone (Chernykh 1992).

With the Timber Graves culture, we again encounter attempts to identify an archaeological entity with a distinct ethnicity. Many scholars, for example, A.I. Terenozhkin (1976) and B.N. Grakov (1977) identified the culture with the Cimmerians, a group of ancient people who lived north of the Caucasus and the Black Sea and historically attested to a time-span between 714 and *c.* 500 BC. Historical records regarding the Cimmerians are vague and sketchy. Here, as in many later cases, the testimony of Herodotus is particularly important. Herodotus, who is often referred to as the 'Father of History', was born in 484 BC, probably in Halicarnassus, a Greek city on the southern Aegean coast of Asia Minor. His *Historia* described the expansions of the Persian empire. Book IV relates in great detail the unsuccessful campaign waged by Darius against the Scythians. To collect the necessary information for his book, Herodotus undertook numerous voyages to various parts of the Persian empire: Egypt, Libya, Syria, Babylon, Susa. He journeyed up the Hellespont to Byzantium, went to Thrace and Macedonia, and crossed the Danube. He voyaged along the northern shores of the Black Sea, visited Olbia, the largest Greek city in the Dniepr-Bug estuary, and went further inland up some of the rivers. The information collected by Herodotus and recorded in his book contains priceless observations about the geography of Scythia and the ethnology of local tribes. Herodotus wrote:

> The land which is now inhabited by the Scyths was formerly inhabited by the Cimmerians. On their [Scythian] coming, the natives [the Cimmerians], who heard how numerous the invading army was, held a council. At this meeting, opinion was divided, and both parties stiffly maintained their views. But the Royal tribe was braver. While the others urged that the best thing to be done was to leave the country and avoid a contest with so vast a host, the Royal tribe advised them to remain and fight for the soil to the last. As neither party chose to give way, one determined to retire without a blow and yield their lands to the invaders, but the other, remembering the good things which they had enjoyed in their homes, and picturing to themselves the evils which they had to expect if they gave them up, resolved not to flee, but rather to die and at least be buried in their fatherland. Having thus decided, they drew apart in two bodies, the one as numerous as the other, and fought together. All the Royal tribe was slain and their people buried near the river Tyras, where their grave is still to be seen. Then the rest of the Cimmerians departed, and the Scythians,

on their coming took possession of a desert land. . . . Scythia still retains traces of the Cimmerians: there are Cimmerian walls and a Cimmerian ferry, and also a tract called Cimmeria and the Cimmerian Bosporus. It appears likewise, that the Cimmerians, when they fled into Asia to escape the Scyths, made a settlement in the peninsula, where the Greek city of Sinope was afterwards built . . .

Hence, one may see a colourful and, beyond any doubt, partly fictitious account of the final stages of the Cimmerian history. Herodotus, based on much later records, provides an exact location for the Cimmerians (the Pontic steppe and the Crimea), reports their internal division, their strife with the Scythians, their defeat and departure from the historical scene. Based on different sources, Strabo, the Greek historian and geographer who was born in 64/63 BC and died after AD 23, reports the Cimmerians as dwelling in the eastern Crimea and in the neighbouring Taman peninsula, in northwestern Caucasus. He also mentions that the Cimmerians took part in the assaults on Asia Minor, moving through Caucasus.

The Assyrian cuneiform texts repeatedly mentioned 'the people of Gamirra' who, on several occasions, invaded the northern frontiers of the state of Urartu and penetrated further south into Assyria and Asia Minor. The initial appearance of the Gamirra was reported between 722 and 715 BC. Grakov (1977) argued that the Gamirra were the Cimmerians. In 679–678 BC, the Gamirra-Cimmerians were defeated in Asia Minor, after which they are often mentioned in the Assyrian texts. In 676–674 BC, together with the Urartians, they assaulted Phrygia. In 647 BC they captured Sardis in western Anatolia. Assurbanipal, the last 'great' king of Assyria, defeated them in Cilicia after 654 BC. They last appeared in Asia Minor and their final retreat (probably resulting from the Scythian débâcle) occurred in 614–611 BC. After that time, they virtually disappeared from the written sources.

Scholars still argue about the language of the Cimmerians. There are very few available records. Several proper names (such as Kob) were reported by the Greek historians and these sound like Thraco-Phrigian; others (Teushpa, Dugdamme, Sandakashtru) are of the Iranian character.

The Scythians were the next historically and archaeologically identifiable cultural group to appear in the South Russian Plain and they made a substantial impact on the entire ancient world. The Scythians (and Scythian-related groups), often under different names, are mentioned in various written sources: in cuneiform-written Assyrian, in Urartian and Babylon inscriptions, in biblical texts, and even in Chinese chronicles. They are often mentioned by various Greek sources. Among the latter, the testimony of Herodotus, contained in Book IV of his *Historia* and based on first-hand information as well as on the accounts of the dwellers of Olbia (or Olbiapolites), is particularly valuable.

Summing up the available evidence, one may assume the following essential facts in the history of the Scythians. For a long time the Scythians, alongside the Cimmerians, took an active part in the conflicts of the Middle East. In the course of these conflicts, the Scythians scored a victory over the Medes and reached the borders of Egypt. Biblical texts provide a vivid description of the terror caused by the Scythian invasion. Later, as the Medes' allies, they inflicted a heavy defeat on Assyria and took part in the sacking and destruction of Niniveh. For no less than twenty years the Scythians were a dominant force in considerable areas of western Asia; they controlled vast areas in Urartu and western Iran. Still later, the Median king Kiaxar slew the Scythian chieftains during a drinking feast, after which the remaining Scythian groups retreated to the Pontic steppes where they turned their arms against the Cimmerians.

In 514–512 Darius I, the Achaemenid king of Persia, waged a campaign against the Scythians. The expedition (the 'Scythian War') was colourfully and poetically described by Herodotus in Book IV of his *Historia*. According to Herodotus's account, Darius and his army crossed the Hellespont into Thrace and attacked the Scythians from the rear. The Persian campaign proved to be a complete failure. The Scythians adopted a scorched earth tactic. Evading open clashes, they retreated deep inland, breaking up wells and destroying food and fodder. Exasperated, Darius eventually decided to withdraw. The Scythians harassed the retreating Persians and Darius was just able to get his troops back to the bridge across the Danube which opened the way to safety.

During all that time, the Scythians maintained largely peaceful relations with the Greek colonies that had emerged along the Black Sea coast. In the fourth century BC, the Scythians had to meet a new threat, that of the Sarmatians, who encroached on their lands moving from the east. It is generally accepted that the Sarmatians shared basically the same language (Iranian), and a similar culture and style of life as the Scythians. Nevertheless, their relations were far from peaceful. Increasing Sarmatian pressure had induced the Scythians to move further west. In 346 BC, the Scythian king, Aertes, led his people across the Danube into the Dobruja. The move brought conflict with the Macedonian King, Philip II. A battle was fought close to the Danube; Aertes was killed and the Scythians agreed to peace terms.

In the following year Alexander the Great sent a punitive expedition against the Scythians. This time the Scythians routed the Greek forces and killed Zepyrion, the governor of Thrace. The Crimea now emerged as a centre of the Scythian power. Scyluris, the Scythian ruler, established the first Scythian kingdom, with Neapolis (near the present-day Simferopol) as its capital. The Scythians tried to gain command over the Greek cities, aiming to assume control over their foreign trade. In 100 BC Scyluris had his own coins struck in Olbia. Later he attacked another large Greek city, Chersonesos. Mithridates, the king of the Pontic empire, defeated the Scythians on land and at sea (the Scythians had a fleet of their own manned by the Greek sailors). Still later, the Scythians joined forces with Mithridates in an attempt to resist the Roman domination of the Black Sea. These attempts were futile, and soon the entire Pontic area found itself under the Roman protectorate. At the same time the Scythians suffered a severe defeat at the hands of the Sarmatian warriors, who increasingly pushed them towards the west. Much weakened, the Scythian state still existed in the second and third centuries AD, but it eventually succumbed to the assault of new waves of nomads.

The first excavations of Scythian antiquities in southern Russia and Ukraine date back to 1763 when General A.P. Melgunov opened some magnificent barrows near the town of Elizavetgrad (Kirovograd). In 1830 P. Dubrux discovered and excavated the stone burial chamber at Kul-Oba barrow, near the town of Kerch in eastern Crimea. Intensive excavations of Scythian barrows at the turn of the century were carried out by N.I. Veselovsky while the settlements and hill-forts in the forest-steppic zone were studied by A.A. Spitzyn and V.A. Gorodtsov. In Soviet times large-scale excavations of both barrows and settlements were conducted by A.I. Terenozhkin, B.M. Mozolevsky, V.P. Shilov, P.D. Liberov, I.B. Brashinsky and others. The problems relating to the origin, ethnicity and social pattern of Scythian groups were discussed by M.I. Rostovtseff, V.I. Ravdonikas, M.I. Artamonov, B.N. Grakov, A.I. Terenozhkin, P.D. Liberov, A.M. Khazanov and other scholars (Melyukova 1989; Terenozhkin and Il'inskaya 1986).

Three main groups of Scythian sites have been distinguished in the Pontic steppes: (1) Central steppic; (2) Lower Don; and (3) Steppic Crimean. The Scythian burials in the steppic areas consisted mainly of barrows (kurgans), which started to emerge at the turn of the seventh/sixth centuries BC from the Danube to the Don. Starting with 450–400 BC, the barrows tend to cluster in the Lower Dniepr, the Lower Southern Bug and in the Dniestr-Danube interfluve. At that time the number of 'rich' barrows increased. The greater part of the so-called 'royal tombs' belong to the fourth century BC. The highest barrows are: Alexandropol (21 metres); Chertomlyk (19 metres); Oguz (20 metres); Bol'shaya Tsymbalka (15 metres); and Kozel (14 metres). To the medium group belong: Melitopol (6 metres); Tolstaya Mogila (8.6 metres); and Gaimanova Mogila (8 metres). The barrows of common tribesmen are usually less than two metres in height and less than 100 metres in diameter; they form cemeteries consisting of 10–15 (up to 100) barrows.

The barrows usually contained either rectangular or oval-shaped graves. Timber burial chambers and catacombs were also in use, the latter becoming particularly complicated in the royal tombs (Fig. 32). Inhumation was the predominant burial rite. The dead were usually laid on the back, rarely in a contracted posture, on the right or left side. The head was directed either to the west or northwest. About 80 per cent of the burials were single graves. Multiple burials started to occur only after the fourth–third centuries BC. The body was placed on a bed of reed, grass, bark, or occasionally on skin or fur. Coffins or sarcophagi were found only in the richest tombs (at Chertomlyk, Melitopol, Tolstaya Mogila, and Oguz). The burial inventory of common tribesmen usually included a quiver and

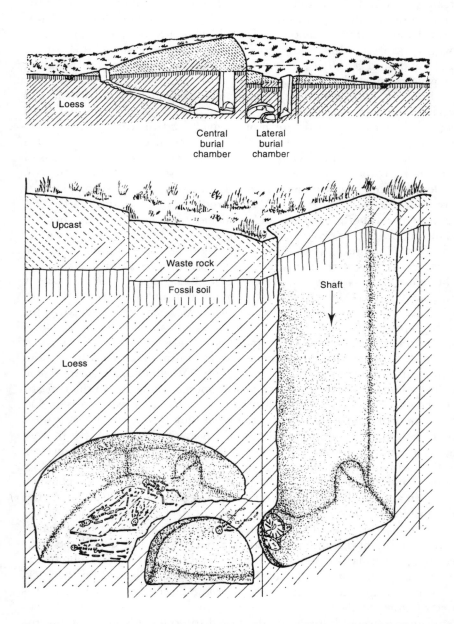

Central burial chamber

Lateral burial chamber

Upcast

Waste rock

Fossil soil

Shaft

Loess

Loess

Fig. 32 Cross-section of the Scythian 'royal' barrow. Tovstaya Mogila, Ukraine. *Source.* R. Rolle, M. Müller-Wille & K. Schietzel, *Gold und Steppe. Archäologie der Ukraine.* Schleswig: Archäologisches Landesmuseum der Christian-Albrechts-Universität.

arrowheads, and occasionally, one or two spears; more rarely still, a sword, dagger or armour were found. In exceptional cases, elements of horse gear were encountered. Female common graves contained clay or plumb spindle-whorls and various ornaments. Of common female graves 25–27 per cent contained weapons (arrows, spears, swords or daggers, and occasionally a belt with gold plaques). Both male and female graves contained a meal as evidenced by the bones of sheep, cattle or horse. The cemeteries situated close to Greek colonies often contained Greek-made drinking vessels.

The rich burials show a considerable social differentiation. Starting in the fifth century, the richest tombs were often accompanied by the burials of horses and human attendants. In some cases (Strashnaya Mogila, mound 1) horse and human burials were found in tombs with not particularly rich inventories. The horse burials more often accompanied male tombs, but in some cases also female rich graves (Khomina Mogila, Gaimanova Mogila, Solokha, Alexandropol). In some cases (Chertomlyk) the graves of servants contained rich inventories (including gold and silver implements). The burials of intentionally murdered women, at Chmyreva Mogila and Gaimanova Mogila, were made in separate chambers and contained an inventory comparable in richness to that of the 'king'. All royal tombs contained numerous gold plates (up to 2000) which evidently were sewn on the clothing. Both male and female tombs contained plate bracelets and gold pendants. The number of ritual vessels varied from one or two to ten; these were mostly Greek-made amphorae, kitchen vessels or bronze cauldrons with the remains of a ritual meal (horse, goat or cattle). The tombs of rich warriors contained goryti with arrows, trimmed quivers with arrows, one or several swords, and hatchets. The graves of noble Scythian women usually had mirrors, glass and gold beads, various ornaments of precious metals, and bronze and ivory ornaments, predominantly of Greek workmanship.

The archaeological records are corroborated by Herodotus's evidence. He wrote that when a Scythian ruler died he was embalmed, placed on a wagon and carried around to visit the various tribes over which he ruled. After the completion of this ceremony, the king's body was brought to the grave. In an open space around the body of the king, one of his concubines was buried, having previously been killed by strangulation, together with his cupbearer, cook, groom, lackey, messenger, some of his horses, and other possessions such as golden cups. After that, the tribe set to work to raise a mound above the grave. The grisly ceremony was continued a year later. This time fifty young men were killed, along with fifty horses, and the dead horses and their riders were mounted around the royal tomb. Based on this evidence, Scythian society may be viewed as a polygamist tribal chiefdom.

Stable settlements started to appear in the steppic area in the late fifth century BC. The largest settlement, Kamenskoe, on the River Dniepr opposite Nikopol, reached the size of 12 sq. km. The settlement had a large citadel and was protected by earthen defence walls and ditches. Bronze and iron tools and blacksmith's implements were found around practically every house.

It is generally acknowledged that the economy of Scythian groups was essentially based on nomadic stock-breeding. This picture basically concords with Herodotus's evidence: 'Having neither cities nor forts, and carrying their dwellings with them wherever they go . . . and living not by husbandry but in their cattle, hay waggons are the only house they possess, how can they fail to be unconquerable and unassailable even?' Indeed, faunal remains showed the predominance of cattle and horse. However, new evidence has demonstrated that in some areas, such as that of the Lower Dniepr and the Lower Don, a fallow system of agriculture based on the cultivation of rye, Italian millet and emmer, was in existence. In these areas stable settlements have emerged. The settlement of Elizavatovskaya, situated on one of the islands in the Don delta, was populated mostly by the Scythians. This site, which emerged at the turn of the sixth/fifth centuries BC, was encircled in the fourth century by a system of defence walls and ditches. The settlement soon developed into an important centre of maritime trade and crafts.

The social, cultural and trade contacts with the Greek cities were extremely important for the Scythian groups. The Scythian social élite provided a ready market for Greek craftsmen. The flow of goods from the Greek cities included metal-works, high-quality pottery, jewelry, as well as wine and olive oil in containers (amphorae). The opposite flow consisted mostly of raw materials and perishable goods: salt, honey, meat, hides, furs and slaves.

The origins and language of the Scythians remain the object of debates. In his *Historia*, Herodotus mentioned three versions of the origin of the Scythians:

> According to the account which the Scythians themselves give, they are the youngest of all nations. . . . A certain Targitaus was the first man who ever lived in this country, which, before his time, was a desert without inhabitants. He was a child of Zeus and a daughter of Borisphenus. Targitaus, thus descended, begot three sons, Leipoxais, Arpoxais, and Colaxais. . . . From Leipoxais sprang the Scythians of the race called Auchatae; from Arpoxais, the middle brother, those known as the Catiari; from Colaxais, the youngest, the Royal Scythians or Parlatae. All together are named Scoloti, after their king. The Greeks, however call them Scythians. . . . The Scythians add that from the time of Targitaus to the time of the invasion of their country by Darius, is a period of 1000 years . . .

And here is the second version:

> The Greeks, who dwell about the Pontus, tell a different story. According to them, Heracles, when he was carrying the cows to Geryon, arrived in the region which is now inhabited by the Scyths but which was then a desert. . . . While he slept, his mares, which he had loosened from his chariots to graze, disappeared. He went in quest of them and, after wandering over the whole country, he came at last to the district called the Woodland where he found in a cave a strange being, between a maiden and a serpent. . . . At least, when the

creature gave up the mares she said to him, 'When your mares strayed hither, it was I who saved them for you; now you have paid a reward, for I bear in my womb three sons of yours'. . . . The woman, when her children grew to manhood, first gave them severally their names. One was called Agathyrsus, one Gelonus, and the other, who was the youngest, Scythes. In obedience to Heracles' orders she put her sons to test. Two of them, Agathyrsus and Gelonus, proving unequal to the task enjoined, their mother sent them out of the land. Scythes, the youngest, succeeded and he was allowed to remain. From Scythes, the son of Heracles, were descended the kings of Scythia.

Herodotus also related the third legend in which 'he was inclined to put more faith than in any other'. According to the later story:

The wandering Scythians once dwelt in Asia, and they warred with Massagatae, but with ill success; they therefore quitted their homes, crossed the Araxes [the Volga] and entered the land of Cimmeria.

Hence, in Herodotus's three legends one may distinguish three different concepts of the Scythian origin: an autochthonous development (the first); an immigration from outside (the second) and the mix allochthonous/autochthonous development (the third). Ironically, all three concepts may be found in the contemporary scholarly discussions.

Rostovtseff (1922) suggested that the Scythians were an Iranian group which arrived in the Pontic steppes from inner Asia. This hypothesis was developed further by Terenozhkin, who argued that this group had originated in the steppic belts of Central Asia. A second school of thought (Tallgren 1926; Artamonov 1974; Grakov 1977) links up the origin of the Scythians with later waves of the proliferation of the Timber Grave culture, which bearers partly swept away, partly assimilated the local Cimmerians. This theory was later developed by the scholars who supported the concept of autochthonous development, and argued that the Scythians emerged from the local groups of the Timber Grave culture. This hypothesis is strongly advocated by the anthropologists Debets (1971) and Konduktorova (1972). Based on the physical anthropological evidence, these scholars argue that Scythian skulls are similar to those found in the Timber Graves and are quite distinct from those of the Central Asian Sacae. The hypothesis which argues that the language of the 'Royal Scythians' was an Iranian dialect was first advanced in the 1860s. Later, basing his conclusions on the linguistic analysis of proper- and place-names, Abayev (1949) convincingly proved this. He also proved the affinity of the Scythian language with modern Ossetian.

Archaeologically, the Scythian culture is distinguished by the combination of three types of artefact: weaponry, horse gear and the 'animal style' (a so-called Scythian triad). The animal style, which is one of the most spectacular peculiarities of the Scythian culture, is conspicuous in various forms of decorative art. It is characterized by the animals rendered in dynamic poses: with dangling legs and head, with rear legs folded forward

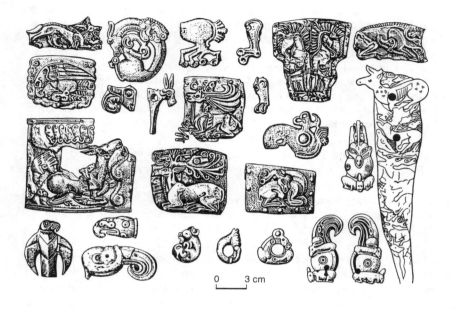

Fig. 33   Scythian 'animal' style.
     Source. A.I. Melyukova, *Stepi evropeiskoi chasti SSSR v skifo-sarmatskoe vremja.*
Moscow: Nauka, 1989.

over the front legs or curled into a circle. No less common are the compositions showing one or more creatures linked in combat. A typical example is a wooden rython from the Seven Brothers barrow in Kuban (northern Caucasus) which is decorated with four gold plaques showing a bird or a carnivorous animal attacking a herbivorous one (Fig. 33). Scythian works of art, which were often manufactured by Greek artisans, obviously reflected a common Scythian mythology.

It is important to emphasize that the 'Scythian triad', including the animal style, spread well beyond the proper Scythian ethnicity, which was basically restricted to the group of Royal Scythians. The Scythian culture, including the mythology and its material manifestations, was transmitted to the entire Scythian socio-cultural network, which consisted of a large number of loosely related chiefdoms. The Scythian-related complexes with the manifestations of animal style were found far to the east, in southern Siberia: a group of five large barrows in the eastern Altai mountains, Gorno-Altai Republic (southern Siberia), Russia, was discovered by S.I. Rudenko in 1924 and excavated by him in 1929 and 1947–49. The earthen mounds were covered by cairns of rocks, under which a lens of frozen soil was formed soon after the interments. Due to the permanent refrigeration, all organic matter such as objects of wood, leather, fur and textiles, as well as the mummified bodies of humans and horses, were uniquely preserved.

The rectangular tomb-shafts under the barrows, oriented east–west, contained human burials in a log chamber, with horse burials in the northern part of the shaft. The finds included a four-wheeled carriage, a large felt carpet, and various art objects. The barrows were constructed for the social élite of the local Scythian-related nomadic group and date from the fifth–fourth centuries BC.

Another large royal barrow, Arzhan, that lies in the valley of the Uyuk river in the Republic of Tuva (southern Siberia), was discovered and excavated by M.P. Gryaznov in 1971–74 (Gryaznov 1980). The burial chamber under the cairn contained the burials of the 'king' and the 'queen', the skeletons of fifteen human attendants and 160 horses. The horse gear, weapons and works of art, made in the typical animal style, leave one in no doubt that this complex belongs to the Scythian culture. The barrow dates from the eighth–seventh centuries BC.

A group of Scythian-related sites in the forest-steppic zone of the Russian Plain is particularly important for the present study. Eight local groups were identified there: Middle Dniepr (Kiev-Cherkassy); East Podolian; West Podolian; Vorksla; Seim; North Donetsian; Sula; and Middle Don (Fig. 34) (Grakov 1977; Terenozhkin and Il'inskaya 1986). The sites of the Middle Dniepr catchment are particularly well studied. They included both fortified and unfortified settlements as well as cemeteries. It was noted that unfortified settlements appeared earlier, by the end of the seventh century BC. These settlements were usually located on top of the upper river terraces. Several settlements were of a considerable size; the largest one, Tarasova Gora, covered an area of 43 hectares. It included no less than twenty dwellings of semi-subterranean type, 5 by 10 metres, with clay-covered walls supported by posts. Fortified settlements (hill-forts or *gorodishche*) started to appear in the second half of the sixth century BC. They were built on top of hills, or on promontories in river valleys. The fortifications consisted of turf ramparts with the remains of timber walls, often revealing traces of fire. The largest hill-fort, Bol'shie Valki (near the town of Kanev on the Dniepr), reached an area of *c.* 500 hectares. It was surrounded by a rampart, 3–4 metres in height, and a ditch. The settlement included thirty-five dwellings, both surface and semi-subterranean ones, with walls supported by posts. A structure containing a large number of lustrous vessels of Villanovan type is thought to be a sanctuary.

The burials in Timber Graves were the dominant type of sepulchre. At the early stage the dead were buried in an extended posture, on the left or on the right side. The graves of male 'commoners' always included arrow- and spearheads, and often horse gear. Rich male burials had more diversified inventories: bronze cauldrons, bronze swords, often golden weapons, as well as skeletons of horses and human attendants. The grave goods in female graves included numerous ornaments: pins, ear-rings, beads, bracelets, bronze mirrors, and also loom weights, indicating weaving. In all cases the grave goods included ceramics, mostly hand-made pottery. At the later stage

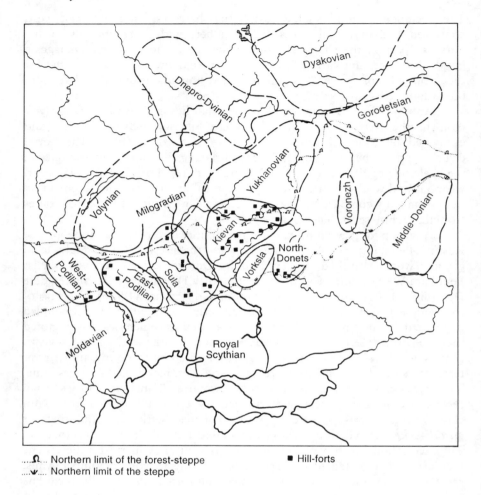

....Ω.... Northern limit of the forest-steppe   ■ Hill-forts
....v.... Northern limit of the steppe

Fig. 34 Forest-steppe 'Scythian' groups.
    After. A.I. Melyukova, *Stepi evropeiskoi chasti SSSR v skifo-sarmatskoe vremja.*
Moscow: Nauka, 1989.

rich graves contained imported Greek-made vessels. Rich graves of the
Catacomb type appeared at the final stage, in the third and second centuries BC.

    Russian and Ukrainian scholars stress that the bulk of the pottery
corpus indicates direct analogies to the preceding Chernoles culture of the
third–sixth centuries BC. Yet the impact of the Scythian culture was
considerable. This was particularly apparent in the weaponry and horse
gear, and in the brilliant examples of the animal style that are also known.
At the same time other types of ornament point to contacts with the west,
for example, the spiral pins find analogies in the Lausitz culture.

128

The most significant aspect in the subsistence of the Scythian-related forest-steppic groups was their heavy reliance on agriculture. Large amounts of charred grains found at the site of Ivane-Puste in western Podolia and at several other sites included barley (*Hordeum vulgare*), hulled wheats (*Triticum dicoccum, T. monococcum*), naked wheats; millet (*Panicum miliacetum*), and rye (*Secale cerale*). Pulses were also found: bitter vetch (*Vicia ervilia*), field pea (*Pisum sativum* var. *arvense*) and flaw (*Linum usitatissimun*). It is also important that, when describing various Scythian tribes, Herodotus specifically mentioned that several of them practised agriculture. Describing two tribes, Callipidae and Alizones, Herodotus wrote: 'Both these people resemble the Scythians in their way of life and also grow grain for food, as well as onions, leeks, lentils and millet. North of the Alizones are agricultural Scythian tribes, growing grain not for food but for export...'. This highly significant testimony by the Greek writer is corroborated by the archaeological evidence, which clearly indicates trade contacts between the Greek cities on the Black Sea coast and the forest-steppic groups. The Greek-made goods, mostly pottery, and often Ionian vessels, were usually present in the rich graves. The amount of Greek imported goods increased in the sixth and fifth centuries BC, and included the bronze mirrors manufactured in Olbia and bronze containers (the find of a gold-gilded cauldron was particularly impressive). Especially numerous were the finds of amphorae.

The emergence and development of Greek colonies along the Black Sea coast was yet another important element in the social development of the southern Russian Plain in the first millennium BC. The Greek expansion overseas was a part of the accelerated social development of mainland Greece that had followed the period of economic and social decline in 1100–1000 BC (the Greek 'Dark Ages'). A number of city-states (*poleis*), emerged in various parts of mainland Greece in the early centuries of the first millennium BC. Their expeditious rise was due to a combination of social and geographical factors. Among the latter, one should mention the mosaic pattern of Greek landscapes with the rapid transition from river valleys and depressions to hills and mountains, leaving little space for arable land. The long and sinuous coastline was highly suitable for seafaring, which is attestable at the earliest stages of the Greek civilization. Insufficiency in land resources is often quoted as one of the main motives for the Greek expansion overseas. As elsewhere in Europe, settled agriculture in Greece largely depended on forest clearance. Beyond limited arable land, valley pastures were used for grazing cattle and horses and mountain pastures for breeding sheep and goats. Judging from the testimony of contemporary Greek writers, the yield in archaic Greece was modest, not more than three or four to one. Cereals had to be imported to make up for the deficient food supply. At the same time, vines and olives were cultivated on a sufficiently large scale, apparently for export.

Various political factors were no less important. For example,

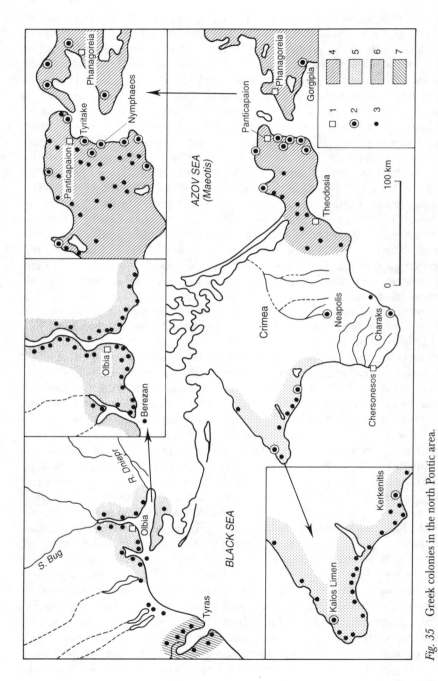

Fig. 35 Greek colonies in the north Pontic area.
Key. 1 – Metropolis; 2 – Secondary urban centres; 3 – Agricultural settlements; 4 – Agricultural hinterland of Bosporan Kingdom; 5 – Agricultural hinterland of Chersonesos; 6 – Agricultural hinterland of Olbia; 7 – Agricultural hinterland of Tyra.
After: S.D. Kryzhitsky, in *The Landscape in Flux*, J. Chaplam & P. Dolukhanov, eds, Colloquia Pontica, Oxbow Press (in press).

Herodotus reported that repeated attacks by the Gyges and their allies in Lydia had effectively blocked the landward frontier of the Ionian cities in the coastland of Asia Minor, and thus instigated the Ionian overseas expansion (Cook 1962). The Ionian cities, particularly Miletus, were particularly active in their drive overseas. Miletus was said to be 'mother' of no less than ninety colonies scattered in various seas. It has been suggested that the Ionians had already learned of the curiosities and richness of the Black Sea (in the form of the Argonaut legend) in the eighth century BC. Yet the first firmly attested acquaintance with the great northern sea occurred in the seventh century BC. At that time, the Greek poets started to mention the Istros (Danube), the Borysthenes (Dniepr) and the savages of the Salmydessian coast. Later, in the middle of the seventh century, the peoples of other Greek cities, such as the Dorians of Megara, entered in the competition. Between the seventh and the fifth centuries BC a string of Greek city-states emerged along the northern shores of the Black Sea. Among the most important ones were Tyras in the Dniestr estuary, Olbia in the Dniepr-Bug estuary, a group of sites in the Crimea (Chersonesus near Sebastopol, Theodosia in the southeast), Panticapaeum near the modern town of Kerch, and Gorgippia, near Anapa on the Caucasian coast (Fig. 35).

Olbia was an important Greek (Ionian) colony, later a city-state, situated on the Bug-Dniestr liman (estuary) near the town of Ochakov in Ukraine. The site has been excavated by Russian and Ukrainian archaeologists since the 1850s: A.A. Uvarov, B.V. Farmakovsky, E.I. Levi, S.D. Kryzhitsky and others in recent times (Kryzhitsky 1985). The earliest Greek settlement emerged on the island of Berezan in the Bug-Dniestr estuary in the late seventh century BC. The initial Greek settlement on the mainland appeared in the mid-sixth century. The city flourished especially in the fifth–fourth centuries BC, when a network of agricultural settlements appeared in the hinterland. The density of Greek settlement declined in the late third century BC. The city further declined in the second–first centuries BC when it was controlled by the Scythian kings. There was further progress in the second century AD when a Roman garrison was stationed there and the area became part of the Roman province of Lower Moeosia. The city which became an important trade centre, was again devastated in the third century AD by Goths. The city died out completely in the fourth century.

Chersonesus was another Greek colony in the western part of the Crimea, three kilometres west of the modern city of Sebastopol (Shcheglov 1978). The first excavations at Chersonesus were undertaken in 1827 and the site has been continuously studied ever since. As follows from archaeological and historic documents, the city was founded in 421 BC by the Greeks coming from Heraclaea Pontica, a city on the southern shore of the Black Sea. The Heraclaeum peninsula, where the city was founded, was initially inhabited by the Tauri, a tribe related to the Cimmerians and hostile towards the Greeks. In the third century BC Chersonesus controlled a considerable area of the western Crimea. In the second century BC, the

Scythians made an attempt to seize the city. The citizens turned for help to Mithridates Eupator, the king of Pontus. The Scythians were repulsed, the city passed under Midridates's control, and after his death became part of the Bosporan kingdom. Later on the Romans occupied the city. In the second century AD Chersonesus became the centre of Roman administration. It is highly significant that throughout this period the population of Chersonesus was of a mixed ethnic composition. This is shown by the materials of a large cemetery, north of the city, which contained the evidence of various burial rites.

Several Greek colonies grew up in the Cimmerian Bosporus, around the straits of Kerch, separating the Crimea and Caucasus: the Kerch and Taman peninsula. Panticapaeum, on the Crimean side of the straits, was the most important one. Phanagorea was the settlement which arose on the eastern, Caucasian shore. Myrmecium, Tyritace, Nymphaeum and several minor cities were located both north and south of Panticapaeum, along the coast (Gaidukevich 1949). The first Greek settlements appeared there in the sixth century BC. By 480 BC a Bosporan state was already in existence, ruled by the aristocratic family of the Archaenactids. Later they were replaced by the dynasty of Spartocids. In the fourth and third centuries BC, the polytechnic state of Bosporus included the Kerch and Taman peninsula, the low stretches of the Kuban river, the Don Delta and the shores of the Azov Sea. The economic and political crisis of the late third–second centuries BC, brought about social unrest. The intervention of the Mithridates Eupator led to the loss of the political independence and the inclusion of the cities into the Bosporan kingdom. A prolonged period of political instability followed. The political dependence on Rome in the first century AD coincided with a new upsurge of economic activity and urban development.

Agriculture constituted the basis of the economy of the Greek cities in the Pontic area. Naked two-row and six-row barley, wheats (bread wheat and spelt, followed by club wheat and hard wheat), as well as millet remained the dominant crops throughout the classical era. Rye started to appear in Chersonesus in the first half of the third century BC. Onions and garlic, the staple ingredients in the Greek diet, were also grown.

Throughout the northern Pontic area the Greeks implemented their traditional system of mixed farming with winter and spring ploughing and the use of manure. Wooden ploughs were fitted with iron shares; the oldest iron shares were found in the fourth century BC deposits at Chersonesus. Due to the favourable climate and availability of land resources, the yield was much higher than in mainland Greece. According to Blavatsky's estimate (1953), the average yield was six or seven to one for wheat and five to one for barley. Bosporus was the main producer of grain. Strabo reported that Bosporus, under the reign of Leucon I, was exporting to Athens no less than 16,000 tons of grain annually. Grain was also exported to other Greek centres, especially to Mytilene and Rhodes.

Vines were cultivated in Pontica from the fifth century BC. Viticulture and wine-making later developed into one of the most profitable branches of the economy of the Greek cities, mainly due to the occurrence of a large market, both at home and in Scythia. Large Greek vineyards were established at farmsteads in the western Crimea and on the Heraclaeum peninsula, near Chersonesus. Wine-making gained particular importance in Bosporus where several small cities, notably Myrmecium and Tyritace, specialized in the import of wine. Four wine-producing assemblages have been discovered at Olbia.

Animal husbandry played an important role in the farming economy. At all classical sites, sheep and goat make up more than 50 per cent of the total faunal remains. There are indications that sheep and goats were also exported to mainland Greece.

The Greek Pontic cities were important craft centres. Iron metallurgy and iron-working developed in Olbia from the sixth century BC. Later, similar crafts appeared in Panticapaeum and other Bosporan cities. Since the fourth, and particularly in the third–second centuries BC, gold was widely used for the manufacturing of various ornaments, also for the Scythian market. At a later stage, gold-working and jewelry developed into an independent craft. Among other crafts, glass-working, weaving, leather craft, and, particularly pottery-making, were significant. Potters' quarters were established in practically all the major Greek cities in the area.

The Greek Pontic cities were important centres of trade. Commercial links connected these cities with major centres on mainland Greece, the Aegean islands and Asia Minor. As the analysis of the amphorae has shown (Brashinsky 1980), the direction of trade links was changing throughout this time, being mostly dependent on the changing political situation and the availability of a market. Chios first became prominent in the fourth century BC but by the sixth century BC had become the most important trading partner. Later trading partners included Thasos, Menda, Lesbos, Rhodes and the southern Black Sea cities of Heraclaea Pontica and Sinope. Grain and salted fish were the main items exported to the Greek centres. The goods imported from Greece included wine, oil, ceramics, marble and terracotta sculpture, etc. No less significant were the trade links that had bound together the Greek cities with the Scythian, and later Sarmatian, communities in the north.

Now let us try to assess the general politico-economic situation which had emerged in the Russian Plain by the end of the first millennium BC (Fig. 36). The greater part of the forested north was taken up by the groups whose subsistence retained its predominantly foraging character although there are also indications of animal husbandry and metallurgy based on the exploitation of local ore. Large areas in the central and western parts of the Russian Plain included various groups whose economy was based predominantly on stable stock-breeding, supplemented by swidden cultivation. By trade links, these groups were increasingly included in the network of Iron Age communities in the west and south. South of these

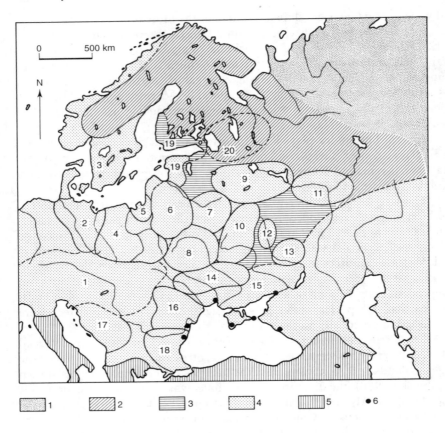

Fig. 36 Eastern and Central Europe in the first millennium BC.
Key. 1 – Hunter-gatherers; 2 – Hunter-gatherers with elements of stock-breeding; 3 – Hunter-gatherers with elements of swidden-type agriculture; 4 – Groups of farmers and stock-breeders; 5 – Early states; 6 – Greek colonies.
Cultural groupings: 1 – La-Tène; 2 – Jastorf; 3 – South Scandinavian; 4 – Pomorian; 5 – West Baltic; 6 – Stroked pottery; 7 – Dniepr-Dvinian; 8 – Milogradian; 9 – Dyakovian; 10 – Yukhnovian; 11 – Gorodtsovian; 12 – Voronezhian; 13 – Middle Don; 14 – 'Agricultural' Scythian; 15 – 'Pastoral' Scythian; 16 – Getean-Dacian; 17 – Illyrian; 18 – Thracian; 19 – East Baltic; 20 – Kargapolian.
Source. M. Zvelebil & P. Dolukhanov, *Journal of World Prehistory*, v. 5. Plenum Press, 1991.

groups, in the South Russian forest-steppe, lay the area occupied by the 'agricultural Scythians': the only area (with the exception of the Greek colonies), with a sufficiently developed agriculture. As we remember, the local tribes produced the grain not only for the domestic use, but also for export. The Royal Scythians, with an economy predominantly based on nomadic stock-breeding, were located to the south, in the steppic zone. The

Greek cities and their substantial agricultural hinterland formed the most economically advanced area, although it was restricted to the coastland of the Black Sea.

Now we may embark on a more difficult task: the interpretation of the available evidence in terms of languages and ethnicities. Two elements in this equation are more or less clear. First, the large area of the north, with its predominantly foraging population, consisted, in all probability, of various Finnish-speaking groups. Second, the Royal Scythians, predominantly nomadic groups, spoke northern Iranian dialects.

When one looks at the groups in the area of mixed forests and forest-steppe, two archaeologically established features are particularly obvious. On the one hand, their local origin: practically all Russian and Ukrainian scholars are unanimous in stressing that these groups developed locally, without any major influx from outside. On the other hand, during the Iron Age the previously homogenous zone, in the economic sense, had obviously disintegrated. The economy of such 'cultures' as 'stroked' pottery, Dniepr-Dvinian and Milogradian was based on stock-breeding-cum-swidden cultivation, whereas that of the 'agricultural Scythian' groups was based on developed agriculture. The distinction between the two is of fundamental importance. I have suggested that the area of Corded Ware cultures in central and eastern Europe belonged to groups which spoke as yet undifferentiated Germanic-Baltic-Slavic dialects. Using the same system of arguments, one may suggest that the eastern European groups which had developed on the Corded Ware basis in the Bronze Age (East-Baltic, Sosnitsian, Komarovian, and possibly Pozdniakovian) supposedly used the proto-Baltic-Slavic dialects. There are serious linguistic arguments for the existence of an undifferentiated Baltic-Slavic language in the past (see Chapter 5).

The disintegration of the previously homogenous area into two economic zones, that of stock-breeding-cum-swidden cultivation and that of the 'agricultural' Scythian, may be viewed as a formation of two distinct socio-cultural networks where different communication media, that is different languages, were in use. It is tempting to link this up with the disintegration of the proto-Baltic-Slavic language into the Slavic and Baltic ones. In that case, the areas taken up by such archaeological cultures as that of 'stroked' pottery, Dniepr-Dvinian and Milogradian should be seen as populated by the predominantly Baltic-speaking groups. This suggestion was made by Sedov (1970b), who substantiated this conclusion by the analysis of place-names. This leaves us with the 'agricultural' Scythians, who, in that case, should be viewed as proto-Slavs. This conclusion is not entirely new. In recent years it was spelled out by B.A. Rybakov (1979).

In his book, Rybakov based mainly on the analysis of Herodotus's texts, has attempted, like many historians and archaeologists before him, to correlate his testimony with the archaeological evidence. Herodotus on several occasions mentions various tribes, which, according to his information, inhabited the northern Pontic area. Describing the area north of Olbia and stressing that 'no one has any accurate information about what lies beyond that region', Herodotus nevertheless, enumerates several ethnic groups. These were: 'the Graeco-Scythian tribe called Callipidae' in the middle of the Scythian coastline; the Alizones, 'their neighbours to the east'; the 'agricultural Scythians' north of the Alizones; beyond these, the 'Neuri'; and north of them, as far as Herodotus knew, 'the country was uninhabited'. Further west, along the river Hyspanis (that is the Southern Bug) lived the Borysthenites. Further north, beyond the great tract of uninhabited land, lived yet another tribe, the Androphagi.

In his analysis of the Herodotus text Rybakov makes a very serious conclusion. He argues that first, both 'the agricultural Scythians' and Borysphenites mentioned by the Greek historian corresponded to archaeological forest-steppic 'Scythian' groups – Middle Dniepr (Kiev-Cherkassy); East Podolian; West Podolian, etc. – and secondly, that all these groups were 'proto-Slavs'.

One may not agree with the other arguments of Rybakov, such as the direct identification of all groups mentioned by Herodotus with various archaeological cultures. For example, the Neuri have been identified with the Milogradian and were thought also to be Slavs; the Androphagi have been equated with the Dniepr-Dvinian, etc. Yet the principal conclusion that the forest-steppic agricultural network may have used the proto-Slavic language as a communication medium seems to be highly significant.

Chapter 7 ···

The Slavs, Balts and Finns

Apart from archaeology, there are three main sources of information pertinent to the origin and early history of ethnicities of the Russian Plain: written records of ancient writers, linguistics and physical anthropology. Now we shall review briefly all this evidence in relation to the Slavs and some of their immediate neighbours, starting with written sources.

Ptolemy (c.AD 100–178) was the first to mention the Slavs. In his *Geography* he used the name '*Soubenoi*'. According to the ancient geographer, the whole area of northern Scythia, 'near the unknown land and before the Imaos mountains [the Urals]', was inhabited by three peoples, namely Scythian Alans (Sarmatians), 'Soubenoi' and Alanorsi (Ptolemy, *Geography*, Book VI: 14, 9). After a prolonged absence, the Slavs reappear in the sixth century AD. The Byzantine historian Procopius mentioned them in the form '*Sklavenoi*' when discussing the Gothic Wars of AD 536–537. In Procopius's account, the Slavs are mentioned as invaders in the Lower Danube region. Jordanes, the contemporary Roman historian of Gothic origin, also discussed the Slavs (*Sclavini*). In his account, they are placed between the Carpathian mountains, the Vistula and the Dniestr.

It is significant that ancient writers also used different names to designate the Slavs: Jordanes mentioned the names of *Antes* and *Sclavini*, as two components of the same populus, *Venedi*. He especially stressed that they both spoke the same language. Indicating the area of Venedi as to the east of the Sclavini, he wrote: 'The Sclavini and the Antes do not differ in appearance: all of them are tall and very strong, their skin and hair are neither very light nor dark, but all are ruddy of face. They live a hard life of the lowest grade just like Messagetae, and are just as dirty as they.' Actually, the Antes are mentioned in the written records even earlier than the S(c)lavini. Pliny the Elder, in his *Natural History* (Book VI: 35), written in the first century AD, placed the Antes, among other peoples, in an area between the Azov Sea and the Caspian Sea. The third name, *Venedi*, was mentioned in the first century AD by Tacitus. The Roman historian referred to them as 'robber-like vagabonds' who carried out raids in the forests and mountains between the area of Peucini (Germanic Bastarnae) in the eastern Carpathians and that of Finni. Tacitus stressed that in contrast to the habits of Sarmatians, who were nomadic horse-riders, the Veneti fought on foot and built houses (Tacitus, *Germania*: 46).

As one may see, written records relating to the early Slavs are both fragmentary and contradictory. Any attempts to locate their place of origin based entirely on the evidence of written sources are futile: the areas mentioned in ancient texts cover practically the entire zone of early Slavic settlement. The only conclusion to be made is that the Slavs, under different names and in some poorly defined areas of the Russian Plain, were known to the ancient writers from the first centuries AD.

Now we should address the linguistic evidence. Slavic (or Slavonic) languages belong to one of the largest branches of the Indo-European family. The total number of speakers at the present time is estimated at 268 million. According to a widely accepted classification, Slavic languages consist of three groups with sub-groups:

(1) *Southern Slavic* (with sub-groups: (1) *Serbo-Croatian-Slovenian*: (2) *Bulgaro-Macedonian*);
(2) *Western Slavic* (with sub-groups: (1) *Czech-Slovakian*; (2) *Lekhic*; (3) *Sorbian*);
(3) *Eastern Slavic* (with sub-groups (1) *Russian*; (2) *Ukrainian*; (3) *Belorussian*).

Old Slavonic (or Old Bulgarian), the dead language which is known from texts dating not earlier than the eleventh century AD, is now generally acknowledged as initially belonging to the Slavs of Macedonia from the second half of the ninth century AD (de Bray 1969). All Slavic languages, those both extinct and currently in use, have developed from Common Slavic or Proto-Slavic. The reconstruction of Common Slavic, based on a common vocabulary and systemic regularities in the evolution of individual languages, forms one of the most promising trends in contemporary linguistics (Birnbaum 1983).

Slavic languages feature a number of common phonological characteristics. All Slavic phonological systems are rich in consonants, particularly spirants and affricates (that is, consonant sounds that begin as stops with complete stoppage of the breath stream and are released as fricatives with incomplete stoppage). This and associated phenomena are thought to be related to 'palatalization', the process by which the pronunciation of an initially nonpalatal sound is changed by raising the tongue towards the hard palate. This was originally connected with the adaptation of a consonant to a following vowel within a syllable.

There are certain distinct features in the grammar of Slavic languages. All these languages are synthetic: they express grammatical meaning through the use of affixes (prefixes and suffixes) and grammatical inflections.

Another feature is that verbal categories retain their archaic character. At the same time, due to inflections, the word order in Slavic languages is much more flexible than in modern western (Germanic and Romance) Indo-European languages.

The adherence of Slavic languages to the Indo-European family was first recognized in the early nineteenth century. At that time Franz Bopp, the German scholar, classified the Slavic, Baltic (Lithuanian and Latvian), and several extinct (Persian and Sanskrit) languages into the '*satem*' group of Indo-European languages, in contrast to the western or '*centum*' group which included Celtic languages. The latter classification, which was based on the reflexes of original palatal velars (*k'*, *g'*) in such words as the Latin for '100', is now considered of secondary importance (Birnbaum 1983: 16). Apart from that, all Slavic languages share a number of other important features. Together with other eastern Indo-European languages, they show a regular change of Indo-European palat sounds. Thus, *k'* and *g'* consonants, modified by bringing the front part of the tongue up to the hard plate, change into spirants of the *s* and *z* type. Other innovations (also shared by the Baltic languages) include a regular change of the Indo-European syllabic *r*, *n* and *m* into *ir* and *ur*. One also notes a similar pattern of stress in nouns and verbs, and the same reshuffling of the verbal system.

As we shall see later, Slavic languages show the closest affinities to the Baltic branch of Indo-European languages. Less clear is their relationship to Early Germanic (especially Gothic) and Indo-Iranian (particularly Iranian) languages. Scholars note certain common elements in Germanic, Slavic and Baltic languages, for example, the '-*n* suffixation'. Based on this and other similarities, certain linguists (Georgiev 1959; Senn 1954) spoke about a 'Baltic-Slavic-Germanic unity' that might have existed in the past. However, one should bear in mind that it is often hard to decide whether the common elements were jointly inherited from a common Indo-European source or were later borrowings due to social or cultural interactions (Birnbaum 1983: 17). Thus, the observed common elements in certain Slavic (or even Balto-Slavic) and Indo-Iranian languages (such as the sound 'γ' currently present in Ukrainian and certain South-Russian dialects) were ostensibly limited to lexical borrowings which had penetrated into Slavic from Iranian (Scythian or Sarmatian) languages.[1]

The most obvious parallels are observed between the Slavic and Baltic languages. These include a great number of lexical items exclusively characteristic of Slavic and Baltic (Trautmann 1923), the double or parallel reflex (*ir/ur*, *ju/jau*, etc.), striking similarities in accentuation, a similar formation of collective numerals, similarities in nominal derivations, specific parallels in verbal derivations and several other features (Birnbaum 1983: 19–21).

---

[1] It was suggested that the standard pronunciation of the word 'Boγ' (God) as 'Box' has resulted from the typical South-Russian pronunciation of monks in the Kiev-Lavra monastery.

It has been noted that Slavic languages show particularly strong affinities to Old Prussian, as well as to Lithuanian and Lettish (Latvian) or, rather, their dialects. Based on the observed affinities, several scholars suggest the existence of a hypothetical common Balto-Slavic proto-language that developed from a common late proto-Indo-European base (Birnbaum 1983: 18). There are indications of isogloss integrations with other Indo-European languages, such as Greek, Armenian, Hittite and even Toharian. There are also controversial judgements about common elements of Slavic languages with non-Indo-European languages, notably, Finnic and Altaic (Turcic). If these common elements are real, they should have resulted from the cultural and social interactions of Slavic groups with their Finnish and Turcic neighbours at various stages of their common history.

The use of the anthropological evidence is severely restricted by the scarcity of available materials: since the cremation was the dominant burial rite among early Slavs, their earliest graves contained very few remains suitable for analysis. Yet several anthropologists based on their studies of craniological materials from the ninth–fourteenth centuries, spoke about a considerable homogeneity of the Slavic population (Alexeyeva 1973; Mikic 1986). This general conclusion seemed to contradict craniometric evidence which pointed to large variations among medieval Russian groups. They also contradicted the evidence for a considerable variability of the somatic characteristics of various contemporary Slavic groups, for example, the difference between fair-haired northern Russians and Mediterranean-like southern Slavs is apparent. Support for the concept of the genetic homogeneity of the Slavs came from yet another source, namely the ABO blood-group system (Bunak 1969). Alexeyev (1974) noted that populations in the Slavic area (referred to by him as 'Central-Eastern European') feature a small Mongoloid admixture which tended to increase in the easterly direction.

Craniometric data show a strong variability among several Slavic groups. Noticeable differences are particularly recognizable between western, southern and eastern groups of Slavs. Using several craniometric indices in her studies of medieval Slavic materials, Alexeyeva (1973) distinguished a dolichocephalic group, which included broad-faced varieties (several early medieval Slavic tribes: Volyniane, Drevliane, Krivichi), as opposed to the mesocephalic group (Dnieprian Slavs). She stressed that a similar combination of craniometric variables was typical of certain Baltic groups (Semigalians, Latgallians, and Zemaitians). Benevolenskaya (1985) also reported remarkable similarities of several later Russian groups in the Pskov district to Baltic groups, particularly, Prussians and Yatvyagians. This similarity was attested both in blood systems (A and M) and craniological measurements.

Alexeyeva (1973) equally noted considerable morphological similarities between eastern Slavs and eastern groups of narrow-faced Finno-Ugrians. Substantial craniometric affinities were recognized between western Slavs and neighbouring Germanic groups, while the southern Slavs showed similarities to several Balkan groups. On the other hand, Alexeyeva acknowledged considerable similarities of Slav groups in the south of the Russian Plain to pre-Slav entities, to the Chernyakhov culture and Scythian forest-steppic groups.

Now we should turn our attention to the nearest neighbours of the early Slavs. In doing so we begin with the Balts, whose contacts with Slavs are well attested linguistically. The term 'Balts' is a neologism which was used from 1845 to designate several peoples speaking 'Baltic' languages in the eastern Peribaltic area. Only Lithuanian and Lettish languages are currently in use, spoken by Lithuanians and Latvians respectively. Written sources retained records of several other Baltic groups and their languages: Old Prussian, Curonian, Semigallian and Selian. All these languages disappeared between 1400 and 1600.

Gimbutas (1963) argued that the Balts, under the name *Aestii*, were first mentioned by Tacitus in his *Germania*, dated AD 98. The Roman historian mentioned the *Aestii*, *gentes Aestiorum*, a people living on the eastern shore of the Baltic Sea, who were collectors of amber and more energetic cultivators of crops and fruits than the neighbouring Germanic people, although resembling them in appearance and customs. Jordanes also mentioned the Aestii, 'a totally peaceful people living east of the mouth of the Vistula, on the long stretch of the Baltic coast'. Einhard, in the *Vita Caroli Magni* (c. 830–840) also located the Aesti, the neighbours of the Slavs, on the eastern Baltic coast. The name of Old Prussians ('*Bruzi*') was first mentioned in the ninth century.

Physical anthropology of the Balts was thoroughly studied by Denisova (1975) who based her conclusions on craniometry. She suggested that the initial Baltic population consisted of dolichocranial and moderately broad-faced groups inherited from the Late Palaeolithic groups. An 'oriental' component, with a flattened face, appeared later, in the fifth–fourth millennia BC. Still later, at the beginning of the third millennium BC, the Mongoloid (Lapponoid) element became stronger, mainly in the north-eastern Baltic region. The latter was allegedly associated with pit-and-comb pottery and Finno-Ugric speakers. The appearance of a new dolichocranic moderately broad-faced population was originally associated with the penetration of Corded Ware groups. In her later work, Denisova (1985), stressing the similarity of Corded Ware and Narvian anthropological types, suggested a local development of the former. Basing her conclusions on the materials of the Bronze Age Kivukalns cemetery, Denisova (1975) argued that a massive dolichocranial narrow-faced component appeared only in the late second millennium BC.

Česnys (1985) based on the multivariate analysis of craniometric measurements, identified several clusters among groups of Baltic population. The western cluster, featuring hypermorphy, dolichocrany, a narrow face and a sharp facial profile, was considered the oldest, traceable from the beginning of the first millennium AD. At that time it covered the entire East

Prussia, Lithuania and a considerable part of Latvia. By the second half of the first millennium, this group was restricted to East Prussia, Žemaitia in Lithuania, and Semigallia and Kurzeme in Latvia. The eastern cluster featured more pronounced hypermorphy, dolichocrany, a broad and high face and a sharp facial profile. This group, which had consolidated only by the fifth century AD, embraced only some peripheral parts of Latvia (Aukštainia, Semigallia and Selonia). It was basically similar to several of the Fatyanovo groups indicated by Denisova (1975). The 'first southeastern cluster' was considered as a variant of the eastern one; it included groups of the 'Stroked' pottery culture of the first millennium BC. The 'second southeastern cluster' included Latgalians from Kivti and featured mesocrany and a flattened face which were interpreted as reflections of a 'Finnish substratum'.

The Finns were the northern neighbours of the Slavs throughout their lengthy common history; they consisted of numerous ethnicities speaking languages belonging to the Finnic group of the Finno-Ugric branch of the Uralic languages. No less than fifteen ethnical groups have been identified, predominantly in the forested zone of northeastern Europe.

The Finns (in the form *Fenni*) were first mentioned by Tacitus in his *Germania*. It is generally acknowledged that in this case the Roman historian was referring not to the Finns proper, but to the Lapps. Ptolemy of Alexandria already distinguished two groups of Finns: one in the north of Scandinavia (presumably, Lapps), and another along the Vistula.

Linguists, basing their conclusions on similarities between the existing languages, proceeded in the reconstruction of a hypothetical Proto-Uralic language which had preceded the emergence of individual languages (Hajdu 1975; Vuorela 1964). This proto-language, featuring the properties shared by a great many Uralic languages, included several phonological character-istics. Among these was the stress, automatically put on the first syllable in such languages as Finnish, Estonian, Hungarian and Komi, and also a distinct vowel harmony.

Among the common grammatical characteristics of Uralic languages, one should especially note certain structural similarities, such as the use of a negative structure, the lack of specific conjunctions between words, phrases or clauses, inflections of nouns of number, and the use of case endings to show the function of words in the sentence. The case system of the Uralic languages is particularly original. The cases are numerous: 14 in the Finnish; 16–21 in Hungarian. They include such cases as that of separation (ablative), of direction (locative), and many others.

The problem of the Lappish language remains one of the most important in Finno-Ugrian linguistics. According to the majority view, Lappish is an independent Uralic language with close affinities to the East-Finnic group. In the view of certain linguists (Korhonen, cited after Hajdu 1975), both Lappish dialects and East-Baltic languages have developed from a common proto-language: Early Finnish (or Early Lappish).

Anthropological studies of Finnish groups are largely related to the determination of the Mongoloid (or Lapponoid) element which tended to increase in the easterly direction. The difference between long-headed groups in the west and round-headed, broad- and flattened-faced ones in the east of Estonia was noticeable by the end of the Neolithic period (Mark 1970, 1972; Schwitetzky 1986). Basically similar differences are acknowledged between contemporary groups of western and eastern Finns (Mark 1972; Bunak 1976). The latter groups show considerable similarities with Slavic populations further to the east. In this respect, the precise anthropological definition of the Lapps becomes particularly important. This group of small people with a dark pigmentation of skin, broad and flattened faces, currently living in the extreme north of Fennoscandia, forms a sharp contrast with the surrounding groups of northern Europeoids. The flattened face and nose are typical of the Lapps in much earlier times (at least since the first century BC), although both broad- and narrow-faced varieties were distinguishable.

An original theory regarding the origin of the Lapps was developed by Gokhman (1986). Basing his conclusions on the carinometry of both ancient and contemporary populations, Gokhman distinguished two different anthropological types: (1) individuals with broad and flattened (particularly obvious in the upper part) faces, genetically unrelated to Mongoloids; and (2) authentic flat-faced Mongoloids. The first variety, according to Gokhman, was basically similar to the 'Cro-Magnoid group' identified at Oleni Island and several Mesolithic cemeteries in southern Ukraine. This anthropological type belonged to the oldest population of the Russian Plain and was dominant through the Mesolithic and Early Neolithic periods. The second type started to emerge in the 'forest Neolithic', and was presumably related to the pit-and-comb pottery culture. This anthropological type, which had first emerged in the area of the northern Urals, later led to the formation of an 'Uralic race' with distinct Mongoloid features. If one accepts this theory, one may further suggest that the initial population of the Russian Plain included groups essentially similar to a 'Cro-Magnoid group' who spoke dialects of the Uralic language; Lapps, in this case, should be seen as relics of this ancient population stratum.

Relations of Uralic and Indo-European languages remain open to discussion. Hajdu (1975) quoted several words which are common in Proto-Uralic and proto-Indo-European. They included such concepts as 'name', 'water' and 'house'. A number of coincidences were also found between Uralic and Indo-Iranian languages.

Finno-Ugrian languages include numerous Baltic loan-words. These words relate to such activities as stock-breeding and agriculture, but they also include names of plants and animals, family relations, parts of the body, colour, time, religion, etc. In some cases these words were present in Proto-Baltic only; they disappeared from the modern Latvian or Lithuanian. Yet the greater part of these loan-words are not older than the first millennium BC. It is important that Baltic loan-words are identifiable not only in western-Finnic languages, in which contacts with the Balts are fairly obvious, but also in eastern groups, such as Mari, Mansi, Cheremyss and Komi-Zyryan (Serebrennikov 1957). Thus, these borrowings date to a period when a Baltic-Finnic interaction occurred in a much wider area of the East European Plain. The toponimic evidence is particularly transparent in this sense. Toporov and Trubachev (1962) identified no less than a thousand river names in the Upper Dniepr catchment which are unquestionably of Baltic origin. Certain scholars (Gimbutas 1963) report Baltic place- and river-names in a much wider area, including the Upper Volga-Oka catchment in central Russia. In that area, Baltic toponims contacted Finno-Ugric ones. According to Vasmer (1932) and several Russian linguists (Popov 1948; Nikonov 1964), the boundary between the Baltic and Finno-Ugric toponims runs from the Riga Gulf to the southeast, to the upper stretches of Western Dvina and Upper Volga, thence to the south, to the Oka and Moskva rivers, and further to the south reaching the upper stretches of the Don catchment. Yet linguistic contacts of Finno-Ugric and Proto-Slavic languages remain questionable. These contacts are assumed by several linguists but rejected by others (Birnbaum 1983).

The interaction of various groups of Slavic and Finno-Ugric languages is notable in certain phonological characteristics, particularly palatalization. This feature is present in a number of Slavic languages: Russian, Ukrainian, Belorussian, and a greater part of the Polish and East Bulgarian dialects. Among Finno-Ugric languages it is present in Mordovian, Mari, Udmurt, Komi-Zyryan, certain Lappish dialects, as well as eastern dialects of Finnish and Estonian, and southern dialects of the Karelian language (Jakobson 1985). In other words, this phenomenon is typical of ethnic groups which experienced intense cultural and social interactions in historic times.

In summing up the evidence of written sources, linguistics and physical anthropology one has to emphasize yet again that, in their own right, they fail to provide a reliable basis for a solution to the problem of Slavic origin. This may be viewed as one of the reasons why scholarly opinions about the time and location of the 'initial Slav' settlement are so widely different. The oldest tradition links the area of Slavic origins with the Danubian Plain. This theory is essentially based on the oldest East Slavic chronicle, *The Tale of Years Bygone*, compiled in the eleventh century, which says:

> For many years the Slavs lived beside the Danube, where the Hungarians and Bulgarians now live. From among these Slavs, parties scattered throughout the country and were known by appropriate names . . . Moravians, Czechs, White Croats, Serbs, Khorutanians. . . . When the Vlakhs attacked the Danubian Slavs, settled among them, and did them violence, the latter came and made their homes by the Vistula, and were then called Liakhs. Of the same Liakhs, some were called Polianians, some Lutichians, some Mazovians. . . . Certain Slavs settled also upon the Dniepr and were likewise called Polianians. Still others were called Drevlians, because they lived in the forest.[2] Some also lived

between the Pripet and the Desna and were called Polotians. . . . The Slavs also dwelt about Lake Ilmen, and were known there under their appropriate name. . . . Still others had their homes along the Desna, the Seim and the Sula, and were called Severians. Thus the Slavic race was divided, and its language was known as Slavic.

Certain Polish scholars tended to locate Slavic sources in an area of present-day Poland: Lehr-Splawinski (1946) identified Proto-Slavs with the Trzciniec culture; Hensel (1966) identified them with the Lausitzian. Other scholars preferred to see this area in the Czech Lands where the first authentic Slavic assemblages were found. There are other scholars who saw Poless'e (the Pripet valley) as a possible domain of the earliest Slavs: this particular area is thought to be the 'uninhabited country lying north of the Neuri' referred to by Herodotus. No less numerous are the proponents of the theory which tended to locate the earliest Slavs in a forest-steppic area in the South Russian Plain. I share one of the variants of the latter theory, which will be discussed in the next chapter.

---

2 'Drevo' or 'Derevo' means 'tree' in Russian.

Chapter 8 ....

The Slavs in Europe

Pax Romana

This chapter deals mainly with the events that took place during the first millennium AD. In the palaeoclimatic chronology, based on pollen records, this time-span is referred to as the middle part of Sub-Atlantic.

As in the previous case, the pollen data pertinent to the climate at that time are increasingly supported by the evidence of written records and other historic testimonies. All this evidence indicates that after a pronounced cooling, which prevailed between 900 and 300 BC, the climate steadily grew warmer. Roman records show that after 100 BC the cultivation of the vines and olives spread northwards, to an area where this had been previously impossible due to austere climatic conditions (Gribbin 1978). The temperature was steadily increasing during the whole of the first millennium AD. There exist various kinds of evidence suggesting that, starting with the fifth–sixth centuries, this was accompanied by an increase in precipitation. The combination of high temperature and precipitation eventually led to the establishment of a 'Little Climatic Optimum' around AD 1000–1200 (see Chapter 9).

This period is comparatively well studied by climatologists, who used geological, geophysical, historical and archaeological data. It seems obvious that the general characteristics of this period were basically similar to those of the main Climatic Optimum of the Holocene. At that time, cultivation of the vine in western Europe extended 2–5 degrees further to the north. This alone suggests that the average summer temperature was at least 1°C greater than today. This evidence is supported by Scots pine tree-ring records for northern Scandinavia, which indicate that the peak summer temperature in that area between 1150 and 1200 AD was *c.* 1°C above the 1951–1970 average (Roberts 1994).

In historical terms, the rise of the Roman Empire was the most important process, which greatly shaped the destinies of the whole of western Eurasia for many centuries. The rise of Rome to the level of world power had already started in the second century BC, when she conquered Carthage and, in the words of Rostovtseff (1926), entered the family of Hellenistic empires. Yet, the real consolidation of the world empire was achieved only after 31 BC, under the Julio-Claudians, and started with the establishment of the principate of Augustus.

The balanced domestic and foreign policy of Augustus created the conditions of *Pax Romana*, which effectively brought together all parts of the huge empire. The suppression of piracy and the construction of military roads provided safe arteries for commerce. This, combined with a stable currency, aided the economic growth perceptible in both agriculture and manufacturing. Such products as textiles, pottery, glass, tiles and papyrus were not only consumed locally, in fast-growing urban centres, but were also exported over great distances, often beyond the frontiers of the empire. Trade was conducted by merchants, mostly Levantines, who freely travelled everywhere.

As Rostovtseff wrote, the Roman Empire never was, nor tried to be, a world-wide state 'of a national type' (1926: 242): it held together various local entities that differed widely in their culture and social development. In Augustus's time, Italy remained economically dominant. Yet the eastern provinces, devastated by prolonged civil wars, were rapidly recovering. These Greek-speaking regions in the east retained their cultural identity. The northern provinces – Spain, Gaul and, later, parts of Germany and Britain – were less developed, but they also rapidly proceeded along the road of social and economic progress. The civilizing mission of Rome in all parts of the empire consisted mainly in urbanization:

> The town became the basis of social and economic life in all parts of the Roman Empire: in Gaul, Germany and Britain where the native population led a tribal life; in Spain, where towns of the Greek and Phoenician type existed only on the south and east coast – and the same is true of Gaul; in Africa, where the Phoenician cities belonging to the period of Carthaginian supremacy were built chiefly on the coast; on the Danube and in the northern part of the Balkan peninsula, where, as in central Europe occupied by Celts and Germans, the scattered tribes of Illyrians and Thracians lived in villages; and in the vast spaces of the Near East, where the Hellenistic powers had began to build cities before the Romans came, and to reclaim from the rudeness of tribal life the remote districts of Asia Minor and Syria (Rostovtseff 1927: 243).

The second period of stabilization, often referred to as the heyday of the Roman Empire, was achieved in the second century AD, under the Flavians and Antoninines. At that time the Empire formed a conglomerate of peoples and races with different cultures and languages, and imperial policy was restricted to the imposition of some common political and cultural norms, transcending ethnic differences. Yet there was a substantial Romanization, under the influence of urban life, in the western provinces in particular. It often took the form of the spreading of Roman citizenship that was bestowed on a higher social class. By the second century, latinization occurred in the west and in the Danube region. The east, however, where Greek remained an official language, retained its cultural autonomy. There are indications that Rome even encouraged the Hellenization of the entire eastern area.

Romanization and political stability (*Pax Romana*) substantially enhanced economic development. Considerable technological novelties much improved the general economic performance. Banking and credit facilities were at the disposal of merchant communities. Merchants and goods moved yet more freely along the commercial arteries crossing the empire and going far beyond. Yet the disproportion in the economic development (some eastern and western provinces were developing faster than Italy), combined with the general inefficiency of a slave-based economy, and the maldistribution of wealth, created a strain which eventually led to a decline and collapse of the Roman world system.

An important aspect of the social and economic development of Europe, particularly noticeable during the first millennium AD, was the deep impact that Roman civilization exercised on ethnic groups beyond the Roman frontiers, running in an unbroken line from Britain to the Black Sea:

> These frontiers were not merely a breast-plate to defend Roman civilisation, but also served to promote that civilisation in the most backward parts of Roman dominion. Those military camps and towns which later developed from them became important frontier markets from which Roman goods and Roman cultural knowledge spread far afield (Rostovtseff 1927: 253).

> In peaceful times their streets and shops were thronged by people from the neighbouring villages, and also by traders from near and remote districts inhabited by independent tribes – German, British, Iranian and Celtic. Some of these visitors spent long periods in such centres of civilisation, where they learned to speak Latin or, in the East, Greek, acquired an external polish or culture, and became better acquainted with their enemies. Then they would go home, with their habits changed and their minds stored (sic), and thus contribute to the gradual diffusion of Graeco-Roman civilisation (Rostovtseff 1927: 255).

As a result of all this development, a chain of local cultural entities, variously affected by the Graeco-Roman civilization, emerged on the fringe of the Roman Empire. Some of these entities, or socio-cultural networks, are well attested by archaeological materials.

The Zarubintsy and Chernyakhovian

One of these entities, known as 'Zarubintsy culture', is found predominantly in the Middle Dniepr catchment. This culture was first identified in

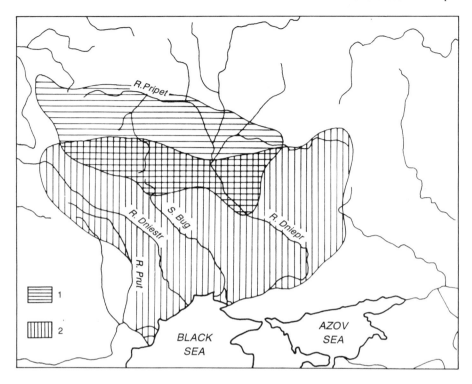

Fig. 37 Zarubintsy (1) and Chernyakhovian (2).
   After: P.N. Tretyakov, *Finno-ugry, balty i slavjane na Dnepre i Volge*. Moscow:
Nauka, 1966.

1899 by V.V. Chvojka (Khvoika), the Ukrainian archaeologist of Czech origin who found a hand-made vessel filled with burnt human bones and iron implements at Zarubintsy, near Kanev, on the Dniepr. Similar finds forming 'urnfields' were later discovered by Chvojka and other archaeologists in the surrounding areas. Summing up available materials, Chvojka came up with a suggestion that Zarubintsy and similar sites dated to the second–first centuries BC and belonged to an 'Early Slavic culture' (Chvojka 1913).

   Zarubintsy sites have been intensely studied since the 1930s (Kukharenko 1961, 1964; Tretyakov 1966; Pobol' 1970). A particularly dense concentration of these sites was found in the Middle Dniepr catchment, between the River Desna in the north, and the Ros' in the south (Fig. 37). In that area alone more than thirty dwelling sites and twenty cemeteries were encountered on both banks of the Dniepr and its tributaries. Dwelling sites were usually located on elevated areas, often on easily defensible hills or on top of high river banks. Dwellings were either of

149

surface or semi-subterranean types, with posts supporting the walls, a hearth in the middle of the living area, and large conic storage pits located nearby.

Numerous cremation graves comprise two main varieties: cremated remains were either placed in an urn, usually a large hand-made ceramic vessel; or were placed in a large pit and surrounded by vessels containing remains of food and ornamental implements with traces of fire. Ceramics formed the bulk of archaeological assemblages, both in settlements and in burial sites, polished vessels being more common in the graves. Ornamental items, which were also more numerous in the graves, included bronze spiral bracelets and fibulae of Middle and Late La-Tène type. In contrast to ornaments, working tools, including iron points and ceramic spindle-whorls, were more common in habitation sites.

Zarubintsy sites were also found further to the north, particularly in the Pripet catchment area. One of the largest settlements, Chaplino, reached an area of 0.6 hectares (Tretyakov 1959). This settlement was surrounded by turf ramparts which were repeatedly rebuilt during the life-time of the site. The Chaplino settlement is particularly remarkable for the richness and variety of its iron implements, which included axes (celts), sickles, spear- and arrowheads, as well as ornaments and elements of horse-gear. A large urnfield situated nearby bore evidence of advanced social stratification. One of the rich burials contained weapons: daggers, knives, spearheads, as well as burnt glass beads. Based on this unusual combination, it has been suggested that this was a double burial, containing the remains of a warrior and a concubine.

Scholars discussing the external contacts of the Zarubintsy culture are unanimous in stressing its close relationship with the Scythian world. Numerous Scythian artefacts found at Zarubintsy sites included daggers, knives, spear- and arrowheads, horse-shoe-shaped fibulae, nail-headed pins, bracelets, pendants, spindle-whorls, as well as distinct types of ceramics. Imported materials also included ceramic amphorae and glass beads manufactured in Pontic workshops. No less intensive contacts are attested with the Celtic (La-Tène) world. These are especially indicated by numerous La-Tène-type fibulae. At the Chaplino urnfield three different chrono-logical classes of burials were distinguished, each containing specific types of fibula, corresponding respectively to Early, Middle and Late La-Tène periods. Based on the presence of these fibulae, the greater part of the Zarubintsy sites can be dated to the time-span between the first century BC and the first century AD. The occurrence of Late La-Tène (provincial Roman) fibulae suggests that the age of the later stage of Zarubintsy culture is the second–early third centuries AD. Other La-Tène materials included iron spearheads, celts, and specific types of bracelet, and, in rare cases, La-Tène ceramic pottery.

The economy of Zarubintsy settlements was based on productive agriculture, which is well documented by numerous finds of sickles of various types. A millstone was found by the side of a grinding stone in a storage pit at the site of Abidna in Belorussia. Pobol' (1970) suggested that agriculture techniques showed a transition from swidden to plough-type cultivation. The evidence for stock-rearing is abundant; animal remains included the bones of sheep, goat, cattle, horses and pigs. Strongly developed iron and bronze metallurgy, based on the local 'marsh' ores was yet another important segment of the economy. Apart from black-smith workshops, which were identified at practically every settlement, a number of specialized centres of iron metallurgy were also found (for example at Ljutezh in Belorussia).

Opinions of scholars in relation to the origin and ethnic affiliation of Zarubintsy culture differ widely. The suggestion first made by Chvojka in the late nineteenth–early twentieth centuries, that Zarubintsy sites belonged to the early Slavs, is still shared by many Russian, Ukrainian and Belorussian archaeologists. Much more diversified are the opinions about its sources: Kukharenko (1961, 1964) opined that Zarubintsy culture emerged in Poless'e and Volhynia as a result of the penetration of the Pomeranian (Pomorian) group of the Lausitz culture from the Vistula basin. Other archaeologists have suggested a local origin of the Zarubintsy culture. Terenozhkin (1955) hypothesized that it had developed from the Belogrud and Chernoles cultures of the Late Bronze Age in a forest-steppic area. Pobol' (1970) argued that it had grown from the Milogradian culture which had developed in the same area during the Bronze Age. Tretyakov (1966: 217), basing his conclusions on the analysis of miscellaneous archaeological and linguistic records, suggested that the Zarubintsy culture resulted from a 'cultural-ethnic integration' of various local Iron Age groups.

In my opinion the Zarubintsy 'culture' was a poli-ethnical entity which resulted from the transition of various Middle Dniepr groups to a plough-type agriculture and their inclusion into an agricultural forest-steppic 'Scythian' network. In its turn, this led to the gradual inclusion of these groups into the sphere of provincial Roman-Celtic interaction. It is very probable that this conglomerate of local ethnic groups used Slavic dialects as a means of communication. Hydronymic data are often used as arguments in that sense. Toporov and Trubachev (1962) showed that the oldest Slavic river-names tended to be located in the eastern Middle/Upper Dniepr catchment. Based on the regular occurrence of old Slavic river names, linguists have suggested that Slavic groups were moving from the south, the catchment of Dniestr and the Southern Bug, to the north, along the Dniepr and its tributaries.

Yet an even stronger controversy stems from the problem of the ethnical affiliation of another culture which appeared in the south of the Russian Plain at a later stage. This culture was also initially identified by Chvojka; it took its name from the village of Chernyakhov, which was the site of a cemetery excavated by Chvojka in 1900–01. Based on his studies of this and similar sites, as well as on the digs conducted at the same time by his colleague, K. Gadachek, Chvojka distinguished the Chernyakhovian culture in the Middle Dniepr, Upper Southern Bug and Upper Dniestr catchment and dated it to the second–fifth centuries AD. Later, the same culture was identified in eastern Romania under the name of Sîntata de Mureş. A large and rich cemetery was excavated in that area at the beginning of this century. Later, culturally related sites were found in the whole of eastern Romania, between the Prut, the Lower Danube and the Eastern Carpathian Mountains. Presently, the corpus of Chernyakhovian antiquities in Ukraine only includes more than 100 dwelling sites and fifty cemeteries.

Chernyakhovian sites are usually located within the valleys of small rivers, often on slopes of elevated terraces and rarely on hills within river floors. Dwelling settlements were large, in most cases stretching over a distance ranging from 0.5 to 1.2 km along the river, their total area varying in size from 2–4 to 15–20 hectares. Often, several settlements were scattered over the range of 1–2 km forming clusters. Each settlement comprised no less than 28–30 dwellings, often rebuilt over and over again. Houses were usually arranged in two or more rows along the lanes. Dwelling structures were of two main types: either wattle and daub houses, or semi-subterranean dwellings of oval or rectangular shape with twig-woven walls. In most cases the dwellings of both types included an open hearth, usually located on the floor, either in a corner or in a niche behind the wall. Large houses with two or more rooms and tempered clay floors were discovered at ten sites in Ukraine and Moldavia. Living rooms had a hearth in the middle, one of the rooms allegedly being reserved for animals. Masonry structures were established at a number of Chernyakhovian sites in the Pontic area. Apart from that, the settlements contained buildings reserved for various economic purposes – granaries, barns and stables – their number often exceeding that of living houses. In at least three cases the settlements were fortified either by turf ramparts with a palisade or stone walls supplemented by a ditch. One of these hill-forts lies near Dniepropetrovsk (Bashmachka) and two can be found near Nikolaev (Alexandrovka and Gorodok).

One of the important features of the Chernyakhovian culture was the bi-ritual character of its cemeteries; both cremation and inhumation graves were found side-by-side in the same graveyards. In several cases, cremated remains were placed in an urn; in others, they were disposed of in special pits. In the case of inhumation, the dead were buried in simple rectangular graves, in extended posture on the back, the head directed to the north or west. Rich women's graves usually contained one or two fibulae, glass, beads of amber or other semi-precious stones, and combs. In contrast, male graves included belt clasps, fibulae and (occasionally) knives. Exceptionally rich graves were rare. In one such case, at Rudki near Kremenec Podol'ski in Moldavia, the grave contained two silver spurs, a silver knife, several Roman-made bronze vessels, a silver bow fibula, a Roman glass cup, a dice of glass paste, and several wheel-made dishes and vases.

Plant and animal remains leave one in no doubt that the economy of Chernyakhovian groups was solidly based on developed agriculture and stock-rearing. According to botanical evidence (Pashkevich 1991), emmer wheat was the most popular crop. Other wheat species including einkorn, spelt and club wheat. Remains of barley were much rarer. Among other crops identified were rye, millet, oats, and pulses including lentils, field peas and horsebean. Details of iron ploughshares were found at several Chernyakhovian sites. A variety of agricultural hand tools – axes and sickles – were common finds at dwelling sites. Cattle usually made up over 40 per cent of animal remains; in several cases it was firmly attested that cattle were used as draft animals. Other domestic animals included sheep and goat (24–25 per cent), pig (6–24 per cent) and horse (10–21 per cent).

Iron metallurgy was the most important craft. Traces of iron smelting were identified in more than forty cases. Cylindrical smelting furnaces were discovered at several sites in western Ukraine and Moldavia. Locally manufactured iron and bronze implements included agricultural tools, weapons, horse-gear and ornaments. Bronze was mainly used for implements: brooches, pendants and beads.

Pottery-making was an equally important craft. Complex potters' ovens were found at more than twenty sites; they produced large amounts of various types of ceramic vessels, for both local and regional consumption. The remains of a glass factory were found at the site of Komarov near Chernovcy in western Ukraine. This factory, presumably manned by Roman craftsmen, produced a variety of Roman-type glasswares.

Archaeological materials clearly show that Chernyakhovian groups were actively involved in political and socio-economic interaction with the Roman world. Numerous finds of Roman coins are but one indication of this involvement. Chernyakhovian sites produced more than a thousand hoards as well as isolated finds of Roman coins, the greater part of which date to the first and second centuries AD. In the third century their number declines, probably due to the monetary crisis in the Roman Empire (Kropotkin 1967). This was accompanied by a marked increase in the volume of imported Roman and Greek goods, reaching a peak in the fourth century. These goods, which included wine and oil in ceramic containers, glass and red burnished ware, precious stones, tissues and other items, originated mainly from Asia Minor and other centres of the eastern provinces of the Empire. The evidence for such imports occurred at practically all Chernyakhovian sites, but the bulk of imported items were deposited in the 'contact zone' which included the northwestern Pontic area, the Lower Danube and Moldavia. The percentage of imported amphorae which is 3–5 per cent on average at all Chernyakhovian sites, reached 20–30 per cent in the Pontic area.

To assess the socio-economic structure and ethnic affiliation of the Chernyakhovian network, it is necessary, first of all, to dwell on the general ecological situation of the steppic and forest-steppic areas. As we have noted earlier, the entire first millennium AD featured a gradual increase in temperature, which, during the first half of the millennium, was accompanied by a stable aridity. The combination of high temperature and aridity created the situation of ecological instability. Agriculture in this high-risk area became less and less predictable. Constantly recurring droughts also severely affected nomadic stock-breeders. One should bear in mind that biological productivity and steppic and semi-desert landscapes are prone to colossal fluctuations mostly depending on the availability of water. Unmerciful droughts, and the resulting insufficiency of food resources, together with the adverse impact of intensive grazing (a 'pastoral depletion'), inevitably increased the dynamics of pastoral groups (Masanov 1970). Easily transformed into numerous bands under a strict military command, nomadic groups moved over huge distances in quest of reliable resources of food and security. Rich, albeit much less organized agricultural communities, became an easy target of hungry hordes of war-like steppic nomads.

Ecologically induced social instability in the 'steppic corridor' coincided with a deep social crisis which struck at the Roman Empire and became particularly acute in AD 235–270. Writing about the causes of this crisis, Soviet Marxist-oriented historians (Bokshchanin and Kuzishchin 1981) especially stressed the following factors: the decline of the labour force due to epidemics and the constantly increasing recruitment into the army; the depletion of arable land; the drop in overall agricultural productivity, resulting from the abandonment of intensive viniculture and olive cultivation in favour of extensive crop production; the demise and decline of manufacturing productivity; the disruption of commerce and the ensuing monetary crisis. Rostovtseff also eloquently described the process.

> The history of the ancient centres of civilisation becomes more and more a history of dissolution and decay. The old institutions are replaced by utterly primitive conditions: in social, economic and intellectual matters there is unbroken reversion to barbarism. ... The complete change of agricultural methods is remarkable throughout the empire. Scientific cultivation, backed up by capital and intelligence, disappears utterly and is replaced by a system which merely scratches the surface of the soil and sinks lower into primitive routine. ... To provide labour for the land became the chief anxiety of the state and private owners. ... There was no longer any possibility of basing the industry on servile labour; the scarcity of labour is a clear indication that the population of the empire was no longer rising but falling. ... The drift of labour to the towns was arrested by the decline of trade and industry. ... The labouring classes were dying out as fast as their social superiors; and their place was filled by new-comers and foreigners – barbarians from over the Rhine and the Danube, Germans and Iranians, reinforced later by Slavs ... (Rostovtseff 1927: 352–3).

Various parts of the Empire were differently affected by the crisis. Commerce remained active in the west, between Spain, southern France, Italy and north Africa, the latter retaining its links with Ostia, Rome, Syria and Egypt.

Rapid social evolution, notable among the groups on the fringe of the Roman world, was in some cases enhanced by the ecologically induced shrinking of their economic resources. This combined with the socio-economic crisis of the Empire, and resulted in an increased belligerency of the 'barbaric' tribes, who were attracted by the apparent richness and vulnerability of neighbouring Roman provinces. Germanic tribes, who had a long record of armed resistance to Romans, were the first on the move. Among various Germanic tribes participating in the barbaric invasions, the role of the Goths was particularly important for the early history of the Slavs.

The initial movements and the later history of the Goths are known principally because of Jordanes, the Roman writer of the mid-sixth century. Himself a Goth, Jordanes was not a professional historian. His book, *De origine actibusque Getarum* (On the origin and deeds of the Getae) or *Getica*[1], written in 550–551, was based mainly on the twelve-volume history of the Goths by another Roman writer, Magnus Aurelius Cassidorus, whose work was lost. According to Jordanes's account, the Goths were an eastern Germanic tribe who had originated in Scandinavia. From there they made a long trek, via eastern Pomerania, the Vistula and thence to the Black Sea. As Jordanes wrote:

> From this island of Scandza [Scandinavia], as from a factory of tribes or a womb of peoples, the Goths are said to have migrated long ago under their king Berig. As soon as they had disembarked from their ships and had set foot on land, they gave the place a name; for even today it is said to be called Gothiscandza. From there they soon advanced against the settlements of the Ulmerugi, who at that time lived on the shores of the sea, made war upon them, engaged in a battle, and drove them from the land. At that time they subjugated their neighbours, the Vandals, and by their victories forced them to join the Gothic tribe . . .

In the following chapters Jordanes describes the subsequent trek of the Goths from Gothiscandza to the Black Sea:

> . . . the army of the Goths together with women and children left on the decision of King Filimer. Soon they passed through a vast swamp [Poless'e?]. While crossing the river [Pripet, Dniepr?] the bridge they used collapsed and split the people forever. Some stayed behind, while others, who had already crossed the river, moved on, invaded the territory of *Spali*, and settled in an area of *Oium* ('rich meadows') on the shore of the Sea of Azov.

Wolfram (1988), from whose book this citation was borrowed, using the Slavic etymology of Vasmer, suggested that *Spali* meant 'giants' (*ispolin*), a term 'typically used to label foreigners', and referred to the

---

1   This title was based on a confusion, since the Goths and Getae are different ethnicities.

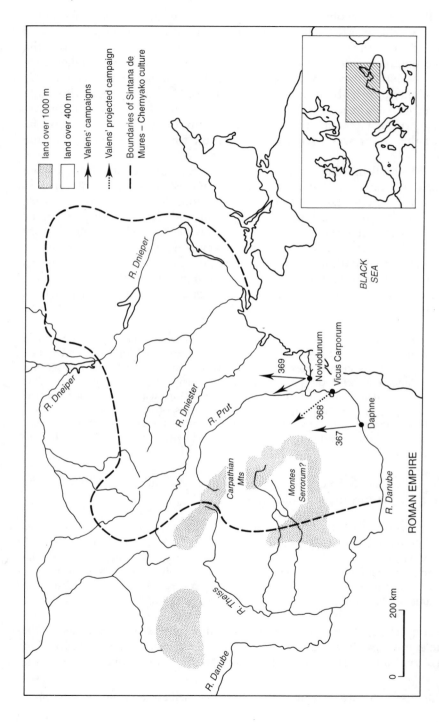

Fig. 38 Gothic wars

Source. P.J. Heather, *Goths and Romans*. Oxford; Clarendon Press, 1991. © Oxford University Press. Reprinted by permission of Oxford University Press.

'Iranian-Sarmatian peoples'. Shchukin (1989) and Kazansky (1991) viewed the 'culture of Wiebark' (dated to the first–fifth centuries AD) as an archaeological document reflecting the southbound movement of the Goths. This culture, first restricted to the Vistula catchment and Pomerania, later spread over greater Poland, the Western Bug and western Belorussia. Its assemblages contained Germanic objects, including Runic inscriptions (one such inscription on a lance found at Suchichno in Belorussia, read: 'attack!').

From the time when the Goths had reached the Black Sea they were divided into two tribes: the Visigoths, west of the Dniestr, with the Balthi as their ruling house, and the Ostrogoths, east of the Dniestr, with the Amali at their head. Both the Amali and Balthi were families of 'kings and heroes' who personified their respective peoples. The Amal genealogy reported in the *Ortogo Gothica*, another important source on Gothic history, gives three eponymous tribal ancestors amounting to 'Scandinavian Gauts'.

By the mid-fourth century, the eastern Goths, who included two substantial political groupings, the Teregingi and Greuthungi, had established themselves as the dominant force in the Pontic area (Heather 1991). The socio-political structure of these groupings is not sufficiently clear. Various independent sources mentioned that pre-eminent figures among the Tervingi were the *iudex*, not kings but judges, whose office was hereditary; yet their real power is hard to assess.

The relationships of the 'Gothic state' with Rome are sufficiently reflected in contemporary sources. For a long time (*c.* 332–365) these relationships were regulated by a peace treaty concluded between Constantine and the Goths. The treaty was signed soon after the construction of a bridge over the Danube in AD 328, which considerably strengthened the strategic position of Rome. Reporting on this agreement, Jordanes stressed that it was a *foedus*, a union confirming special relations; under its provisions the Goths were obliged to send special troops (*foederati*), 40,000 strong, to help the Empire when required.

The treaty was in force until the 360s, when the first Valens's Gothic wars was fought (Fig. 38). According to another Roman source, Ammianus Marcellinus, this war was conducted in three campaigns, none of which was decisive. In 367 the Goths withdrew to the Carpathians; in 368 a major flooding of the Danube prevented a convincing attack by the Romans; in 369 the Goths, under Athanric, lost the engagement with the Roman forces, yet escaped total defeat. The Goths, although undefeated, nevertheless suffered considerable losses. They were deprived of major resources: their harvests were destroyed and commercial links were disrupted. In the terms of a new agreement, concluded in 369 and again called a *foedus*, the Goths consented to submit themselves to Roman rule. In 376 the Huns invaded Gothic lands for the first time. In the summer of that year, they crossed the Danube and unexpectedly attacked Atyhanaric, the Gothic 'judge'.

As Wolfram (1988: 115) noted, from the beginning the Amali kingship had a character of a 'military kinship'. Also they never formed a majority in their 'kingdom' and were therefore culturally absorbed by various local groups. Wolfram also spoke about a 'Scythization' of eastern Goths, who became 'armoured lancers, covering large distances and fighting on horseback'. Their habits included the practice of hunting with falcons, shamanism, and they used a Sassanian royal vestment; in short, they adopted the life-style of the steppic peoples.

The mixed ethnic composition of the Gothic 'state' in the Pontic area included various components, some of which are identifiable in assemblages of Chernyakhovian culture. The Goths nevertheless clearly established themselves as a ruling élite and a dominant force in this ethnic conglomerate. One finds evidence of this in *Getica*: Jordanes, describing one of the Gothic rulers, Ermearic, mentions that he ruled over 'all Scythian and German nations'. The Germanic elements of the Chernyakhovian culture are particularly visible in some of the burials containing weapons. Other Germanic elements are discernible in the structure of houses, which included living rooms and space for animals (so-called *Wohnstallhäuser*); certain types of hand-made pottery and combs also have parallels in Germanic cultures. Still more conspicuous are the finds of implements with runic inscriptions, such as spindle-whorls and pottery at the cemetery of Letčani. Yet Germanic elements were never preponderant and in no case determined the overall character of this culture. Sarmatian elements were no less transparent; they included such features as the cranial deformations noticeable in certain burials, the use of a platform for the placement of grave-goods, and certain types of jewelry. Other elements included those indicative of Daco-Gaetans (some of whom were Romanized). Yet there exists indisputable archaeological evidence proving that the peoples who made up the bulk of the agricultural population of the east Gothic 'state' were Slavs. Shchukin (1994) recently advanced a new hypothesis, according to which the earliest Slavs are identifiable with 'Kiev-type' sites of the third–fourth centuries AD, synchronous with the Chernyakhovian and located in the middle-upper Dniepr.

During the final stage of the existence of their 'state', the Goths in the Pontic area became increasingly harassed by the Huns, nomadic tribes who originated in the semi-deserts of Central Asia. Cemeteries of the early Huns in Tuva (the Sayan mountains in southern Siberia) contained skeletons of medium-sized people belonging to 'a transitional Europeoid-Mongoloid race' (Bogdanova and Radzyun 1991). Over a short period of time, the Huns spread over the entire steppic corridor and started penetrating deep into civilized areas of China, Central Asia, India and Transcaucasia. Local rulers, like in India and Sassanid Iran, often took Huns into their service, using them against rebel tribes. When this happened, the Huns often became incorporated into the ruling élite. For about thirty years from AD 500, western India was ruled by a Hun who assumed royal power.

The first written account made by Ammianus Marcellinus in AD 395 described the Huns as primitive pastoralists and accurate mounted archers in command of horsemanship; they knew nothing of agriculture and had no settled homes. Their loose social units were headed by 'big men' or primates. In the third century, the Western or 'Black' Huns destroyed the Ostrogothic kingdom between the Don and Dniestr rivers. Ermanric, the last Ostrogothic king, committed suicide, having lost a decisive battle in AD 376. Following this defeat, the Ostrogoths and all other ethnic groups which made up the Gothic 'state', submitted to the Huns.

By 432, Rua (Rugila) centralized various groups of Huns under his rule. Later, he was succeeded by his two nephews, Bleda and Attila. In 441 Attila crossed the Danubian frontier and started active operations against the Roman Empire. In 445 he murdered his brother and seized absolute power. He established his capital on the Danube, in the present-day Hungary. The 'empire' of Attila, which also included heterogeneous ethnic groups, at the peak of his power stretched over a huge area of the Eurasian steppes, at least as far as the Caspian Sea. Attila at the helm of his army, attacked in succession the Balkans, Gaul and Italy north of the Apennines. After his sudden death in 453, the 'empire' was rapidly broken up by internal strains and rebellions.

During following years, further advances of various 'barbarian' ethnic groups proceeded. They included the Alani, yet another nomadic group from Central Asia, as well as various Germanic tribes: Vandals, Suebi, Burgundians, Alemanni and Franks. Consecutive waves of these tribes crossed the Rhine and swept through Gaul, Spain and Aquitania. The proclamation of Odoacer, a German chief, as king of Italy in 476, marked the end of the Roman Empire in the west. The imperial power and Graeco-Roman civilization in a specific oriental Christian facet survived much longer in the east, in the political form of Byzantium. It had a profound affect on the socio-political and cultural development of various peoples in eastern Europe, and particularly the Slavs.

Throughout its existence the economy of the Hunnic 'state' was largely based on the merciless exploitation and expropriation of the wealth of conquered nations, particularly agricultural ones. Groups that submitted to the rule of the Huns included a strong Slavic presence, which had a certain influence on the Hunnic culture and language. Jordanes, describing the Huns, mentioned several words in their language, such as millet (*proso*), honey (*médos*) and funeral feast (*strava*), which are obviously of Slavic origin.

The poli-ethnic character of the Hunnic 'empire' is well attested. In some cases, the peoples involved in this conglomerate totally lost their own ethnic identity. Priscus mentioned a Greek who, graduating from slavery to freedom as a warrior and marrying a Hunnic wife, became 'legally' a Hun while retaining his Greek culture. Yet even the ruling élite, apart from the Huns, included easily identifiable alien elements: German, Sarmatian and Slavic. Accounts by Roman historians indicate a cosmopolitan character at Attila's court, with the presence of Romans, and a particular role was played by Ostrogothic and Gepid kings.

At the time of the Hunnic conquest, predominantly Germanic Gothic entities retained their position in the Crimea (Crimean Goths) and northwestern Caucasus (Tetraxites); they remained numerous in the Cimmerian Bosphorus. Kazansky (1993) mentioned the spread of an apparently Germanic female costume (that included large silver brooches) among the predominantly Hunnic élite in south Russia, the Crimea and north Caucasus: this was evidently an imitation of the 'Danubian mode' that was in use among mainly Germanic élites of the 'empire' of Huns in the core area. This mode was largely unknown in the areas to the north which were presumably occupied by Turco-Bulgarians and Slavs.

The rise of the Slavs

The sixth century saw the dramatic rise of the Slavs, who made a sudden appearance on the European historic stage. Byzantine historians report how the Slavs (or *Sklaveni* as they called them) crossed the Carpathians and, passing through the fertile lands of Moldavia and Walachia, invaded former Roman provinces in the Balkans. Soon after Justinian ascended to the imperial throne (AD 527), Slavic warriors crossed the Danubian frontier and, by the end of the century, reached Greece, Peloponnese, the Aegean Islands and Asia Minor. In AD 626, the Slavs, jointly with the Avars, a Mongoloid people, besieged Constantinople, but without success. In the course of the sixth–seventh centuries, the Slavs settled in the Balkans.

In 679, the Bulgarians (or Bulgars), a Turcic-speaking nomadic group originating in the Central area, burst into the Lower Danube catchment and conquered the eastern part of the Balkan peninsula. Written sources referred to them as warlike horsemen governed by khans and boyards. In 635 Khan Kurbat organized an independent tribal confederation which dispersed after his death in 645. The Slavs gradually assimilated Turco-Bulgarians and took part in the creation of a so-called Bulgarian 'empire' in 681. At a later time they waged wars with the Byzantines.

In the northwest, the Slavs, during the sixth century, penetrated to the central Elbe basin, where they entered into direct contact with the Germans. Later, in the eighth century, the Slavs reached the Elbe estuary in the north, and moved into Bavaria in the south, but were stopped by the empire of the Franks. The German-Slavic frontier became stable for three and a half centuries, running along the line of the Elbe, Saale and the Bohemian forests, and being protected by a system of *marks*, special frontier units (Gojda 1991).

Archaeological materials that may be authentically associated with the early Slavs and dating to the fifth century were first identified in the Czech Lands in the form of the so-called 'Prague pottery' by Borkovský, the Czech archaeologist (1940). At the present time, scholars (Sedov 1982) distinguish

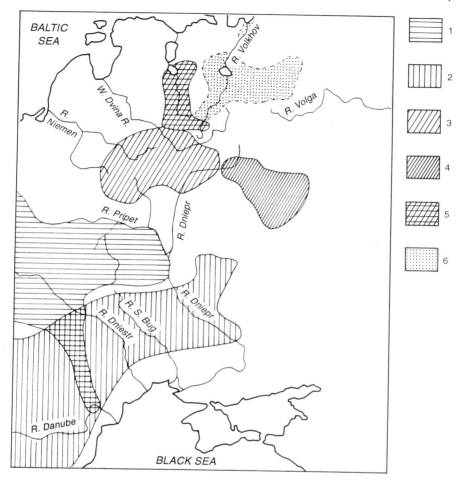

Fig. 39   The East European Plain in the first millenium AD.
    Key. 1 – Prague-Korchak sites; 2 – Prague-Pen'kovka sites; 3 – Tushemlya-Bancerovshchina-type sites; 4 – Moshchiny-type sites; 5 – Long barrows; 6 – *Sopkis*.
    After: V.V. Sedov. *Vostochnye slavjane v VI–XIII vv.* Moscow: Nauka, 1982.

among them two main distinct entities: the Prague-Korchak and Prague-Pen'kovka groups.

The former group is easily identifiable from a particular type of ceramics. Prague-Korchak-type pottery consists of hand-made pots, up to 20 cm high, widening towards the top, with rounded shoulders, vertical or out-turned rims, made of paste tempered with sand and crushed ceramics. Prague-Korchak sites are known over a wide area of central and eastern Europe, from the Elbe to the Dniepr (Fig. 39). They are numerous in the

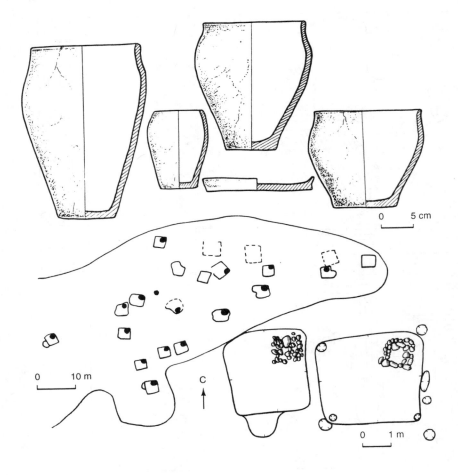

Fig. 40 Pottery, settlement and dwellings of Prague-Korchak type.
From: V.V. Sedov, *Vostochnye slavjane v VI–XIII vv.* Moscow: Nauka, 1982.

west, in the upper catchment of the Elbe and Vistula, in present-day Poland, East Germany and the Czech Lands (Herrmann 1968). In the east, these sites are found in Poless'e (the Pripet valley), in the upper catchment of the Southern Bug, Dniestr, Prut and in Carpathian Ukraine.

Unprotected dwelling sites (*selishche*) were the most common type of settlement. They were usually stretched along the slopes of southern or eastern terraces of small rivers, in size being usually 120–200 x 40–60 metres. In the Pripet valley, Prague-Korchak sites usually formed clusters consisting of three or four settlements at a distance of 2–5 km. Zimnov in western Volhynia is one of the few examples of a fortified settlement. This settlement, which is located on a high promontory of the River Luga, a

162

tributary of the Southern Bug, was protected by a rampart with a timber palisade.

All Prague-Korchak settlements included randomly placed surface-type square timber houses, the necessary features of which were large heating facilities: stone-made ovens, 1 x 1.8 metres in size. A different variety of sunken or semi-sunken house was identified in Poless'e and Volhynia. The foundation of these houses, usually 3 x 4 metres in size, was sunk into the ground, often to the depth of 1 metre. The floors of these timber-walled houses were laid with wooden planks. Ovens, usually made of stones, were placed in a corner facing the door.

The pottery which included Prague-Korchak wares, dominated the archaeological material; other ceramic objects included spindle-whorls, 'frying pans' and enigmatic objects reminiscent of loaves of bread. Iron tools included various agricultural instruments, mostly sickles and scythes, weapons (knives, daggers, spear- and arrowheads) and ornaments. Among the latter, brooches and buckles of various types are particularly numerous. The occurrence of Late Roman iron fibulae specifies the date of the largest part of the Prague-Korchak sites as the late fifth–early sixth centuries AD.

Burial sites belonging to the Prague-Korchak culture comprised both flat graves and barrows (kurgans). In both cases, cremation was a dominant burial rite. Flat graves formed small cemeteries (less than twenty graves); burnt bones were placed into urns and covered by small overturned vessels. The same type of urn was found beneath the barrows, which were usually small, of circular contours and surrounded by shallow ditches. Cemeteries normally contain 10–50 such barrows.

The second group of Early Slavic antiquities, Prague-Pen'kovka, lies to the south of the former in the forest-steppic Dniepr-Danube interfluve, the Low and Middle Danube and the Balkan peninsula. The main distinctions are found in ceramics. Whereas Prague-Korchak pots bellied in their central part and were narrow both at the top and bottom, biconical vases with ribs in the central part form the second variety.

The most common occurrences of Prague-Pen'kovka sites are restricted to the Middle Dniepr catchment, from the Ros' river to Zaporozhe, the Southern Bug and the Dniestr-Bug interfluve. In both the Dniestr and Danube catchment, the two types of early Slavic pottery, the Prague-Korchak and Prague-Pen'kovka, are often found together at the same sites. Unprotected settlements (*selishche*) were usually located within river-floors of small rivers, often on hill-tops. The size of the Prague-Pen'kovka settlements in Volhynia was usually 1.5 hectares; they were slightly larger in Moldavia. As in the previous case, settlements formed clusters, consisting of 5–10 units scattered at a distance of up to 2 km. Each settlement comprised 2–25 living structures. In most cases they were randomly scattered; rarely they formed two or three small groups, or rows along river banks.

Semi-subterranean, square-shaped houses were the only type of

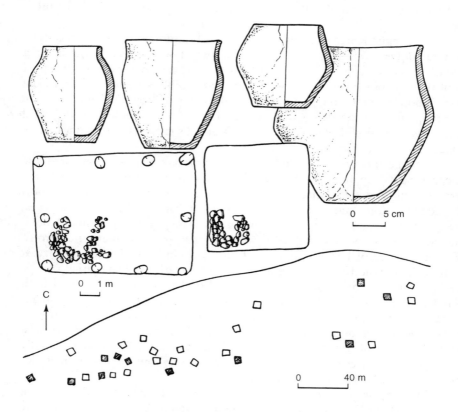

Fig. 41 Pottery, settlement and dwellings of Prague-Pen'kovka type.
Source. V.V. Sedov, *Vostochnye slavjane v VI–XIII vv.* Moscow: Nauka, 1982.

dwelling established at Prague-Pen'kovka sites. These houses were usually small, their size varying from 12–20 sq. m. At an early stage, earthen walls were lined with wooden planks and supported by posts; timber walls dominated later stages. As at Prague-Korchak sites, stone ovens were a dominant feature of the houses. In the case of Prague-Pen'kovka, they were usually located in a corner, opposite the door.

The site at Pastyrskoe on the Tyasmin river (in the Southern Bug catchment) seems to be particularly significant. This Early Slavic site was located on top of a previous settlement which dates to the Scythian epoch. The later settlers, who used the old ramparts, turned the site into a major craft centre. It contained remains of a large blacksmith's shop with fragments of furnace and numerous blacksmith's tools: hammers, anvils and tongues. Iron tools manufactured at Prague-Pen'kovka sites included coulters, sickles, chisels, axes, and spearheads. Metal ornaments were found mostly in hoards; they included various types of fibulae, bead, brooch, belt-buckle, ear-ring, spiral ring, and anthropomorphic figurine. One of the hoards, at Martynovka, on the River Ros', contained approximately 100 items of silver ornaments, mostly adornment of rich female costumes, as well as two silver vases with Byzantine stamps, anthropomorphic and zoomorphic figurines. Scholars (Goryunov and Kazanski 1978; Sedov 1982) attached particular weight to so-called finger-type and anthropomorphic fibulae. These items, dating to the sixth–eighth centuries, were the necessary elements of rich Slavic women's costume; they emerged in the Middle Dniepr area under a strong Byzantine- Balkan influence.

The economy of both groups of Early Slavs was based on productive plough-type agriculture and stock-rearing. Pashkevich (1991) noted that at that time, in addition to the previously existing spectrum of domesticates, naked wheats became the dominant crop; the rapid rise in the importance of rye is equally significant. Archaeological assemblages of these sites show common occurrences of iron ploughshare, various types of sickle, scythe and millstone. The rapid development of agriculture in these Early Slavic areas was at least partly due to the adoption of the progressive provincial Roman technique, with its advanced types of plough, manuring and a field-system with the rotation of crops. Domesticates formed more than 80 per cent of animal remains: cattle and pigs were the dominant species, sheep and goat being less important. It is significant that the agricultural character of Early Slavic settlements is also reflected in written records. Thus Pseudo-Mauricius, the Byzantine writer, in his *Stratericon*, mentioned that the 'Sclavini' possessed a large number of cattle and their houses were full of grain, particularly wheat and millet.

Discussing the origin of the Prague-Pen'kovka culture, Sedov (1982) stressed that both the pottery and types of house, with their characteristic heating facilities, have direct analogies in the preceding Chernyakhovian complexes. Shchukin (1994) argues that the so-called 'Kiev-type sites', synchronous with the Chernyakhovian ones and located in the Middle-Upper Dniepr, played a particularly important role in the emergence of several cultural groups of early Slavs.

One may envisage the following scenario for the spread of Slavonic cultures in eastern and central Europe during the fifth–sixth centuries. The increasing aridity of the climate in the forest-steppic zone caused a considerable decline in agricultural productivity in that area. At the same time, this area became the target of repeated invasions on the part of various nomadic groups (the Huns and many others). Pushed by droughts and hunger, these groups imposed a political domination over Slavic-speaking agricultural communities, subjecting them to harsh exploitation and depriving them of basic living commodities. The combined effect of ecological crisis and political forfeiture led to a gradual outflow of agricultural groups to the north and the west, to the fringe of the former Roman provinces, leaving a kind of power vacuum. The Slavs gained

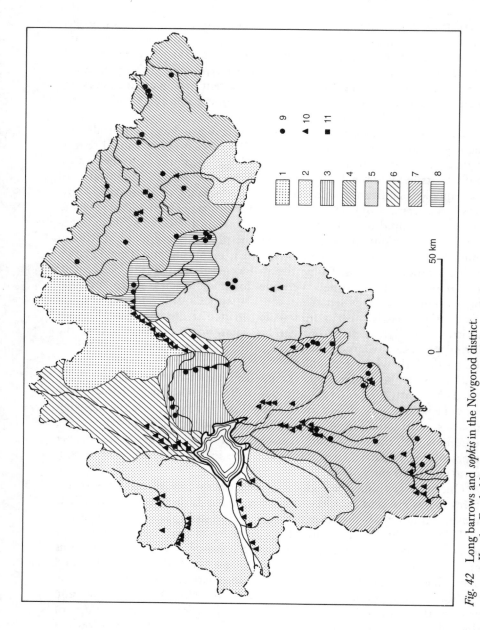

Fig. 42 Long barrows and *sopkis* in the Novgorod district.

Key. 1 – Eroded loamy moraine; 2 – Eroded carbonate-rich moraine; 3 – Sandy fluvio-glacial plain; 4 – Undulated sandy fluvio-glacial plain; 5 – Morainic uplands; 6 – Eroded sandy moraine; 7 – Terraced fluvio-glacial plain; 8 – Submerged fluvio-glacial plain; 9 – Long barrows; 10 – *Sopkis*; 11 – Dwelling sites.

substantial political and military experience in their dealings with their warlike nomadic assailants, emerged as a dominant force and established a new socio-political network in the entire area of central and southeastern Europe. The acceptance of the progressive ploughing technique, which included the use of wheeled plough, manuring, and a field-system with crop rotation, resulted in a rapid increase of agricultural productivity. One may suggest that economic power stood at the bottom of this newly emerged Slavic socio-political network. An intensive exchange of goods and cummunication, as in all similar cases, bound together various ethnic groups involved in this network. The Slavic language functioned as a common information medium. The participation of local tribes is particularly remarkable in Prague-Korchak assemblages: Sedov (1982) noted the similarity of certain types of ceramic and the burial rite of Prague-Korchak sites with those of the local Przeworsk culture.

It was often suggested that agricultural groups, to whom both Prague-Korchak and Prague-Pen'kovka assemblages belonged, spoke a common (not yet diversified) Proto-Slavonic language. This suggestion is substantiated by several linguistic observations. For example, the word 'plough' (*plug*) is common both in Slavic and Germanic languages, and the word for the oldest variety of ard (*ralo*) is common in all Slavic languages.

The Slavs in the north

Beginning with the sixth century, sites allegedly associated with the Slavs appear in northwestern Russia. Burials, which make up the greater part of these sites, fall into two main categories. The first category is referred to as 'long barrows'. These are mounds 1–2 metres high , 12–40 metres long, and 5–10 metres wide; they are usually found in cemeteries, together with 'spherical' mounds of a later age. These sites were first identified by Spitzyn in 1903 and have been intensively studied ever since; more recently, all available evidence on these sites was summed up by Sedov (1974). The dense concentration of long barrows is found mostly in the catchment of Lake Pskov (Peipus), and the Velikaya river, which runs into it from the south (Fig. 42). Each barrow included several burials, their number varying from two to twenty-two. Cremation was the dominant rite, funerary fires usually being located beside the barrows. In about 23 per cent of all cases, burnt bones and accompanying funerary goods were placed into urns, although in most cases bones were found scattered in various parts of the barrow. Hand-made pottery made up the bulk of funerary goods; one may distinguish simple flat-bottomed pots with vertical walls, and large S-profiled jars. Other goods included iron knives, awls, ceramic spindle-whorls, and in rare cases iron sickles, fishhooks, spearheads, as well as moulds for beads, pendants and buckles. Based on the occurrence of specific brooches and other datable artefacts, 'long barrows' were dated to a time-span from the sixth to the tenth centuries.

The second type of burial sites, also found in northwestern Russia and equally associated with the Slavs, is referred to as 'conic barrows' (*sopki*). These are artificial hills of substantial proportions with steep slopes: the most impressive barrows are up to 10 metres high and up to 40 metres in diameter, yet in the majority of cases their height is less than 5 metres and they are often encircled by boulders. In some cases conic barrows are found in isolation, yet more often they form small groups consisting of 4–12 barrows. Conic barrows were first recognized in northwestern Russia in the 1870s. At the turn of the century, they were excavated by several prominent archaeologists, including Spitzyn and Nicholas Roerich, the famous Russian artist and orientalist. The available evidence was summarized first by Chernyagin (1941) and later by Sedov (1970a).

As in the case of 'long barrows', cremation was the dominant rite: burnt bones were either placed into urns or in pits or deposited in ash layers. Grave goods included iron knives, arrowheads, buckles, iron and bronze elements of horse-gear. Ornamental items included beads of glass and semi-precious stone, pendants, bracelets and buckles. Low and broad hand-made vessels with out-turned rims were the most numerous ceramic items. Based on the typology of certain artefacts, conic barrows are dated from the eighth to the tenth-eleventh centuries (Nosov 1981a).

Roerich (1903) was one of the first to note that the two types of burial site are usually found in different landscape settings. To check this observation, I and E.N. Nosov, the archaeologist from St Petersburg Institute of Archaeology, carried out an intensive survey in areas with a dense concentration of sites (Dolukhanov and Nosov 1985; Dolukhanov 1986). As a result of these investigations, it was shown that cemeteries with long barrows are normally concentrated on undulated fluvio-glacial plains covered with sandy soils and pine forests. As for conic barrows, they are usually located on the fringes of end-morainic hills, with predominantly clay soils. Until recent times, these hills were covered with mixed forests with a considerable participation of broad-leaved species (lime, oak, and maple). Podzolic soils developed in these areas and are sufficiently fertile. The most fertile, sod-carbonate variety is particularly common along the western and southwestern shores of the Lake Ilmen, south of Novgorod, where this soil developed on top of carbonate-rich morainic till. The high concentration of carbonate and the low acidity makes this soil the most productive in the whole of northwestern Russia. Yet the high content of gravel considerably diminishes its agricultural potentiality; it has been acknowledged that the cultivation of these soils necessitates the use of iron ploughshares and a substantial investment of labour (Kozlova 1978). This area, often referred to as Novgorod Lake-district (Poozer'je), includes an extraordinary dense concentration of 'conic barrows'.

Based on our investigations, we concluded that the population which left 'long barrows' practised predominantly a swidden-type cultivation, supported by hunting and fishing. As is well known from ethnographical records, these soils may produce high, yet unstable harvests. At least in several cases it was proved that settlements were situated in exactly the same landscape setting as cemeteries, for example, the settlement and long barrow cemeteries at the karstic lake of S'ezzhee in the Mologa catchment (Nosov 1981c).

On the other hand, the economy of 'conic mounds' groups was based on intensive forms of plough-type agriculture. This suggestion is based on several finds of iron parts of ploughshares in the related settlements (Nosov 1981a). Apart of this, 'plough-marks' under a stone circle were identified under the group of barrows at Kolomo (on the southwestern shore of Lake Ilmen). Based on this evidence, it was suggested that plough agriculture and a forest-fallow field-system were dominant among 'conic mounds' groups.

Hence one may conclude that in this case we are dealing with two sufficiently different socio-economic networks simultaneously developing in the northwestern Russian area. The two networks were closely interrelated, as evidenced by the common occurrence of several groups of artefacts, particularly in the styles of ceramic vessels. Both networks were bound together with agricultural communities in the south, from where the main elements of agricultural technology have come. Yet no less important were the links with preceding cultural units, which allegedly belonged either to Baltic or Finnic speakers. These links are attested in several classes of artefacts, notably again in pottery vessels (Sedov 1982). Nosov (1981c) has shown that in several regions of the northwest, particularly in the Volkhov catchment, an uninterrupted local development of the rite of 'long barrows' may be followed; in some cases long barrows were clearly preceded by flat graves in the same area.

Consequently, here one may visualize two ways in which local ethnic groups integrated into the Slavic agricultural network: a 'slow' and a 'fast' lane. The slower model, exemplified by 'long barrows', features a longer survival of basically egalitarian units retaining swidden-type cultivation. The faster socio-economic development corresponded to the areas of 'conic barrows'. The cultivation of fertile, albeit heavy, soils necessitated a much more complex social organization and advanced technical equipment, yet produced much more sizable yields. This social organization was allegedly of a chiefdom type, with its stringent control over manpower, and the procurement and distribution of wealth. 'Conic mounds' in this sense may be viewed as a later northern replica of Bronze Age steppic kurgans: symbols of regional power of group-oriented chiefdoms.

One may easily guess that the latter groups were much more actively involved in the 'Slavic network' with its intensive interchange of goods and ideas. In both cases we are dealing with basically similar local substrata, differently affected by socio-economic change and differently involved in the new network, with different cultural and linguistic implications. Hence the entire process of Slavic dispersion may be viewed as an acculturation or an expansion of a socio-economic network based on productive agriculture and covering a large number of local ethnic entities. The Slavic language was functioning as a common communication medium which bound together various groups involved in the network. In this respect it is worth recalling what Trubetskoy, the Russian-born linguist, wrote long ago, that 'continuing contacts, mutual influence and word borrowing' were extremely important in the emergence of Indo-European languages in all their diversities (Trubetskoy 1939).

If one accepts this model, the emergence of modern Slavic languages may be seen as resulting from an interaction of a new Slavic *lingua franca* with various pre-Slavic substrata. The forest-steppic area in the south of the Russian Plain, the oldest agricultural zone, may be viewed as the core area where proto-Slavic was established after the splitting of the Balto-Slavic entity during the Iron Age. It roughly corresponds to the main area of modern Ukrainian language. The greater part of Russian dialects resulted from the interaction of Slavic speech with various Finnic dialects. The Belorussian language correspondingly resulted from the interaction with the Baltic substratum. Western Slavic languages may have resulted from the interaction of various Germanic (in the north) and Celtic languages (in the south). With regard to south Slavic languages, one may suggest a much more complicated pattern that involved interaction with the Illyrian, Thracian and maybe even Turcic languages.

The above-cited model is obviously an oversimplification: in reality the process of the formation of Slavic languages was much more complex and involved considerable displacements of population. Yet I am convinced that, essentially, this model is correct; one may find convincing arguments in its favour in the fields of archaeology, anthropology and linguistics. For example, the interaction and subsequent assimilation of various Finnic groups in northern and northwestern Russia are well attested; in historical times Finnic groups, such as Vodj, Chud' and Izhora, totally lost their own ethnic identities, but traces of their language are nonetheless identifiable both in modern Russian dialects and in archaeological sites (Ryabinin 1990). On the other hand, existing archaeological and linguistic evidence suggests that Baltic dialects regularly occurred in a considerable part of Belorussia until at least the fourteenth century (Zinkjavičus and Gaučas 1985).

The Vikings and the Rus

The Little Optimum

The events which are discussed in this final chapter focus on two interrelated processes, namely, the emergence of towns and the emergence of the first Slavic state in the Russian Plain. Both events occurred during the final centuries of the first millennium of the Christian era.

In climatic terms this time corresponded to the Little Climatic Optimum. Mean summer temperatures in temperate Europe increased by at least 1°C , which considerably enhanced the agricultural productivity of arable lands. More than that, the retreat of pack ice in the North Atlantic made this area more available for seafaring.

The socio-political environment was developing at that time at a different pace and with varying intensity in different parts of Europe where at least three major areas may be distinguished: Western Europe, the Mediterranean world and Central and Eastern Europe. Social structures, which arose in the greater part of the former western Roman Empire after the collapse of imperial power, were described by Mann (1986: 376) as a 'multiple acephalous federation' consisting of 'small crosscutting interaction networks'. At a later stage, the concentration of power in a pyramid of feudal hierarchy led to the emergence of weak feudal states; the Carolingian 'Frankish' empire in western Europe is the most discernible example. In this, as well as in numerous minor 'Germanic' kingdoms, German invaders, who formed a ruling élite, remained a separate military caste, alienated from the majority of the local population.

The situation in the Mediterranean world was quite different. The socio-political unity of that area was temporarily attained during the reign of Justinian who ascended to the imperial throne in Constantinople in AD 527. Using all available resources, Justinian restored imperial power and the remains of the Graeco-Roman civilization in the ideological configurations of Oriental Christendom. His empire was based firmly in the Mediterranean basin and included Italy, northern Africa and the southern part of Spain. Yet his empire was short-lived. Soon after Justinian's death in 565 the greater part of his acquisitions were lost; the Visigoths regained control in southern Spain; the Lombards took over Italy; the Slavonic tribes, who often combined their efforts with the Avars, resumed their pressure on the Danubian frontier.

In the East, however, a new focus of power soon emerged when the prophet Muhammad united the various Arab tribes of the Arabian peninsula under his religious and military authority in the seventh century. In less than a hundred years his successors, the khalifs, started a stalwart expansion that resulted in the creation of a huge empire, stretching from Gaul and Spain to northern India. The strength of this empire was largely based on the powerful ideology of Islam and on the comparatively high cultural standards of the invaders. The breakdown of 'Mediterranean unity' and the disruption of established trade routes by the Arabs are often quoted as the motifs for the social and political turmoil in Europe during the following centuries. It seems more justifiable, however, to speak about a re-orientation of these routes: Arab merchants created new trade networks different from those which had been in place before. Arab goods and merchants penetrated to various corners of Europe and Arab travellers left colourful descriptions of various European towns and market-places.

Events of no less importance were under way in the vast area beyond the 'limes'. In the early ninth century the steppic corridor had produced a new wave of nomads: Magyars, a Finno-Ugric group originating in an area west of the Urals, 'regained their homeland' in Middle Danube lowland and started plundering neighbouring areas – northern Italy, Germany and even France. Yet another unit, a powerful Turco-Bulgarian 'empire' with a considerable Slavic presence, and generally hostile to Byzantium, became prominent in the eastern part of the Balkan peninsula. In the mid-seventh century another powerful 'state', the Khazar kaganate, arose in the eastern steppic area. Turcic-speaking Khazars formed a conglomerate of nomadic groups originally located in the north Caucasus. At a later stage the Khazars clashed with another Turkic group, the Bulgars, who, as a result, split in two parts: the first moving west to the Balkan peninsula and the second driving north to the Middle Volga, where yet another state, Volga Bulgaria, arose. The remaining Bulgars were included in the Khazar conglomerate. By the 680s the Khazars controlled a vast steppic area between the Azov and Caspian Seas including the eastern Crimea. In the eighth century, the Khazar state showed the basic properties of a feudal state with the hierarchy of social power, and became an important political force – a rival to Byzantium and the Khalifate of Baghdad. Armed conflicts with the Arabs, visibly instigated by Byzantium, were particularly numerous. A considerable part of the poli-ethnic population of Khazaria was involved in agriculture, crafts and trade. Itil, its capital on the Lower Volga, grew into an important centre of administration and commerce, controlling a large stretch of an important trade-route along the Volga. In the early seventh century, Judaism became an official religion of Khazaria. The Jews, who never formed a majority of the 'kaganate' population, were nonetheless active in both trade and administration.

The Vikings in Europe

The remaining areas in the east and north of Europe were affected by less spectacular, albeit no less important development. Discussing the socio-economic progress in that part of Europe, J. Herrmann, the German Marxist archaeologist, wrote that it was largely determined by the 'decomposition of tribal-gentile social structures and the transition to a class society, resulting from the rise of productive forces and stable increase in the surplus value' (1982: 11). Herrmann quotes several indications of this, the progress in agriculture being the most important. The botanical records show that by the seventh–ninth centuries, rye became a dominant crop. Being much more prolific in the natural environment of the European North, rye guaranteed the general increase of agricultural productivity. This was particularly remarkable in Scandinavia, where agricultural settlements concentrated mainly in southern and middle Sweden (Västergötland, Östergötland, Uppland), southwestern Norway and Jutland. The population was rapidly expanding beginning in the seventh century and reaching a peak by the tenth. Lighter soils on sand and moraine were practically all taken up; in Norway farms were built even on mountain heaths.

The development of crafts, and particularly metallurgy and metal-working, was yet another aspect of economic progress in Scandinavia. The local iron metallurgy, which was based on the local deposits of 'marsh iron', rapidly grew in previously thinly populated areas of Småland, Gästrikland and Dalarna in Sweden. Soon, specialized centres of iron-working emerged, a considerable part of locally manufactured iron implements being intended for the export trade.

The situation of overpopulation, the scarcity of available resources, as well as the growing social hierarchy, led to the gradual emergence of a military establishment and military élite. The first indication of this was the appearance of military camps. One of these camps was brought to light at Trelleborg on the west coast of Zealand. It was a circular encampment surrounded by a bank with a palisade and a ditch; inside the camp were found boat-shaped houses carefully laid out in groups of four around a central courtyard (Arbman 1961).

The emergence of professional military casts was still more apparent in the burial rite. In Scandinavia where, during the Iron Age, the dead were usually cremated and buried under mounds, a new type of 'boat grave' appeared in the sixth and seventh centuries. This new burial rite was complex: a boat was lowered into a large hole, the dead man was laid in it on a bed of grass accompanied by his weapons and domestic equipment; then a stallion and an old greyhound were laid beside the boat and killed. The boat was covered with planks, which included sledge-body side-rails, and covered with earth. In other boat graves women were buried. In one of such boat graves, at Tuna in Västmanland, an elderly lady rested on a bier in the form of a straw mattress wearing a pearl necklace with a pendant; the bow contained bowls of wood and clay, a frying pan, dough-trough, and a birch-bark box; the oars were ranged on the bulwark.

At the same time, Scandinavia became increasingly involved in the world trade. This was not a completely new phenomenon. Artefacts of Scandinavian origin occurred in various parts of the Russian Plain at least since the Bronze Age, yet only by the end of the first millennium AD did long-distance trade become firmly established.

The emergence of regional political power, the accumulation of wealth and the creation of increasingly active market-places catering for long-distance trade were the main factors behind the emergence of the first urban centres in Scandinavia, starting in *c.* AD 800. Hedeby in southern Jutland was one of the first to arise (Randsborg 1980). Surrounded by semi-circular earthworks, it stood on the banks of the River Treenem, which flowed into the River Eider and was easily accessible from the Baltic Sea. Initially a small town, it expanded considerably by the tenth century and included dwelling houses, workshops and warehouses; each merchant's house was enclosed by a fence of plaited hurdles. Hedeby was frequented by Saxon and Frisian merchants, and an Arab traveller left a colourful description of the town.

Goods from Hedeby often came to Birka, another trading town situated in Sweden, on the island of Björkön in Lake Mälar. Surrounded by ramparts, 6 feet high and 20–40 feet wide, and situated at a considerable distance from the main buildings, Birka was a merchant town with markets operating in both summer and winter (Fig. 43). The traded items included silver and silk from the Orient, and salt, clothes and household luxuries from western Europe. Among various objects found at the site weapons, mail-shirts, shield-bosses, knives, spear- and arrowheads dominated, while very few feminine articles were reported. Birka was a town of males – merchants and warriors. The crystallization of the two social groups, warriors and merchants, which very often were indivisible, formed a fundamental feature of the Scandinavian social pattern. Arbman (1961) wrote about two types of merchant: 'merchant-skippers' and 'merchant-yeomen'. The former were professional full-time merchants with no fixed place of business; the latter, being no less skilled seamen and salesmen, had their own estates and worked at least half their time as yeomen farmers. Both varieties of merchants increasingly handled locally manufactured products of craftsmen, selling them both to domestic consumers and abroad.

The second important aspect of social life in Scandinavia consisted of

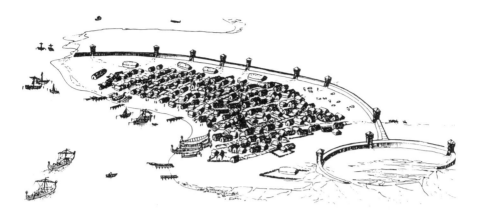

Fig. 43   Birka in the tenth century AD (reconstruction).
Source. J. Herrmann, ed., *Wikinger und Slaven*. Berlin: Akademie Verlag, 1982. (Russ. edition, Moscow: Progress, 1986).

the disintegration of traditional clan societies based on communal property on land and kinship or *aett*. Considerable strata of armed peasants, belonging to free communities (bonds) increasingly entered in conflict with the new élite of landowners. Such conflict often resulted in their expulsion beyond the 'sacral' limits of the communal territory (Lebedev 1985). These groups of dissatisfied yet warlike free peasants formed the core of the groups of Vikings.

Yet, if initially Viking attacks took the form of piratical raids carried out by comparatively small groups (although, such raids are known also at later stages), they soon acquired the form of a large-scale military expansion which gradually became headed by the land-owning élite. Lebedev (1985: 65) wrote about 'Viking movement' in the ninth–eleventh centuries as a national phenomenon that encompassed considerable social strata, including the ruling classes of Scandinavia. The success of the Vikings' seaborne expeditions was largely due to their supremacy in navigation and shipbuilding. Accustomed to seafaring from prehistoric times, Scandinavians were able to design and build fast, mobile and roomy ships capable of transporting considerable armies over long distances. These vessels were technically superior to any contemporary seafaring transport of other peoples. Yet another and even more serious factor in their success was the political and social weakness of the western European states. Multiple 'acephalous confederations' were unable to coordinate any resistance to well-organized and motivated bands of Vikings. Both Britain and Ireland, the prime targets of Scandinavian attacks, were divided countries consisting of a large number of small and weak feudal states.

Scholars are nearly unanimous in claiming that the prime motive behind the Vikings' raids was commercial expansion and control over trade routes. It was constantly noted that journeys in search of new trading opportunities regularly preceded armed onslaughts. Both 'merchant-skippers' and 'merchant-yeomen' readily became merchant-warriors. Paraphrasing the Clausewitz's dictum, one may assert that war in the Viking age was nothing but a continuation of foreign trade with the admixture of different means.

The Viking age is usually counted from AD 793, the year when the monastery of Lindisfarne on Holy Island, off the Northumbrian coast of England was plundered and destroyed by a group of Norwegian raiders. Since that time, the Viking expansion proceeded in two directions: to the west and the east. The western raids were carried out mainly by Norwegians and Danes. The Norwegians concentrated their attacks on the British Isles, Farfoe and Iceland. The Danes raided the rich towns of the Frankish empire along the North Sea coast; their troops moved up the Seine and eventually captured Paris. Later, joining their forces, the Danish and Norwegian Vikings waged successful campaigns in northern France and invaded England.

Starting in *c.* 900 the character of the Viking attacks changes; from marauding and the extortion of tribute they began to appropriate territory and to colonize. In the early tenth century, the dukedom of Normandy emerged as a Scandinavian colony, encompassing the lower Seine and extending to Picardy in the northeast. In 1013 Sveinn of Denmark arrived in England at the head of a Viking army: his purpose was to conquer. Scandinavian possessions in the British Isles varied in size, yet the area of intense colonization, the so-called 'Danelaw' lands, included such communities as the Five Boroughs (Lincoln, Stamford, Leicester, Derby and Nottingham), the kingdom of York and parts of Mercia and Deira, as well as East Anglia. The actual numerical size of Scandinavian colonization, as well as its social and cultural impact on the native population, are open to discussion. In England, the most obvious changes are notable in the social sphere (Richards 1991). The Viking colonization brought about a massive privatization of land, which disrupted the traditional system of landholding. Viking military chiefs divided estates among themselves and their followers and, as a result, many territorial units still bear Scandinavian names. The Doomsday Book records the final division of England in a large number of individual manors, yet it is highly significant that English lords, as well as Danes, took part in this process too, buying land within the Danelaw. Corresponding changes occurred in the settlement pattern: nucleated villages arose in place of numerous dispersed settlements. By contrast, little change is notable in the local administrative system: the main administrative units, the counties, survived unmodified into the post-Conquest period.

There are considerable numbers of Scandinavian place-names in England but their distribution is uneven. They are mostly concentrated in the areas of intensive colonization: the Danelaw. The large proportion of these place-names is often cited as evidence of a massive Scandinavian colonization, although not every historian agrees. Richards (1991: 35) suggested that the English may have adopted Scandinavian words and, as they came into common usage, so used them to name places. More important is that many of the settlements bearing Scandinavian names had been in existence in pre-Viking times, hence these settlements were simply renamed by the Vikings in the process of privatizing the manors. Other arguments relate to linguistic evidence. There are several words in English, particularly in local dialects, that are of Scandinavian origin. They include such nouns as '*lathe*' for 'barn', '*bigg*' for 'barley', '*baorn*' for 'child' and many others. Particularly numerous are the words associated with farming. Richards (1991: 36) rightly acknowledged that the influence of one language on another depends on relative social status. Hence the borrowed words were mainly restricted to the domains of interaction, that is agriculture, social life, weapons and administration. On the other hand, a relative similarity of the English and Scandinavian languages, belonging to the same Germanic family, suggests that the Scandinavians more readily adopted English; the small number of runic inscriptions known in England does not indicate that the Scandinavians continued to use their own language in their own script. The only exception is the Isle of Man where Norse was spoken until the introduction of Gaelic in *c.* AD 1300. Another argument for the comparatively insignificant scale of Scandinavian presence in Britain is the small proportion of Scandinavian burials. There are several thousand Anglo-Saxon cremation and inhumation burials with grave goods of the fifth–seventh centuries, but less than twenty-five pagan burial sites of the ninth–tenth centuries in the area of the Danelaw. As in the case of runic inscriptions, the Isle of Man makes a significant exception. Several boat burials are reported there, including a male laid down on the bottom of a boat and a female nearby. Prominent Vikings were buried under barrows on low hills overlooking the sea (Richards 1991).

If the Danes and Norwegians targeted their raids in the westerly direction, the Swedes, from the beginning, were geographically more attracted by the east. It should be noted that by the beginning of the Viking Age Sweden was socially and politically more advanced than the other Scandinavian countries. A kingdom based in Uppsala was already in existence; royal barrows with rich boat graves in that area contained weapons and goods that included glass beakers and woollen cloth from western Europe.

The Scandinavians and the Slavs

As in all similar cases, Scandinavian military involvement was initially motivated by the expansion of trade. The Russian Plain was crossed by multiple trade routes through which silver and luxury items from the East,

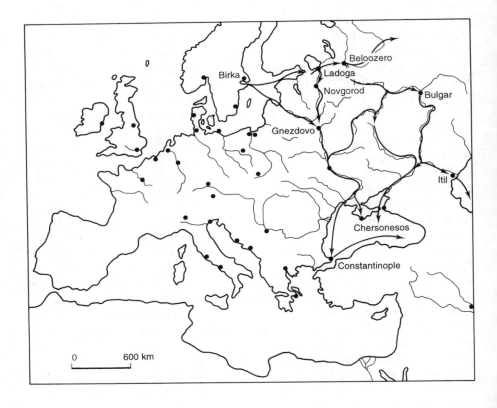

Fig. 44 Trade routes in Eastern Europe in the 9th-10th centuries AD.
After: J. Herrmann, ed., *Wikinger und Slaven.* Berlin: Akademie Verlag, 1982. (Russ. edition, Moscow: Progress, 1986).

furs, honey and slaves from inner Russia reached Scandinavian markets. One of the most notorious trade routes was referred to in Russian chronicles as the 'Road from the Varangians to the Greeks' (*Put' iz Var'jag v Greki*). Judging from the hoards containing Arab coins (*dirhams*), this route was in operation from the end of the eighth century. It ran from the source of the River Neva to Lake Ladoga and via the River Volkhov to Lake Ilmen. From there, via the Lovat' and several smaller rivers, merchants could reach the upper stretches of the Western Dvina, from where boats were portaged to the Upper Dniepr. The way down the Dniepr, which included Kiev and perilous Dniepr rapids, ended up in the Black Sea which gave access to Constantinople and the Crimea. A different path lead to the Volga, to the Khazar Kaganate, on to the Caspian Sea and, via the caravan routes, to the Kaliphate of Baghdad. Yet another route opened ways to the Russian north (Fig. 44).

The socio-economic development in the Russian Plain generally followed the pattern of Scandinavia: the decomposition of a tribal-gentile social structure with the ensuing emergence of an early class society and urbanization. Nosov (1993) has shown how the attitude of Russian scholars towards the problem of the emergence of early cities in Russia has gradually changed. Klyuchevsky (1919) was the first to put forward a holistic concept of the emergence of the Russian town. Linking this process with the development of Early Slavic society as a whole, Klyuchevsky viewed the towns primarily as centres of trade. In Klyuchevsky's view, Russian history started in the sixth century when the first Slavic tribal unions were distinguishable in the Carpathians. The Avars' intrusions in the seventh–eighth centuries caused the displacement of Slavic groups in eastern and northeastern directions. At the same time, there started an intensive disintegration of tribal and gentile leagues. In the course of their colonial movement the Slavs set up individual farmsteads; gentile links increasingly gave way to neighbourhood relationships. A new kind of socio-economic interaction came into play, when trade with the East gained in importance. Participation in trade merged individual farmsteads into larger agglomerations (*pogost*), which eventually developed into important trade centres (towns) with agricultural hinterlands.

Towns, as main centres of trade, developed in the eighth century, primarily serving as points for storage and the dispatch of Russian export goods, and as intermediaries between the Russian hinterland and sea-front markets. Later, in the ninth century, when the towns became fortified, they turned into centres of military power, the protection of trade routes being their main priority. As a result, the urban-controlled areas became further consolidated. At the same time, towns were transforming into centres of political power, which together with their hinterland, became the cores of future states. These emerging cities saw the first appearance of the Vikings in the first half of the ninth century. Soon after, the influx of these and other foreign intruders gained in strength. The Vikings, wrote Klyuchevsky (1919), were actively involved in the emergence of a new social élite, forming a 'military-commercial aristocracy'. In this case, when foreign elements numerically dominated the élite, the town and hinterland acquired the character of a Viking (Varangian) possession.

Later, when Marxist philosophy became the dominant epistemology in Soviet archaeology, towns became increasingly viewed as focal points of feudal socio-economic and production relationships, their prime function being that of catering for feudal land ownership, commercial functions being generally neglected. This concept was first suggested by Yushkov and further developed by Tikhomirov. The latter (Tikhomirov 1956), arguing against Klyuchevsky, wrote that neither trade nor trade routes were directly related to the emergence of towns, being only responsible for the concentration of wealth. According to Tikhomirov, the fortified princely domain (*detinets*) was the core of the emerging towns, which were primarily centres of tribal leagues.

Towns, argued Tikhomirov, developed in densely populated agricultural areas. Although towns were centres of both trade and 'institutionalized craftsmanship', these functions were of secondary importance.

An original concept has been suggested by Grekov:

> When a town emerges within a tribe, the tribe as such no longer exists; hence a town cannot occur in a capacity of 'tribal centre'. . . . The emergence of early towns in Old Rus may be explained in terms of the development of crafts, trade in industrial products, and, especially, foreign trade. . . . Agglomerations that developed into towns, took various aspects: a castle-estate, a fortified refuge, a farmstead situated on a trade-route and later transformed into a market-place, or a hill-fort. Yet, regardless of its origin, the town always featured social division of labour and the high proportion of craftsmen and merchants among its population (Grekov 1949: 92).

In more recent times, a concept of early urban development was elaborated by Kuza (1989) who viewed the Old Russian town as a permanent agglomeration with a considerable agricultural hinterland, which carried out the secondary processing and redistribution of products. Boyars, argued Kuza, stood at the origin of towns, but they were unable to accomplish their functions without merchants and craftsmen, who soon appeared in the towns. The same line was followed by Tolochko (1989), who insisted that Old Russian towns were basically agrarian centres, whose strength was totally based on the productivity of the agrarian hinterland. Yet Old Russian towns, argued Tolochko, emerged primarily as local centres of political and military power, or as provincial administrative capitals.

An original theory was developed by Sedov (1987) who distinguished several stages of urbanization. Initially, in the seventh and eighth centuries, large villages housing professional craftsmen and merchants started to appear in various parts of Old Rus. Later, these villages developed into fortified 'proto-towns', featuring a social stratification, with the occurrence of an élite and a multi-ethnic population. At a later stage, in the ninth century, some of these 'proto-towns' developed into feudal towns, which combined craft-and-trade functions with that of administration and military control. Sedov acknowledged that international trade played a part in the evolution of the proto-town, but denied that this part was decisive. One of the main attributes of a feudal town, according to Sedov, was its bi-partite structure, which included a fortified princely manor (*detinec*) and an unprotected settlement (*okol'nyi gorod*). In one of his papers, Sedov treated this problem in a wider context (1989: 6–55). He noted that non-agrarian, trade-and-craft settlements emerged in the seventh–eighth centuries in areas situated beyond the 'limes', and populated by Germans, Slavs, and Balts who had had no urban traditions in classical antiquity. These settlements developed into proto-towns or *vics* (camps) or coastal trade factories. Although these centres had emerged in areas of dense agricultural population, their further evolution was closely related to commercial links, particularly in the Baltic area.

In yet more recent times, Soviet scholars increasingly broadened the social and geographical context in treating the problem of East Slavic urbanization. Bulkin and Lebedev (1974), while acknowledging that urbanization was one of the manifestations of an early class society, depended on both internal and external factors, and particularly stressed the importance of long-distance trade in the ninth–eleventh centuries. This, combined with the disintegration of the gentile social pattern, ultimately led to the inclusion of Rus, together with Scandinavia, into the network of international trade. Basing their analysis on the study of Russian and contemporary trading centres in western Europe, the scholars encompassed all of them under an umbrella of 'trading camps' (*Handelsplätze* or *vics*). Their main properties were a variable numerical composition of population, a changeable pattern of social roles, a lack of fortifications, at least at an initial stage, a variability of burial rite implying poli-ethnicity, and a limited life-span by the ninth–early eleventh centuries.

In a later work, Bulkin et al., (1978) further elaborated on the evolution of early Russian towns. They argued that these towns developed from the cores of tribal centres in the eighth–ninth centuries. In the ninth–tenth centuries they were surrounded by trade-and-craft suburbs (*posad*). Simultaneously developing special trade-and-craft settlements, they housed poli-ethnic bands of adventurers, who specialized in long-distance trade and military raids, as well as the craftsmen who serviced them. These settlements, which rapidly acquired a cosmopolitan outlook, included an important Viking element. Later, in the late tenth–early eleventh centuries, both types of settlement merged, forming a unified urban pattern.

This was the general social background against which the first Scandinavian traders and warriors made their appearance in northwestern Russia. The role and social implications of the Vikings' presence in Old Russia have been vividly debated since the late eighteenth century. The Viking or Normanist theory, which was initiated by Bayer (1694–1738) and Schlözer (1735–1809), and was shared by a great many western scholars, alleged that the Vikings played a decisive role in the foundation of the first state in Russia. In contrast, many Russian and Soviet scholars argued that the importance of the Scandinavians in early Russian history was negligible. Thus B. A. Rybakov wrote:

> Detachments of Varangians started to appear in far-away confines of the Slavonic world, where the Slavs peacefully lived side-by-side with Finnish and Latvian tribes (Chud, Korela, Let'gola etc.) in the mid-ninth century, when Kievan Rus was already in existence.... Never were the Varangians in possession of Russian towns (1966: 488–9).

To prove or reject their theories scholars often referred to the oldest Russian chronicle, known as the Primary Chronicle, *Povest' Vremennyx Let* (Tale of Bygone Years) which was complied by Nestor, a monk in the Kiev-Pechera monastery in the eleventh century. It was shown (Shakhmatov 1947) that at the base of the 'Tale' lies another chronicle, a so-called *Nachalnyi svod* (Initial Collection) which was compiled in Kiev around 985 with additions from the oldest Novgorod chronicles. The 'Tale' contains the following paragraphs:

(859) The Varangians from beyond the sea imposed tribute upon the Chud, the Slavs, the Merians, the Ves and the Krivichians. But the Khazars imposed it upon the Polianians, the Severians and the Viatichians, and collected a squirrel skin from each hearth. . .

(860–862) The tributaries of the Varangians drove them back beyond the sea and, refusing them further tribute, set out to govern themselves. There was no law among them, but tribe rose against tribe. Discord then ensued among them, and they began to war one against another. They said to themselves, 'Let us seek a prince who may rule over us, and judge us according to the law'. They accordingly went overseas to the Varangian Russes: these particular Varangians were known as Russes, just as some are called Swedes, and others Normans, Angles, and Goths, for they were thus named. The Chuds, the Slavs, and the Krivichians then said to the people of Rus', 'Our whole land is great and rich, but there is no order in it. Come to rule and reign over us'. They thus selected three brothers, with their kinsfolk, who took with them all the Russes and migrated. The oldest, Rurik, located himself in Ladoga (Aldeigjuborg); the second, Sineus, in Beloozero; and the thid, Truvor[1], in Izborsk. On account of these Varangians, the district of Novgorod became the land of Rus'. The present inhabitants of Novgorod are descended from the Varangian race, but aforetime they were Slavs.

The chronicle further accounts that two years later the younger brothers died and the eldest (Rurik) assumed full power, after which he went south and built the town of Novgorod (Holmgar) on the shores of Lake Ilmen. From there the Rus people spread south (Kaiser and Marker 1994; Brøndsted 1960).

Thus goes the chronicle; now we may turn back to the archaeological evidence. The first major site along the 'Road from the Varangians to the Greeks' was Ladoga.[2] The settlements known in the Norse chronicles as Aldeigjuborg lie on the River Volkhov, a few kilometres upstream from its mouth in Lake Ladoga. In that area the deep Volkhov valley, eroded in the morainic till, reaches the underlying limestone of Ordovician age, forming several perilous rapids. This area, at least seasonally, is unnavigable, travellers often being obliged to portage their boats on dry land. The

---

[1] The latter two names are often interpreted as misspelt *'sine hus'* ('his house') and *'tru vaering'* ('loyal army').
[2] The site is usually referred to as Staraya Ladoga (Old Ladoga), yet this name is in use only since 1704 when a new settlement (Novaya Ladoga) arose further downstream, due to the construction of a canal.

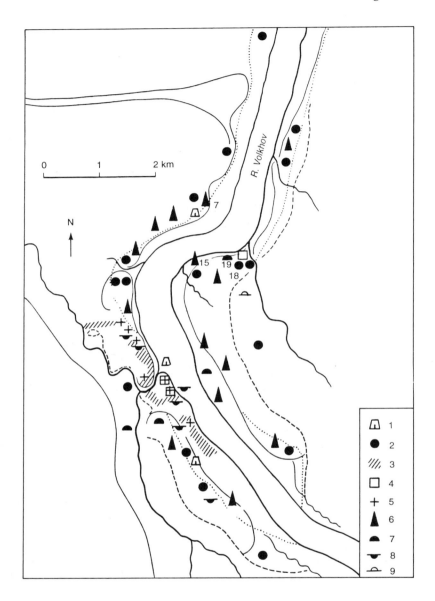

Fig. 45 Volkhov in the Staroja Ladoga area.

    Key. 1 – Neolithic sites; 2 – Unfortified settlements; 3 – Urban area; 4 –
Hill-forts; 5 – Temples; 6 – *Sopkis*; 7 – Barrows; 8 – Flat graves; 9 – Tombs with
stone structures.

    Source. J. Herrmann, ed., *Wikinger und Slaven.* Berlin: Akademie Verlag,
1982. (Russ. edition, Moscow: Progress, 1986).

settlement of Ladoga, which has been excavated for more than 100 years, covers an area of more than 2,000 sq. metres, on the left bank of the Volkhov (Fig. 45), and embraces the time-span between the mid-eighth and tenth centuries. Already at its initial stage, in the mid-eighth–early ninth centuries, Ladoga became a major craft-and-trade settlement with an important agricultural hinterland. Its multi-ethnic population included Slavic, Finnic and Scandinavian elements. The Slavic presence is particularly obvious in the types of house-building (authentically Slavic rectangular timber houses with an oven in a corner) as well as in ceramics and agricultural implements. Finnic elements allegedly associated with the Chud and Proto-Karelians are seen in some classes of pottery and bone implements.

Numerous barrows, dated to the ninth-eleventh century and belonging to local Finnic groups, are found along the lower stretches of smaller rivers flowing into Lake Ladoga from the south. The appearance of this burial rite and some elements of their material culture, detectable in funerary goods, reflect, in the view of Nazarenko (1982), a Scandinavian cultural impact, probably due to the presence of Scandinavian fur merchants. Later, in the twelfth century, the local burial rite disappeared under a strong Russian influence.

Scandinavian implements were identified in all levels of the settlement of Ladoga, starting with the oldest ones. They included various ornaments, and what is more important, objects with runic inscriptions. A wooden rod with a runic inscription, allegedly of a magic character, was dated to the ninth century. Another inscription also of a magic character, made on a copper pendant, dates to the tenth century. Since its early stages, Ladoga developed into an important centre of international trade. Its cultural deposits included several hoards containing Arab coins (*dirhams*), dated to AD 786, 808 and 847. Imported goods included glass beads originating from the eastern Mediterranean area, Baltic amber, Frisian ceramics and incised bone.

The Ladoga assemblage comprises several important burial sites. The oldest among them are conic mounds which are numerous on both banks of the Lower Volkhov; they are dated to the eighth century. Apart from that, there are several long and spherical mounds as well as mounds with cremation and inhumation graves of the Scandinavian type of the tenth–eleventh centuries. A special Scandinavian cemetery (Plakun) is situated on the lower terrace of the right bank of the Volkhov, facing the settlement. This cemetery included no less than sixty barrows; seven (or eight) of which included boat graves with cremations. One barrow, situated at some distance from the main cemetery, contained a boat grave with inhumation. It is generally acknowledged that this was a military cemetery, belonging to a small Viking detachment.

The levels of the mid-ninth century bear traces of a major fire which destroyed the entire settlement. Some scholars tend to link this with the events of AD 859–862, reported in the 'Tale', and which included the

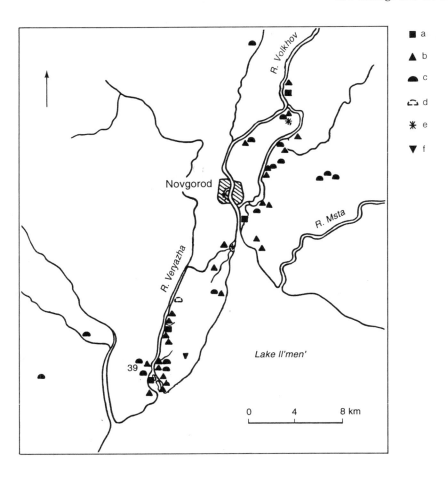

Fig. 46   Archaeological sites in the Novgorod area.
    Key. a – Hill-forts; b – Unfortified settlements; c – *Sopkis*; d – Suggested
location of *sopkis*; e – Pagan sanctuaries; f – Ritual stone.
    Source. E.N. Nosov, *Novgorodskoe (Rjurikovo) gorodishche.* Moscow: Nauka,
1990.

expulsion of Vikings and the ensuing internal strife.

    The next major cluster of settlements encountered by travellers along
their way to the south, was located in the sources of the River Volkhov and
on the shores of Lake Ilmen (Fig. 46) (Nosov 1990). Both the lake and the
rivers belonging to its catchment were formed during the Last glaciation.
The fluvio-glacial plain, with several minor undulations and elevations,
dominates the surrounding area. River valleys here are normally up to 3 km
wide with well-developed river floors. One of the major features of the area

is the great magnitude of seasonal flooding. The area of the Ilmen basin seasonally inundated is no less than 70,000 hectares, reaching 150,000 hectares in exceptional years. The highest flood was recorded in 1966 when the level of the Volkhov reached 7.66 metres above its present one, flooding a considerable part of the town of Novgorod. As a result, numerous hill-tops at the Volkhov sources seasonally turn into islands surrounded by torrential streams. The settlements of the first millennium AD were usually located on top of these hills.

This area includes an extraordinary high concentration of conic mounds. As had been previously mentioned, the Ilmen catchment contains the most fertile soils of the entire Russian northwest. The Lake District (Poozer'je), a narrow band 60 km long, along the northwestern shore of Ilmen is particularly remarkable in this sense. Eight out of nineteen known in the entire Ilmen area are found in the Lake District.

The number of settlements reliably dated to the first millennium AD in the Novgorod area is now estimated as twenty-five. These sites stretch along the Upper Volkhov, as well as along Veryazha and numerous minor rivers; they are also found on the shore of Lake Ilmen. The great majority of these sites were unprotected; fortifications were established only in three cases. One of the fortified settlements, Georgi (St George), dated to the end of the eighth and beginning of the ninth centuries, is located on the terrace of the Veryazha river, 4.5 metres above the river floor. Excavations have revealed the remains of turf ramparts, storage pits and burned stones, presumably belonging to heating devices. The finds included typical Ladoga-type ceramics, fibulae, sickle-like knives, scythes, as well as a bronze knife with an unusual handle, a bronze ring and casting moulds suggestive of local bronze metallurgy. Another fortified settlement, Vassilevskoe, was located on a slightly higher level of the same terrace, 300 metres downstream from the former. Excavations have revealed several storage pits and structures of various origin, their foundations being dug into the ground. The finds included Ladoga-type ceramics, numerous arrowheads, a part of an iron necklace and several glass beads. The latter two artefacts are obviously of Scandinavian origin; the beads may be reliably dated to the late ninth–early tenth century. This date was further corroborated by the radiocarbon measurement of charcoal samples from various structures: the calibrated dates cluster between AD 960±30 and 940±40. Animal remains included cattle, sheep, pig, horse and dog; bones of elk were also found. There were indications of local iron and bronze metallurgy.

Porost' was another major settlement, that was located in the confluence of the Volkhov with one of the minor rivers. This settlement, which included several clusters of buildings, was of a considerable size; its deposits were found stretching over a distance of 500 metres. The finds included glass beads of Scandinavian origin and suggested an age of the eighth–tenth centuries. Another large hill with a flattened top, situated 300 metres off the settlement and known as Peryn', is associated with the location of a sanctuary of Perun, the thunder-god in the pantheon of Early Slavs. According to the Third Novgorod chronicle, this sanctuary included a huge wooden idol of Perun, which was dismantled and thrown to the Volkhov in AD 988. Excavations carried out by Sedov in 1948–53 revealed a circular platform surrounded by a ditch with the foundation of a post in the centre and eight holes, allegedly intended for a ritual fire.

Yet another settlement, Kholopy Gorodok (Serfs' Township or Drelleborch in the Hanseatic documents) lies at the confluence of the Volkhov with another small river, Volkhovets, 14 km upstream from Lake Ilmen. The settlement, which included a fort with ramparts (*gorodishche*) and an unprotected part (*selishche*), was located on an elevated hill amidst the low-lying seasonally flooded plain. The finds made at the site included various objects of Scandinavian origin, such as a boat-shaped bracelet, and a large collection of glass beads. A hoard of oriental coins was found in 1979 in an area of the unprotected settlement; the majority of these coins are dated to AD 810–811. Based on these and other finds, the age of the settlement is estimated as the eighth–tenth centuries. One of the most interesting finds was a hoard which contained a collection of 112 agricultural implements; among them were found elements of ploughshare (similar tools were found also at Ladoga), as well as axes, hoes, knives, a horse-bridle and other objects. The horse-bridle with animal heads has analogies in the south, mostly in Turcic and Avar antiquities of the seventh–eighth centuries.

Rurikovo Gorodishche (Rurik's Hill-fort) occupies a key position among first-millennium settlements at the Volkhov's sources. Situated at a naturally protected location, on an island at the bifurcation of the river, the site was in a position to control the on-going traffic of goods. At the height of its development the settlement reached a considerable size, exceeding 4 hectares, stretching alongside the Volkhov river over a distance of at least 350 metres. The steep slope facing the river was fortified by an artificial escarpment and a ditch at least 4.5 metres deep. As in many similar cases, the settlement included both a fortified and an unprotected segment. The settlement was in existence from at least the middle of the eighth century. The suggested date is substantiated both by archaeological finds and various dating techniques. The dendrochronological analysis of tree-rings has shown that the trees felled in AD 889–948 were used in construction. Radiocarbon measurements of charcoal samples collected at the bottom of the ditch suggest the age of AD 880±20 (calibrated). All these dates, in the opinion of Nosov, provide a *terminus post quem*.

Like all the sites in that area, Rurik's Hill-fort provides abundant evidence for the multi-ethnicity of its population. Nosov (1990) argued that the majority of this population consisted of Slavs. The ceramics which made up the bulk of the archaeological assemblage were obviously Slavic. Among other Slavic implements, Nosov quoted specific types of arrowhead and some other characteristic items such as bread ovens and temple rings. The

Scandinavian presence was transparent from the beginning. The implements of Scandinavian origin included a sword with a characteristic hilt and fibulae confining the heads of a human male and animal. Other Scandinavian objects included a lead dragon's head with an open mouth and upward twisted tongue. Yet, two bronze pendants with identical runic inscriptions remain the most sensational. These inscriptions were allegedly of a magic character. One of the variants of the translation reads: 'Should you not be deprived of your male force!'

The finds at Rurik's Hill-fort are indicative of various activities performed at the site. These activities included agriculture, fishing, hunting and various crafts, which included bronze metallurgy judging from the fragments of moulds. No less important was bone and antler working. The finds of gold wire suggest that gold jewellery items were at least partly manufactured by local goldsmiths. Trade was a substantial aspect of the daily life of the local settlers. Material proof exists in the form of fragments of a balance and numerous weights. One should not forget that the Volkhov was, and remained, an active commercial thoroughfare; five hoards with oriental coins of the ninth–tenth centuries came only from the upper stretches of this river.

Based on the analysis of available archaeological evidence, Nosov (1990) suggested that in the eighth–ninth centuries Rurik's Hill-fort, like Ladoga downstream of the Volkhov, was an important centre of craft and trade which eventually became a military stronghold. Ladoga and Rurik's Hill-fort controlled both ends of an important waterway. Nosov further suggests that both settlements developed into the centres of local tribal leagues even before an active military intervention on the part of Vikings.

Now we may address the problem of the Vikings' presence. As follows from the existing archaeological evidence, there is no doubt about the presence of Scandinavians at a very early stage in the existence of the fortified settlements along the Volkhov. Yet the questions remain, what was the character of this presence, and what impact did it have on the social and cultural development of the local groups? There is a growing trend among Russian scholars to view Nestor's account in the 'Tale' as more or less correctly reflecting the actual course of events. Thus, Lebedev (1985) and several other Russian scholars tended to identify Rurik with Hroekr of Jutland, known from Scandinavian sources to be in possession of large areas in western Jutland and along the coast of Frisia in the mid-eighth century. The invitation addressed to Scandinavians ('Come to rule and reign over us') may have followed internal conflicts which are visible in the traces of the intensive fire at Ladoga that we know occurred some time after AD 864. After several years spent in Ladoga, Rurik returned to the west (870–873); during that time he actively took part in several diplomatic missions. In his absence, power in Ladoga was seized by a local opposition led by Vadim the Brave. On his return to Ladoga, Rurik suppressed the resistance and calmed the opposition by marrying a daughter of a local nobleman.

In contrast to the western countries, the Vikings' conquests in Russia never took the form of a peasant colonization. This was mostly a military intervention which had, nonetheless, greatly enhanced the development of already existing proto-urban centres, turning them into effective market-places and military-administrative strongholds. As Kirpichnikov (1988) remarked, Ladoga, due to its advantageous strategic position, became, albeit for a short time, the capital of Rurik's emerging empire.

After a comparatively short stay at Ladoga, Rurik, according to Nestor's account, moves further upstream, to Volkhov's sources. In the words of the chronicle, '. . . and he came to the Ilmen-Lake and built a town above the Volkhov which he called Novgorod and sat there to reign and distributed *volosts* (estates)'. Nosov (1990: 190), following Tikhomirov, viewed these words as a clear indication of the fact that Rurik actually came not to Novgorod, but to Hill-fort, the former being situated in a low-lying area at a considerable distance from the lake. At the same time, Nosov stressed that Hill-fort was already an important administrative centre and that it was its useful strategic position that had naturally attracted Rurik. Only at a later stage was the administrative centre transferred to a 'new town' (that is, Novgorod) further inland. This suggestion finds support in the archaeological evidence: the earliest levels of Novgorod are dated to AD 1044, hence they are considerably younger than Hill-fort. For a long time the two settlements, the older and younger, coexisted side-by-side, until the former had faded away.

Nosov (1993) noted that the existence of 'paired settlements' was a characteristic feature in the early urban development of eastern and northern Europe. Such pairs were rather common in the east: Gnezdovo/Smolensk, Timerevo/Yaroslavl, Sarskoe Gorodichche/Rostov, Rurik's Hill-fort/Novgorod. They are also known in the western Baltic basin: Hedeby/Slesvig in south Jutland, Birka/Sigtuna. Nosov viewed this as one of the features dictated by the development of long-distance trade.

The character of the Vikings' presence in Russia is further clarified by the linguistic analysis of the word '*Rus*'. As we remember, in the 'Tale' Nestor clearly indicated the Russes as one of the Scandinavian peoples ('. . . these particular Varangians were known as Russes, just as some are called Swedes, and others Normans, Angles, and Goths . . .').

As the convincing linguistic analysis shows (Mel'nikova and Petrukhin 1989), the word 'Rus' is derived from the Finnish '*Routsi*'. This and similar words in Finnish and other western Finnic languages (*Roots* in Estonian, *Rôtsi* in Vodian, *Rôtši* in Karelian) have the same meaning: Sweden. Analyzing the etymology of this word, Mel'nikova and Petrukhin (1989) suggested that its origin may be found in the word 'boatsmen' (Anc. Swedish '*botsmæn*') being transformed into the Finnish '*puosi*'. Hence, as Russian linguists suggest, this word from the very beginning was used by the Finns to denote intruders from oversees of a distinct Scandinavian (Swedish) descent. The transition of Finnish '*Ruotsi*' into the Russian '*Rus*' is quite logical in accordance with phonological laws: '*uo*' is easily transformed into '*u*' and '*ts*' into the palatized '*s*'.

In contrast to this hypotheses, proponents of the autochthonous origin of the name '*Rus*' usually suggest that this name has developed from the river Ros', the tributary of the Middle Dniepr, in an area rich in Chernyakhovian and Zarubintsian sites. Mel'nikova and Petrukhin (1989) noted that the authentic Slavic name of this river is R's (Ръс) the symbol ъ amounting to the Indo-European 'i', which, according to phonological laws, in no case could produce the name '*Rus*'. Similar conclusions follow from the analysis of other written sources. Mel'nikova and Petrukhin (1989) argued that Arab writers who often used the word '*ar-rus*' never attached to it any ethnic significance. They viewed the '*ar-rus*' as warriors and merchants regardless of their ethnic affiliation. The same applies to Byzantine sources which often mentioned 'people calling themselves the Ross' (Rhos), who in reality were groups of Scandinavians accomplishing various missions.

Summing up the existing evidence relating to early urbanization and early statehood in northwestern Russia, one should dwell on the following essential elements. First of all, one should take into account that early urban centres developed in the areas of high concentrations of conic mounds. As I tried at show in the preceding chapter, these areas, which featured an accelerated social development, were actively involved in a Slavic socio-political network, with a great number of small ephemeral chiefdoms exercising power over local groups of people and regionalized resources. The second element was the re-orientation of trade routes and an increasing involvement of northwestern Russia into a new trade network which included markets in Scandinavia. The area of inner Russia, which underwent at that time a rapid socio-economic development and which provided an easy access to flourishing markets in the south, formed a natural attraction for the Viking expansion, which formed the third element of the urban development.

In contrast to the west, this expansion never took the form of a peasant colonization. The Vikings formed a social élite of newly emerging Slavic statehood. They considerably enhanced the process of social development, creating and protecting the infrastructure and establishing new local markets. In the end they succeeded in creating a major arena of social power, knitting together ephemeral chiefdoms into a new kind of social network with themselves at the top. Yet a considerable number of the Scandinavians of a lower social rank were easily inter-mixing with the common locals: one of the early Novgorod chronicles (AD 864) mentioned 'common Novgorodians of Varangian descent'.

Yet the cultural impact of the Scandinavians, due to a greater geographical distance from the core area and the language barrier, was much less conspicuous in Russia than in the west. There are no Scandinavian place-names in Russia, neither can one find any Scandinavian impact on the

Slavic languages. Even the names of early Rurikids, which were definitely Scandinavian at the beginning (Oleg, Olga, probably derived from Old Scandinavian *Helgi* or 'holy'), soon became totally Slavic (Svyatoslav, Svyatopolk, Vladimir etc.).

Oleg the Holy, the prince-priest, succeeded Rurik after his death. Having consolidated his political, economic and ideological power in Ladoga, he, at the head of a predominantly Varangian army, started moving further to the south along the great trade route, first to Novgorod and then to Kiev. The seizure of Kiev marked a new and decisive step towards the creation of early Russian statehood. The geographical situation of Kiev, at least in one respect, resembles that of Novgorod. Situated in the middle stretches of the Dniepr, near its confluence with its main tributaries, including the Pripet flowing from the west and the Desna from the east, Kiev lies at the focal point of a catchment covering a considerable part of Russian water routes. However, there are significant differences. Kiev, situated at the transition of the forest and forest-steppic zone in the classical area of fertile south Russian chernozem, lies at the centre of one of the richest agricultural regions of eastern Europe. The earliest evidence for productive agriculture came from the sixth millennium BC, when early Tripolye settlements appeared there (actually, the eponym site of Tripolye lies now within the confines of Greater Kiev). Since that time, the development of agricultural communities proceeded uninterruptedly, throughout the Bronze and Iron Ages. The area of the Middle Dniepr was part of the forest-steppic zone of eastern Europe where the first Slavic-speaking communities ('agricultural Scythians') are identified.

Kiev was originally located on a high and steep bank of the Dniepr, which formed a flattened loess-covered plateau stretching 14–15 km from the north to the south and 3–4 km from the west to the east. This plateau, crowning the high bluff of the Dniepr, was eroded by numerous streams and small rivers, easily isolating dependable hills and promontories which became the arenas of early settlements. The widening of the river floor notable in the north, forms yet another arena of early settlement, Podol, which includes an easily attainable harbour on the Dniepr (Fig. 47). As we had noted before, the area of Kiev bears evidence for practically uninterrupted agricultural settlements. Several hill-tops – Zamkovaya, Starokievskaya etc. – as well as Podol contained the remains of Zarubintsian and Chernyakhovian settlements. The presence of numerous Roman coins indicated an interaction of these settlements with the Roman provincial world.

Excavation at Zamkovaya (Castle) hill revealed archaeological deposits belonging to the sixth and seventh centuries; these deposits contained Byzantine coins with the effigies of the Emperors Anastasius I (491–518) and Justinian I (518–527). The excavations, initiated in 1909 and only recently completed, brought to light the remains of a large fortified settlement (*gorodishche*) situated on top of Starikoevskaya (Old Kiev) hill and dated to

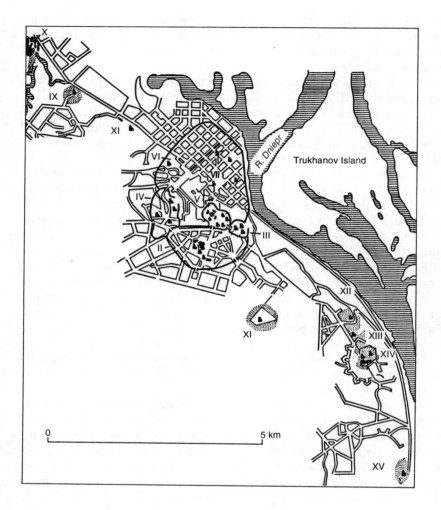

Fig. 47 The Old Kiev.
   Key. Districts: I – Vladimir's City; II – Yaroslav's City; III – Michael's Part;
IV – Kopyrev End; V – Castle Hill; VI – Shchevkovista; VII – Podol; VIII – Khorevitsa;
IX – Dorogozhichi; X – St Kirill Church; XI – Klov; XII – Ugorskoje; XIII – Berestovo;
XIV – Pechera Monastery; XV – Vydubichi.
   Source. V.D. Baran, *Arheologija Ukrainsloi SSR,* v. 3. Kiev: Naukova
Dumka, 1986.

the late fifth–eighth centuries. The settlement was surrounded by a steep
ditch, at least 3 metres deep, and an impressive wall. Inside the protected
area were found numerous storage pits and dwellings, which included the
princely castle, as well as a pottery oven with numerous ceramics. A find of
a spinning-whorl with a trident (now used as a national Ukrainian symbol)

is remarkable. A structure found in the middle of the settlement is interpreted as a pagan sanctuary. This was an oval-shaped clay platform, 4.2 × 3.5 metres with four outstanding edges and was inlaid with closely set sandstone cobbles. A column-like construction made up by interlaying strata of burned clay and ash was found flanking the main structure from the west; this was surrounded by a large number of animal bones and skulls.

Russian and Ukrainian archaeologists tend to identify the site on Old Kiev hill with the earliest settlement mentioned in the old Russian chronicles. As one of these chronicles accounts:

> ... once there were three brothers, one by the name of Kiy, another, Shchek, and the third, Khoriv, and their sister, Lebed' (Swan). They sat on three mountains, Kiy on one where now is Borichev road, Shchek on the mountain now called Shchekavitsa, and Khoriv on the third mountain called henceforth Khorevitsa. And built they a town, and called it Kiev, in the name of the elder brother.

Rybakov (1982), basing his analysis both on archaeological records and on old Russian, Byzantine and Armenian written sources, argued that by the middle of the first millennium AD Kiev, due to its peculiar geographical position and economic progress, came to the fore among contemporary Slavic settlements and became the capital of the Polianian tribal union. Rybakov ascribed the foundation of Kiev to Kyi, the prince 'whose authority extended to the Danube and whose diplomatic connections reached Constantinople.' Tolochko (1983), for his part, suggested that the tribal union centred around Kiev, which in his view soon acquired the character of a 'proto-town' comparable in its importance to those of other early Slavic states: Bohemia, Moravia and Bulgaria. During the ninth century, the Old Kiev settlement spread out to nearby hills – Castle, Bald, Shchekovitsa, Detinka – and soon reached Podol.

Kiev was already a buoyant settlement when it was seized by Oleg and his Varangian 'loyal army'. In his 'Tale' Nestor gives a brief account of this event which he dates to AD 882. According to his account, Oleg first seized Lubech, the town on the Dniepr north of Kiev, than sailed downstream to Kiev itself and captured it, having cunningly killed Askold, the ruler. There is still a place in Kiev called 'Askold's grave'. The year of 882 is often regarded as the beginning of the first Russian state, with Kiev as its capital.

The beginnings of Russian statehood

In the years which followed, the city of Kiev underwent a rapid development. This development was particularly remarkable in the tenth and eleventh centuries when, in the reign of Vladimir and Svyatoslav, Kiev became a large centre of trade and industry, covering the area of about 70 hectares. The urban complex included the fortified core (*detinets*) with the princely manor and several major Christian temples: the Church of the Tithes, the oldest, was built by Byzantine architects in 989–996. The city was considerably enlarged under Yaroslav in the early eleventh century. At that time the majestic St Sophia became the principal temple for the entire Old Russia. This gigantic yet elegant building, with five naves and five apses which survive to this day, was built in an original artistic style, although in the mainstream of Byzantine traditions. Three smaller churches of a similar design were built in close vicinity.

Crafts and industries flourished in early medieval Kiev and in other Old Russian towns (Rybakov 1948). They included jewellery-making, glass-making, house-building and various metal-working enterprises. Kievan artists created icons, carved ivories and made magnificent frescoes: the mosaics of St Sophia with the portraits of Russian princes and their families are among their most outstanding achievements. The craftsmen concentrated mainly in Podol which soon acquired a kind of self-government. There are indications of trade links with practically all the major foreign centres of that time.

Similar developments are notable in minor Russian towns – Chernigov, Pereslavl, Belgorod, Turov, Galich and others. Originally developed from local centres of tribal unions, they became local administrative centres. The situation of Novgorod was remarkable in that sense. It became the administrative centre of northern Russia and soon acquired a special 'republican' status, the princely power being considerably restricted by a 'parliament' – the *veche*, usually dominated by local boyars.

The question of interaction of princely power with local groups deserves special attention. For a long time, as in the west, this was largely restricted to the extortion of tribute. As Nestor wrote:

> In 883 Oleg conquered and taxed the Drevlians, at one black marten for each person. In 884 he conquered the Severians and laid a light tax on them. He did not permit to pay tribute to the Khazars for he said: 'I am their enemy'. In 885 he sent envoys to the Radimichains asking: 'To whom do you pay tribute?' They answered: 'To the Khazars'. Oleg said to them, 'You shall not pay tribute to the Khazars but to me'. And they gave Oleg a shilling each, the same as they paid to the Khazars.

A similar account is given by Constantine Porphyrogenitos, the Byzantine writer:

> At the beginning of November the Rus and all their chieftains leave Kiev and go out on *polud'ye*, which means their rounds to the Slavonic regions of the Verevians and Dregovichians and Krivichians and Severians and the rest of the Slavs who pay them tribute. They are maintained until the departure of ice in April, when they return to Kiev, fit out their ships, and come down to Romania (Byzantium).

Relations of 'the Rus' with local tribes were not always peaceful. A chronicle recounts that the Drevlians, exasperated by an unjustified increase of taxation, attacked Prince Igor and killed him and his 'small escort'. In revenge, Olga, his widow, executed two embassies of the Drevlians (the first group of ambassadors was buried alive, the second was burnt). She then sent a punitive expedition to Irorosten, their main town, and burnt it to the ground and massacred all its inhabitants.

The extent of Scandinavian participation in the Kievan ruling élite and in their army is equally open to debate. Probably, at least initially, the prince's forces contained a considerable Viking presence which is attested by archaeological evidence. The cemetery at Gnezdovo[3] near Smolensk included 600 graves, some of which, particularly rich ones, contained typical Swedish artefacts, mainly weapons, as well as Byzantine goods. Three graves with Scandinavian implements were found near Chernigov; these graves were made in timbered chambers and resembled similar graves in Birka (Arbman 1961). Ibn Rutan, an Arab traveller, gave the following description of a burial of a Viking chieftain in Russia:

> When one of their chiefs dies, they dig for him a grave like a roomy house, and lay him in it. They put in his clothes, gold arm-rings, food, jugs of liquor and coins. They also put in the woman he loved, still living, and close the door of the grave, and she dies.

Nestor included into his 'Tale' a treaty concluded by the Russians with the 'Greek Emperor'; the Russian mission included persons with Scandinavian names: 'we of the Rus: Karl, Ingeld, Farlof, Vermud etc., sent by Oleg, great prince of the Rus . . .'. Yet, as Lebedev noted, not necessarily all of them were Varangians; they could well have been Slavs who adopted 'good old Varangians names' as they came into common usage. The list included at least one Slavic name, Borichev, which sounds similar to the Borichev road, near the hill, where Kiy's initial settlement was founded. This name was mentioned again: the Drevlian ambassadors were buried alive near Borich's house. Hence, the Borichs were probably an old Slavic family whose initial household was located near the core of the emerging city.

The Varangians were rapidly incorporated into the Slav élite, acquiring Slavic names, language and habits, and losing the remains of their Scandinavian identity. In the *Pravda Russkaia* ('Rus' Justice'), a code of customary law enforced in the early eleventh century under the reign of Yaroslav the Wise, the Rus (Rusins) were considered as active members of a military-merchant community, regardless of ethnic affiliation.

Vladimir (980–1015) is often viewed as the authentic founder of the Kievan state. The adoption of Christianity by Vladimir in AD 988

---

[3] A gloomy coincidence: in a nearby concentration camp, at Khatyn, several thousand Polish officers were executed by the Soviet secret police during the last war.

considerably strengthened and consolidated his princely power, adding to it an ideological dimension. Rybakov (1981) wrote that Christianity was epistemologically complimentary to the 'pagan' beliefs of the Slavs, their local traditions being later incorporated into it, thus forming a syncretic religious system. On the other hand, the Christian Orthodoxy in a specific Oriental-Byzantine form created an ideological power base, essential for the consolidation of a centralized state. The adoption of Oriental Christianity further severed the relations of the Russian state with the European north and west, increasingly opening it to the south. The relations of the Kievan state with Byzantium were not always easy. Separated from the Black Sea by the steppic corridor (where at that time there appeared new nomads, the Pechenegs), the Russians nonetheless repeatedly crossed it to find a way further south, across the sea to Byzantine shores. In AD 907, a Russian fleet of Prince Oleg sailed down the Bosphorus. Unable to seize Constantinople, the Russians started to negotiate. The resulting treaty not only established regular trade links between Byzantium and the Rus, but equally provided for Russian participation in the various war efforts of the empire. In following years, Russian troops took part in military operations in Cyprus, Syria and Crete. In AD 914 the Russian fleet again attacked the southern coast of the Black Sea. Only with a great effort could the Greeks beat off this onslaught. Two years later Prince Igor, at the head of a joint Russian-Pecheneg army, appeared on the Danube. The ensuing negotiations ended in another treaty, essentially similar to that of AD 911.

The baptism of Vladimir and the official 'conversion' of the Rus marked the culmination of Russo-Byzantine relations. This ceremony was accomplished in Chersonesos, the Crimean town that was at that time in Byzantine possession. The agreement was sealed by Vladimir's marriage to Anna, daughter of Emperor Basil II. In his 'Tale' Nestor colourfully depicts the events which followed:

> ... When the Prince arrived at his capital, he directed that the idols should be overthrown, and that some should be cut to pieces and others burned with fire. He thus ordered that Perun's idol should be bound to a horse's tail and dragged along Bordichev [again Bordichev!] to the river. . . . And they [the Prince's men] had thus dragged the idol along, and cast it into the Dniepr river.

At least officially, Russia became a spiritual and cultural dependency of Byzantium, the Russian church being headed by a Greek metropolitan appointed by Constantinople. Yet this dependency was more illusory than real and never took the form of a political domination.

Nevertheless, baptism much enhanced the cultural development of Russia; the country became inundated with Byzantine religious missionaries, craftsmen and artists who actively transmitted Byzantine philosophical and artistic values. The original Russian culture emerged as a synthesis of various inner and outer impulses, the role of Byzantium among the latter being considerable. Much later, in the times of Muscovy, the new Russian state pretended to be a spiritual successor to the Byzantine legacy (Moscow being considered as 'the third Rome'); the Byzantine two-headed eagle has recently been restored as the main symbol of Russia.

Monasteries, which started to spring up in Russia, became the centres of culture and literacy. These monasteries often contained rich libraries and monks became the first annalists who copiously reported the legends and events reaching them. Nestor, the author of the 'Tale of Years Bygone' was a monk at Kiev-Pechera (Cave) monastery, established in the early eleventh century.

The consolidation of administrative and ideological power attained in the tenth and eleventh century considerably enhanced the ethnic and linguistic amalgamation of the various ethnicities which made up the Russian state. Both administrative institutions and the church greatly contributed to the spread of Old Russian speech as well as common cultural and aesthetic values, which constituted the new Russian culture. There is numerous evidence for a comparatively rapid and peaceful assimilation of various (predominantly Finnic) groups by the Slavs starting with the ninth century (Dubov 1994).

Yet the Kievan Rus', which in the early eleventh century reached its maximum natural extension covering the entire forest and forest-steppic zones of the Russian Plain, remained a loose confederation of regional arenas of power with strong separatist trends. It was a rural society with a comparatively low degree of urbanization. Towns, which emerged as both administrative and craft-and-trade centres, remained basically local market-places.

Existing evidence also suggests strong regional differences in the socio-economic sphere. Although plough-type agriculture was dominant in the whole of Russia prior to the disintegration of Common Slavic, marked differences are apparent both in the field-system and in the implements of soil cultivation. Two- and three-field systems were used along with the use of the scratch-plough (*ralo*) for the cultivation of light soils and the heavy-plough harnessed by a pair of oxen in the chernozem soils of the forest-steppic area. By contrast, 'the forest fallow', with one of the fields resting for 10–16 years, remained dominant in the forested areas further north, where the light scratch two- and three-toothed plough (*soxa*) remained the dominant implement (Levasheva 1994). In those areas, the pioneering of virgin soils was economically more profitable than the intensified exploitation of existing plots.

The decentralization resulting from the economic disintegration and the strife among regional élites eventually led to the fall of the Kievan Rus' in the thirteenth century and was followed by the prolonged domination of the Mongols. It took more than a century for a new centre of power to form in Russia, this time in Moscow.

Conclusions

The main conclusions which follow from the materials presented in the preceding chapters may be summarized quite simply: the socio-economic development of the peoples who lived in the Russian Plain throughout Prehistory and Early History was following a pattern common to the rest of Europe, with limitations and variations imposed by the physical and social environment. In other words, the Slavs, as well as other peoples of eastern Europe, are, and always have been, an integral part of Europe. But this general statement needs clarification. The intensity of interaction of east European communities with the rest of the continent was changeable during the course of time. The east European or Russian Plain was settled by early humans later than the greater part of southern and western Europe. Although the presence of scattered human groups is well attested in its fringe at an early date, the massive settlement of the Russian Plain started much later, during the middle and final stages of the Last glaciation, c. 40,000–30,000 years ago. At that time a network of Upper Palaeolithic settlements, which arose in the Russian Plain, rapidly attained the economic and cultural levels of central and western Europe. The sources of common European heritage lie there, in the caves and open-air settlements of Ice Age hunters. These groups of anatomically modern humans were essentially similar, by their economy and spectacular cultural attainments, in all parts of Europe. The situation remained basically unchanged during the several millennia that followed the end of the Ice Age. Mesolithic Europe was also essentially uniform in all its parts. There is substantial evidence for the social complexity achieved by Mesolithic groups, particularly in the north and southeast of the continent.

The situation dramatically changed during the postglacial period known as the Climatic Optimum, when the temperature and humidity of Europe became markedly higher than it is today. At that time, at the height of Thermal Optimum, the division of Europe into the west and the east became evident for the first time. A farming economy, which had appeared within the Fertile Crescent area of the Near East and started spreading to Europe a few millennia later, was, for a very long time, effectively restricted to the southeastern, central and western parts of the continent. The frontier between the farming and hunter-gathering parts of Europe, which had been established about 5000 years ago, ran from eastern Poland in the north, along the Western Bug, and further to the southeast, including the forest-steppic Ukraine and the Balkans.

The second, and no less important division, which became apparent at that time divided eastern Europe into two unequal parts: the forested north and the steppic south. The steppic corridor opened the way to and from Inner Asia. During the millennia that followed, numerous groups of nomads, originating in the hills and deserts of Central Asia, moved along this corridor from the east to the west. These movements, rarely peaceful, were nearly always initially targeted at farming communities in the Russian forest-steppe. Weakened or enhanced by these initial contacts, nomadic waves proceeded further west.

The barriers between the agricultural west and the foraging east remained transparent: there is multiple evidence for the occurrence of complex networks, including mutually complimentary elements in both areas. The network of Corded Ware, which was in existence 5000–4000 years ago, is an outstanding example of a complex cultural entity that included a great number of regional centres of power in central, northern and eastern Europe. If our theory is correct, this complex network included a common communication medium, being nothing other than an undifferentiated common proto-Baltic-Slavic-Germanic language.

The next stages in the socio-economic and political history of early Europe saw a gradual rise of world powers centred in the Mediterranean area. These powers gradually increased their influence in the surrounding areas. The Greek civilization was the first to appear. Increasingly infiltrating into the close and distant neighbourhood in the form of multiple colonies, it soon established a network of its own, involving various local groups in an economic and political interaction. The areas lying to the north, and variously affected by the impact of Greek civilization, were essentially following their own evolutionary trajectories. At a certain time, several agricultural groups in the forest-steppic area of the Russian Plain, with its high agricultural potential, ethnically identified themselves as the Slavs. Separated from the Greek Pontic states by the steppic corridor, but nonetheless engaged in multi-faceted relations with them, the Slavs have maintained their own identity ever since, being alienated both from the Iranian-speaking nomadic Scythians in the south, and the Baltic-speaking forest-farmers and stock-breeders in the north.

The next stage in the historical evolution of Early Europe was overshadowed by the rise and fall of the first poli-ethnic superpower, the Roman Empire. Having reached its maximum extent and largely exhausted its resources, the Roman world power started to subside in the first centuries

AD, under the combined pressure of internal tension and an ever-increasing pressure from belligerent tribes beyond the frontiers. The latter resulted primarily from the disintegration of an archaic social pattern, and an acute economic crisis induced by deteriorating ecological conditions. Pushed by the scarcity of resources in the drought-stricken core area, the waves of nomadic stock-breeders moved towards the west in search of stable food and greater security. Exposed and largely defenseless, Slavic agricultural communities were among the first targets on the route of warlike nomadic groups. Partly destroyed and partly subjected to merciless exploitation, Slavic groups were often later involved in further movements, to the west, this time as part of the attacking force.

An increasing pressure on the part of the consecutive waves of nomads coming from the east combined with a declining agricultural productivity of the forest-steppe and led to a larger infiltration of the Slavs into the more fertile and relatively more secure areas in the west and northwest. Eventually, in the middle of the first millennium AD, the Slavs created a major socio-political network covering huge areas on the fringe of the declining Roman Empire. As in all previous cases, it was a poli-ethnic entity, that gradually acquired the Slavic mode of life and cultural-symbolic values. The common Slavic language functioned as the communication medium. Further socio-economic development of initially Baltic- and Finnic-speaking groups in the densely forested areas of the Russian Plain increasingly involved them in an expanding Slavic network. Essentially, this was a process of assimilation and acculturation with only limited displacements of population.

Further social progress, which included the crystallization of towns along major trade-routes and eventually led to the emergence of the state, proceeded mainly along the line of internal evolution. Yet the influence of outer forces was also considerable: first the Viking expansion, and later, the ideological involvement of Byzantium. The amalgamation of the rich traditions of local groups, with Scandinavian political and commercial experience and the Byzantine-Roman legacy created an impressive edifice of Russian culture, which made a remarkable contribution to the common European cultural heritage.

Glossary

Alluvium sediments deposited by running water within river valleys.

AMS (**Accelerator Mass Spectrometry**) the technique of radio carbon dating based on the separation of carbon isotopes (carbon-12, 13 and 14) with the use of sophisticated nuclear physics devices and enabling the achievement of greater accuracy on smaller samples.

Archaeological culture a set of artefact-type categories which constantly recur in assemblages within a limited geographical area (Clarke 1968).

Ard a simple form of plough usually made of wood; includes a share which is dragged through the soil. In use since the Iron Age.

Artefacts natural objects modified by a set of purposeful human actions; archaeologists distinguish *stone a.* or *lithics* (*lithic industry*), *bone-and-antler a.* (*industry*), **pottery**, *metallic industry*.

Assemblage an associated set of contemporary artefact-types (Clarke 1968).

Availability phase a period of time during which farming is known to the foraging groups yet not adopted, however there exists exchange of materials and information between the foraging and farming communities (Zvelebil and Rowley-Conwy 1984).

Awl a stone or metal tool with a strong sharp point intended for perforating or scoring various materials.

Axe *stone a.* large tools manufactured by means of pecking and grinding out of various resistant rocks, particularly widely used since the Late Neolithic, often imitating metallic prototypes. Several varieties are distinguished: *Battle (boat) a.*(a variety: *faceted B.a.*). Metallic axes are made of bronze and include several types: *axes-celts, socketed celts, shaft-hole axes*.

Barrow (**burial mound, tumulus, kurgan**) artificial hill erected over the remains of the dead, particularly common in the Eneolithic and Bronze Ages in the south Russian Plain and Central Europe, and extended over the greater part of that area in the Iron Age. *Long, conic barrow* (*sopkis*) –

specific types of *b*. in existence in north-western Russia in the sixth–eleventh centuries AD.

Blade a long and narrow flake, usually with long cutting edges produced from prismatic core. In the Neolithic Age blades inserted in antler handles were used as sickles, as evidenced by a specific '*sickle-gloss*' resulting from their use for cutting grass, reeds and/or cultivated cereals.

Boat grave a burial rite based on the dead being laid into a boat; largely practised in Scandinavia and north-western Russia in the sixth and seventh centuries AD.

Boyars military and administrative aristocracy of the Old Russian state.

Brachicephalic broadheaded.

Bronze Age period of human prehistory (*c.* 4,000–3,000 years ago) featuring the rapid development of bronze metallurgy, advanced social stratification (particularly in the south), and the intensification of trade links. Several cultural entities are distinguished in the boreal zone of northern Eurasia: *Volosovian, Trzciniec, Komarovian, Abashevian, Pozdnyakovian, Kargapolian, Seima-Turbino* – a transcultural complex. Several cultural entities featuring the kurgan burial rite (*Kurgan cultures*) are identified in the northern Black Sea area: *Pit-Graves (Yamnaya); Catacomb Graves; Timber Graves.* Cultural groups featuring the occurrence of élite tombs developed in the northern Caucasus, e.g. *Maikopian (Maikop).*

Burial rite traditional methods of the disposal of human remains: the *inhumation* acknowledgeable in Europe since the Mousterian and varying in time and in various cultural groups, and the *cremation* with the subsequent placement of ashes in a burial urn, particularly common in eastern and central Europe since the Bronze Age. Archaeologists distinguish *indivdual,* and *collective (multiple) burials*. The burials are also divided by the position of the dead in the grave (*extended, contracted, supine, on the side*), and the construction of the grave (e.g. **flat grave**, under **barrow** etc.).

Burin flake or blade with a narrow cutting edge produced by one or several '*burin blows*' directed along the side of the piece.

Chalcolithic (Eneolithic) a period of human prehistory (*c.* 5,500–4,000 years ago) which featured the initial development of copper metallurgy, the plough-type agriculture, the advanced stock-breeding, the appearance of large settlements, and the kurgan burial rite (at later stages). Several cultural units distinguished in the south Russian Plain and the Balkans include: *Cucuteni-Tripol'ye* (Late Tripol'ye groups: *Vykhvatintsy, Sofievka, Usatovo*), *Boian, Gumelniţa, Sredni Stog.*

Chiefdom a form of organization of pre-class society distinguished by the presence of centres which co-ordinate economic, social and religious activities and the distribution of wealth (Service 1962).

Choppers, chopping tools (pebble tools) the first human tools made of pebbles by means of chipping off flakes from one side (**choppers**) or from two sides (**ch.-tools**).

Cimmerians ancient people living in the steppe area of South Russian plain in the seventh–sixth centuries BC and often identifiable with the Timber Grave culture.

Circum-Pontic network (province) a group of Bronze Age social groups in the basin of the Black Sea bound together by intensive trade, mostly in ore and metallic implements.

Corded Ware (battle-axe) cultures a group of archaeological entities (*c.* 4,500–4,000 years ago) featuring the development of a distinct burial rite and predominantly stock-breeding economies, variously supplemented by farming (in western areas); and predominantly food-gathering strategies with elements of stock-breeding (mostly in the forested areas in the east). Based on the typology of ceramics and battle-axes, several local groups are distinguished: *Single Graves, Thuringian group, Pomorian (Rzuchevo), Fatyanovo, East Baltic, Middle Dnieprian, Carpathian.*

Core the block of stone from which flakes or blades are produced.

Cro-Magnon Man an early variety of modern humans (*Homo sapiens*) flourished in Europe mainly during the **Upper Palaeolithic.**

Cromlech (or Megalithic tomb) a structure consisting of large, often free standing stone slabs (*megaliths*), usually used for multiple burials, spread in the Atlantic Europe, in the Mediterranean area and in the western Caucasus in the Late Neolithic and Bronze Age. Several varieties are known: e.g. *(stone) cist* – a box-like chamber, *dolmen* – a simple arrangement of large stones forming a chamber.

Cultigenes (domesticates) domesticated plants and animals.

Detinets fortified princely domain in Medieval Russia.

Dolicephalic longheaded.

Ethnocultural paradigm a concept which implicitly or explicitly equates archaeological entities (usually '**archaeological cultures**') with distinct ethnical or linguistic units.

Fibula a brooch or a fastener made of bronze or iron; in use since *c.* 1000 BC, and particularly common in the **Iron Age.**

Flake a thin chip of stone produced from a core.

Flat grave inhumation burials made in graves without major superficial constructions (**barrows**).

Fluvioglacial deposits/landforms sediments and relief features resulting from the activity of running meltwater in glaciers and glacial lakes during the course of Ice Age.

Geometric microliths (geometrics) small-size implements largely used in the **Mesolithic Age;** usually elements of composite tools, they are made by splitting or truncating and retouching microlithic blades. Several typological varieties are distinguished: *lunates, triangles, rhombi, trapezes, crescents.*

Glacio-isostasy an uplift or subsistence of large portions of the Earth's crust resulting from an excess or a deficiency of the superficial weight imposed by the ice-sheet.

Gracilization a general trend towards the smoothening of the skull's relief and the diminishment of the main diameters of the face, acknowledgeable during the course of the Upper Palaeolithic.

Handaxe bifacially chipped core or large flake with a butt and cutting edge, in use since the Lower Acheulean.

Harpoon a point made of bone or antler with prominent barbs on one or two sides adapted for hunting fish and sea mammals; appeared in the **Upper Palaeolithic,** and widely in use since the **Mesolithic.**

Hill-fort (*gorodishche*) an Iron Age fortified settlement usually erected on hill-tops, often on a river bank. Fortifications include ramparts, ditches and palisades.

Hoard an intentional deposit of various objects usually of prestigious or symbolic value.

Holocene the last interval of geologic time which lasted since *c.* 10,000 years ago. Includes several climatic periods first identified based on the **pollen** records (the Blytt-Sernander scheme) and later confirmed by other palaeoclimatic records: *Preboreal, Boreal; Atlantic period* (or *the Climatic, thermal optimum*); *Sub-Boreal* and *Sub-Atlantic.* During its course marked changes occurred in the area of the Baltic Sea, where the following stages are distinguished: *Baltic Ice Lake; Yoldia Sea, Ancylus Lake; Litorina Sea.* The latter corresponds to the rise in the sea-level of the Atlantic Ocean (the *Flandrian*) and the Black Sea (the *New Black Sea* transgression).

Homo erectus an early human species (the genus *Homo*), most likely originated in Africa *c.* 1.6 million years ago, and by 1.0 million years ago spread largely in some parts of Europe and Asia.

Iron Age a period of human prehistory and early history, which featured the development of iron metallurgy, an advanced social stratification with the appearance of military élite and military strongholds (**hill-forts**), and the emergence of first 'world powers' in the Mediterranean basins, increasingly influencing the rest of Europe. Traditionally includes two periods: *Halstatt* (750–500/400 BC) and *La-Tène* (500–400–120/100 BC). Several cultural units are distinguishable: *Urnfield cultures; Lausits, Pomorian (Pommeranian*) group; *Stroked pottery, Dniepr-Dvinian, Milogradian.*

Isogloss an area of common linguistic (phonological and morphological) phenomena acknowledgeable in various dialects.

Karst the solution of massive limestone by groundwater resulting in the formation of cavities, sinkholes and underground rivers.

Language families languages supposedly of common origin showing considerable affinities in the vocabulary and structure (*Indo-European, Finno-Ugric, Altaic* etc.).

Levallois technique the production of the flakes of predetermined form by means of careful preparation of the upper surface of the core.

Limes ('path' in Latin) a frontier with a system of natural and artificial fortifications which separated the Roman-controlled areas from unfriendly territory, constructed by the Romans during the first and second centuries AD.

Loess yellowish sediments consisting of silt-size grains deposited during the cold stages of the Ice Age and intercalated with brownish organic-rich levels (*fossil soil*) formed under milder conditions.

Mesolithic (or **Middle Stone Age**) a period of human prehistory in the course of Early and Middle **Holocene** (10,000–8,000/6,000 years ago) which featured the existence of groups of food-gatherers, the use of **geometric microliths, axes, harpoons** and the appearance of large cemeteries. Based on the typological criteria, several archaeological 'cultures' are distinguished: *Kunda, Neman, Grebenikian, Kukrekian* and others.

Metal-working sites sites reserved for metallurgy and metalworking which include the kiln, and a set of special implements (clay or stone moulds, hammers, anvils, tongues).

Moraine, morainic deposit (**glacial till, glacial drift**) sediments and relief features (such as end- moraine ridges) resulting from the stationary position of advanced glaciers during the Ice Age.

Mousterian (or **Middle Palaeolithic**) a period of human prehistory (usually 120,000–40,000 years ago) which included several industrial groups (*Mousterian facies*).

Neanderthal Man (*Homo sapiens neanderthalensis*) a fossil human species originated *c.* 200,000 years ago and replaced by the modern humans in Europe between 50,000 and 30,000 years ago.

Neolithic (**agricultural**) period in human prehistory (in various parts of Europe between 8,000 and 4,500 years ago) which featured the emergence and spread of food-producing economies (farming and stock-breeding), the appearance of large settlements and the initial social stratification. Based on the typological criteria several archaeological cultures are distinguished in southeastern and central Europe, including: *Aceramic Neolithic, Starčevo, Körös, Criş, Linear Pottery, Impressed pottery (Impresso), Funnel Beakers.*

Neolithic (**'forest' N. or Sub-Neolithic**) period in human prehistory in the boreal zone of Eurasia (*c.* 6,000–4,000 years ago) which featured the existence of groups of pottery-producing food-gatherers. Based mostly on the styles of pottery, several archaeological 'cultures' are distinguished, including: *Bug-Dniestrian, Dniepr-Donetsian (Strumel'-Gastjatin), Narva, Upper Volga, Volga-Kama, Sperrings, Pit-and-comb pottery (Lyalovo).*

Network a concept developed in social anthropology which sees society or its elements as bound together by multiple relationships (*socio-cultural, exchange, mating n.*). Several scholars tend to substitute the concept of archaeological culture with that of network (Chapman and Dolukhanov 1993).

Okol'nyi gorod an unprotected area of Old Russian city.

Oppidium large permanent settlement of proto-urban type, administrative, ideological, commercial and industrial centres which arose predominantly in the Celtic areas of Europe in the second and first centuries BC.

Oxygen isotope analysis the measurement of past climate based on the ratio of two isotopes of oxygen, ^{16}O and ^{18}O, in sediment cores.

Palaeolithic Lower (Older Stone Age) the earliest period in human prehistory which started with tool-making and ended with the beginning of the **Mousterian** (*c.* 120,000 years ago); it included various types of **pebble** industries and the *Acheulean* (with subdivisions).

Palaeomagnetic dating the measurement of geologic age based on the residual magnetism of igneous and sedimentary rocks and the comparison of polarity changes (*magnetic epochs*).

Permafrost permanently frozen ground currently occurring in the Arctic area and widespread in the Ice Age.

Pile-dwelling (lake d.) a dwelling erected on piles either in the off- or on-shore area of a shallow lake. This practice was widely use in the Alpine area, in Scandinavia and in the north-western part of the Russian Plain in the Late Neolithic and the Bronze Ages.

Pleistocene (or the **Ice Age**) a geologic period which lasted from *c.* 3–2.5 million to 10,000 years ago and which featured the periodic occurrence of large ice sheets and the emergence of Man.

Pogost an agglomeration of farmsteads in early Medieval Russia which eventually developed into major trade centres.

Point sharp-pointed tools made either of **blades** or **flakes** or by core-technique; largely in use in the **Mousterian, Upper Palaeolithic** and **Mesolithic.** Amongst Upper Palaeolithic p. several varieties are distinguished: e.g. *shouldered (Kostenki) p.; leaf-points (Solutrean, Szeletian);* **tanged points;** *Kukrek.*

Pollen analysis (palynology) the identification of fossil pollen and spores in geologic and archaeological deposits and the reconstruction on this basis of past vegetation and climate.

Polud'e the collecting of tribute by the prince and his army amongst the subjects in the Kievan Rus.

Portable art sculptural representations of humans (*anthropomorphic figurines*, mostly female) and animals (*zoomorphic figurines*) are widespread in the Upper Palaeolithic. Female figurines are numerous in the Neolithic and Eneolithic agricultural communities. In the forest Neolithic animal representations (mostly elk) are more common.

Posad trade and craft suburb of Old Russian city.

Post-framed house a dwelling of rectangular form. Its structure included the posts supporting the roof and the walls: the poles are evidenced by the postholes visible on the living surface.

Pottery (ceramics) various objects, mostly containers, made of paste, usually clay tempered with sand, crushed shells, crushed pottery, organic matter or asbestos; in use since the Mesolithic/early Neolithic. Subdivided into types in accordance with the form and functions: *cups, bowls, 'lamps', beakers* (e.g. *Funnel Beakers*), *amphorae* (two-handled pot with a narrow neck), *pithoi* (enormous jars), the treatment of the surface (*barbotine, impressed pottery*) or the styles in the ornamental pattern (e.g. *pit-and-comb pottery,* **Corded Ware**).

Povest' vremennyh let (The Tale of Bygone Years) a primary chronicle allegedly compiled by Nestor, a monk in Kiev-Pechera monastery in the eleventh century.

Prismatic core technique the production of standard long, thin and parallel-sided blanks (**blades**) from the **core** either by a direct or indirect (through a bone punch) percussion; the technique largely in use in Europe since the **Upper Palaeolithic**.

Prognathism (adj.: prognathous) a face having the jaws projecting beyond the upper face.

Put' iz Variag v Greki (Road from the Varangians to the Greeks) a major trade-route from Scandinavia to Constantinople via Russia in operation since *c.* AD 800.

Radiometric dating the measurement of age of geologic and archaeological objects based on the rate of decay of radioactive isotopes. *Radiocarbon (Carbon-14) dating,* most widely used in Quaternary geology and archaeology, is based on the measurement of the amount of radioactive carbon-14 (or C-14) in organic matter synthesized within the past 50,000 years. The dating of tree rings and varves of known age revealed a considerable departure of radiocarbon (*uncalibrated*) dates from true or calendar age, the former is corrected by the introduction of *dendro-chronological calibration* (hence *calibrated* dates). Radiocarbon dates usually quote the laboratories: HEL-269 (from the lab. at Helsinki University); TA-175 (from Tortu University) etc.

Retouch secondary trimming of flakes or blades by percussion or pressure applied to the surface or the rims of the piece.

Rock carvings (petroglyphs) pictures of Neolithic and Bronze Ages incized or carved on the rocks usually facing the waterways. These pictures obviously of symbolic significance, usually depict the scenes of fishing and hunting. They are particularly common in the Russian north and Fennoscandia.

Scrapers flakes or blades retouched forming an arched 'scraping' end; varieties: *side-scraper* (particularly common in the Mousterian); *end-scraper; double scraper.*

Scythians ancient people (or several culturally related peoples) allegedly of Iranian origin living in the steppe zone of Eurasia in the seventh–second centuries BC. Several cultural groups are distinguished: the *Royal S.* in the Ukrainian steppe and Crimea, the *agricultural S.* in the forest steppe. The latter supposedly included Slavic elements.

Sea level fluctuations the rises (*transgressions*) and falls (*regressions*) in the level of the ocean resulting from the change of the aggregate quantity of water during the glacial/interglacial epochs (the *eustatic* effect).

Secondary product revolution the period in Europe starting with the middle of the fifth millenium BC featuring a dispersed settlement pattern, a greater emphasis on burials, the spread of plough agriculture and dairy husbandry (Sherratt 1981).

Selishche unprotected settlement; such settlements were common in Russia in the 8th–10th centuries AD.

Swidden (slash-and-burn or shifting) cultivation a primitive agricultural method based on the clearing of forests by burning and sowing the seeds into the ashes. Was largely in use in boreal Europe since the Iron Age.

Tanged point cultures a group of late glacial cultural entities in northern Europe (15,000–10,000 years ago), identified based on the occurrence of specific tanged points: *Hamburgian, Lyngbian (Bromme – L.), Ahrensburgian* and *Swiderian.*

Tell a mound formed by the superimposed accumulations of debris of collapsed mud and wattle dwellings in a settled area of a Neolithic village.

Terrace (river terrace) an even or slightly tilted surface extended along the river valley, a former river floor.

Thermoluminescence (TL) the measurement of age of archaeological or geological objects (pottery, bones and minerals) previously exposed to radiation, and based on the emission of light.

Three-age system the division of human prehistory into three stages, those of Stone, Bronze and Iron, first advanced by the Danish archaeologists, C.J.Thomsen and J.J.A.Worsaae in the 19th century.

Toponymy the study of geographical place-names (toponyms), including river-names (hydronyms), as well as the names of lakes, mountains, roads etc.

Upper Palaeolithic the later period of the Palaeolithic (Old Stone Age) – *c.* 40,000–10,000 years ago, identifiable in Europe, Middle East and northern Africa, featuring the large use of **prismatic core technique**, and the appearance of 'mammoth dwellings' and the 'Palaeolithic art'. Based on the typological criteria of lithic and bone-and-antler industries, several 'archaeological cultures' and cultural groups are distinguished: *Chatelperronian,*

Szeletian, Streletskian, Aurignacian, Eastern Gravettian (an obsolete term which covered several 'cultures' including *Kostenkian,* synonyms: *Kostenki – Avdeyevian, Willendorf-Kostenkian*).

Valdai (Last, Wurm, Weichselian, or Devensian) glaciation lasted from 120,000 to 10,000 years ago and consisted of four major stages: *Early* (120,000–70,000), Middle (70,000-25,000), *Last Glacial maximum,* or *pleniglacial* (25,000–15,000) and *Late glacial* (15,000–10,000 years ago. The latter included two mild intervals: *Bölling* and *Alleröd* separating colder stages: *Older, Middle* and *Younger Dryas.*

Varves laminated sediments of various composition and texture forming pairs attributable to seasonal variation of climate.

Veche local parliament in Novgorod.

Vicus (pl. **vici** or **vics**) a small urban-like settlement in the Roman-dominated area, also a proto-urban settlement and the centre of trade in Scandinavia and Russia in the 8th–9th centuries AD.

Bibliography

Abayev V.I. 1949. *Skifskii yazyk i folklor (The Scythian Language and Folklore)*. Moscow–Leningrad: Izd. AN SSSR.

Alexeyev V.P. 1974. *Geografija chelovecheskih ras (The Geography of Human Races)*. Moscow: Nauka.

Alexeyev V.P. 1978. *Paleoantropologija zemnogo shara i formirovanie chelovecheskih ras (The Palaeoanthropology of Human Races)*. Moscow: Nauka.

Alexeyeva T.I. 1973. *Etnogenez vostochnyh slavjan po dannym antropologii (Ethnogenesis of the Early Slavs According to Anthropological Evidence)*. Moscow: Nauka.

Alexeyeva L.I. 1976 *Teriofauna rannego antropogena Vostochnoi Evropy (Mammalian Fauna of the Early Quaternary Period of Eastern Europe)*. Moscow: Nauka.

Allsworth-Jones P. 1986. *The Szeletian and the Transition from Middle to Upper Palaeolithic in Central Europe*. Oxford: Oxford University Press.

Allsworth-Jones P. 1989. The Szeletian and the stratigraphic succession in central Europe and adjacent areas. In P. Mellars (ed.), *The Emergence of Modern Humans*. Edinburgh: Edinburgh University Press, pp. 160–242.

Ammerman A.L. and L.L. Cavalli-Sforza. 1973. A population model for the diffusion of early farming in Europe. In C. Renfrew (ed.), *The Explanation of Culture Change: Models in Prehistory*. London: Duckworth, pp. 358–74.

Anisyutkin N.K. 1978. Varianty srednego paleolita v Pridnestrov'e (stinkovskaja kul'tura) (The variants of Middle Palaeolithic in the Middle Dniestr area, the Stinkian). *Arxeologicheskii sbornik Gosudarstvennogo Ermitazha*, 19: 5–21.

Anthony D.W. 1986. The 'Kurgan Culture'. Indo-European origins and the domestication of horse. *Current Anthropology*, 24/4: 291–313.

Arbman H. 1961. *The Vikings*. London: Thames and Hudson.

Arslanov Kh.A. 1987. *Radiouglerod; geoximija i geoxronologija (The*

Radiocarbon: Geochemistry and Geochronology). Leningrad: Leningrad University Press.

Artamonov M.I. 1974. *Kimmeriicy i skify (The Cimmerians and the Scythians).* Leningrad: Leningrad University Press.

Artëmenko I.I. 1987a. Komarovskaja kul'tura (The Komarovian culture). In O.N. Bader, D.A. Krainov and M.F. Kosarev (eds), *Epoha bronzy lesnoi polosy SSSR/Arheologija SSSR.* Moscow: Nauka, pp. 113–16.

Artëmenko I.I. 1987b. Sosnitskaja kul'tura (The Socnitsian culture). In O.N. Bader, D.A. Krainov and M.F. Kosarev (eds), *Epoha bronzy lesnoi polosy SSSR/Arheologija SSSR.* Moscow: Nauka, pp. 106–13.

Bader O.N. 1965. *Kapovaya peshchera (The Kapovaya Cave).* Moscow: Nauka.

Bader O.N. 1970. *Bassein Oki v epohu bronzy (The Oka Basin in the Bronze age).* Moscow: Nauka.

Bader O.N. 1978. *Sungir'. Varxnepaleolitichskaja stojanka. (Sungrir. An Upper Palaeolithic Site).* Moscow: Nauka.

Bader O.N. 1987. Pozdnjakovskaja kul'tura (The Pozdnyakovian culture). In O.N. Bader, D.A. Krainov and M.F. Kosarev (eds), *Epoha bronzy lesnoi polosy SSSR/Arheologija SSSR.* Moscow: Nauka, pp. 131–5.

Benevolenskaya Yu. 1985. O kranio-serologicheskom parallelizme i differenciacii na territorii Pskozshchiny i Pribaltiki (On the cranial and blood-group similarity in the areas of Pskov district and Baltic states). In I.E. Ronis (ed.), *Problemy etnicheskoi istorii Baltov.* Riga: Zinatne, pp. 5–8.

Berezanskaya S.S. 1985. Vostochnotshineckaja kul'tura (The Eastern Trzciniec culture). In I.I. Artemenko (ed.), *Arheologija Ukrainskoi SSR,* t.1. Kiev: Naukova Dumka, pp. 437–44.

Berezanskaya S.S. and N.N. Cherdnichenko. 1985. 'Srubnaja kul'tura' (The Timber-Grave culture). In D.Ya. Telegin, (ed.), *Arheologija Ukrainskoi SSR.* Kiev: Naukova Dumka, pp. 462–472.

Beug H.-J. 1982. Vegetation history and climatic changes in central and southern Europe. In A.F. Harding (ed.), *Climatic Change in Later Prehistory.* Edinburgh: Edinburgh University Press, pp. 85–102.

Bibikov S.N. 1981. *Drevneishii muzikal'nyi kompleks iz kostei mamonta. (The Oldest Musical Complex Made of Mammoth Bones).* Kiev: Naukova Dumka.

Bintliff J. 1984. Iron Age Europe, in the context of social evolution from the Bronze through to historic times. In J. Bintliff (ed.), *European Social Evolution. Archaeological Perspectives.* Bradford: University of Bradford, pp. 157–226.

Birnbaum H. 1983. *Common Slavic. Progress and Problems of Reconstruction.* Columbus, Ohio: Slavica Publishing Inc.

Blavatsky V.D. 1953. *Zemledelie v antichnyh gorodah Severnogo Prichernomor'ja (Agriculture in Ancient Cities of the North Pontic Area).* Moscow: Izd. AN SSSR.

Bogdanova V.I. and A.B. Radzyun. 1991. Paleoantropologicheskie materialy gunno-sarmatskogo vremeni iz Central'noi Tuvy (The palaeo-anthropological Hunnic-Sarmatian materials from the Central Tuva). In R.F. Its (ed.), *Sbornik Muzeja antropologii i etnografii,* XLIV, St Petersburg: Nauka, pp. 55–100.

Bokshchanin A.G. and V.I. Kuzishchin. 1981. Social'no-ekonomicheskii i politicheskii krizis rimskogo obshchestva i gosudarstva (235–284 gg. n.e.) (The socio-economic crisis of the Roman society and state, 235–284 BC). In V.I. Kuzishchin (ed.), *Istorija Drevnego Rima.* Moscow: Vysshaja shkola, pp. 274–80.

Bordes F. 1981. Vingt-cinq ans après: le complexe mouserien revisité. *Bulletin de la société préhistorique française,* 78/3: 77–87.

Borkovský I. 1940. *Staroslovanskà keramika ve střední Europě. Studie k počátkám slovansk kulturi. (Old Slavic Ceramics in Central Europe. Studies on the Beginnings of the Slavic Culture).* Prague: Archaeological Commission, Czech Academy of Sciences.

Bouzek J., D. Koutecký and E. Neustupný. 1966. *The Knovíz Settlement of North-west Bohemia.* Prague: National Museum.

Braichevsky M.Yu. 1965. Teoretichni osnovi doslidăen' etnogenesu (Theoretical foundations of the ethnogenetic studies). *Ukrain'ski Istorichni Zhurnal,* 2: 46–56.

Brashinsky I.B. 1980. *Grecheskii keramicheskii import na Nizhnem Donu v V–III vv. do n.e (The Greek Imported Ceramics in the Low Don Area in the 5th–3rd centuries BC).* Leningrad: Nauka.

Bratchenko S.N. and O.G. Shaposhnikova. 1985. Katakombnaja kul'turno-istoricheskaja obshchnost (The Catacomb cultural-historical entity). In I.I. Artëmenko (ed.), *Arheologiya Ukrainskoi SSR (The Archeology of the Ukrainian SSR),* t.1. Kiev: Naukova Dumka, pp. 403–19.

Bray de R.G.A. 1969. *Guide to the Slavonic Languages.* London: Dent.

Bräuer G. 1989. The evolution of modern humans: a comparison of the African and non-African evidence. In P. Mellars and C. Stringer (eds), *The Human Evolution: Behavioural and Biological Perspectives on the Origin of Modern Humans.* Edinburgh: Edinburgh University Press, pp. 123–54.

Brøndsted J. 1960. *The Vikings.* London: Penguin Books.

Bryusov A. Ya. 1956. Arxeologicheskie kul'tury i etnicheskie obshchnosti (Archeological cultures and ethnical entries). *Sovetskaja Arheologija,* 26: 5–27.

Bryusov A.Ya. 1961. Ob ekspansii kul'tur s boevymi toporami' v konce III tysjacheletija do n.e. (On the expansion of the Battle-Axe culture at the end of the third milleniun BC). *Sovetskaja arheologija ,* 3: 14–33.

Bud'ko V.D. 1970. Paleolit (The Palaeolithic). In V.F. Isaenko (ed.), *Ocherki po arxheologii Belorussii.* Minsk: Nauka i Tehnika.

Bulkin V.A. and G.S. Lebedev. 1974. Gnezdovo i Birka (k probleme stanovlenija goroda) (Gnezdovo and Birka: the problem of the emergence of cities). In *Kul'tura srednevekovoi Rusi.* Leningrad: Leningrad University Press, pp. 11–17.

Bulkin V.A., I.V. Dubov and G.S. Lebedev. 1978. *Arxeologicheskie pamjatniki Drevnei Rusi IX-XI vekov* (*Old Russian Archaeological Sites of the 9th–11th Centuries* AD). Leningrad: Leningrad University Press, pp. 138–40

Bunak V.V. 1962. Antropologicheskie tipy russkogo naroda i voprosy istorii ih formorovanija (Anthropological types of the Russian people). *Kratkie soobshchenija Instituta etnografii AN SSSR*, XXXVI: 75–82.

Bunak V.V. 1969. Genogeograficheskie zony Vostochnoi Evropy vydelyaemye po gruppam krovi ABO (Gene-geographical zones of Eastern Europe as identified by ABO blood groups). *Voprosy antropologii*, 32: 6–28.

Bunak V.V. 1976. Rassengeschichte Osteuropas. In I. Schwidetzky (ed.), *Rassengeschichte der Menschheit*, vol. 4. Wien: Oldenburg pp. 7–102.

Burdukiewicz M. 1979. Zur problematic des spätpaläolithilkum im südwestern der VR Polen (The problem of late Palaeolithic in south-west Poland). In B. Gromsch (ed.), *Veröffentlichungen des Museums für ur-und frümgeschichte Potsdam*, v. 12, 9–38.

Česnys G. 1985. Paleopopulacionnyi podhod k resneniju voprosa o formirovanii nekotoryh Baltskih plemjon i narodnostei. (Palaeo-populational approach to the problem of the origin of Baltic tribes and groups). In I. Ronis (ed.), *Problemy etnicheskoi istorii baltov* (*The Problems of the Ethnic History of the Balts*). Riga: Zinatne, 30–4.

Champion T., C. Gamble, S. Shennan and A. Whittle. 1984. *Prehistoric Europe*. London Academic Press.

Chapman J. 1993. Social power in the Iron Gates Mesolithic. In J. Chapman and P. Dolukhanov (eds), *Cultural Transformations and Interactions in Eastern Europe*. Aldershot: Avebury, pp. 71–121.

Chapman J. and P. Dolukhanov. 1993. Cultural transformations in Eastern Europe: Theory and terminology. In J. Chapman and P. Dolukhanov (eds), *Cultural Transformations and Interactions in Eastern Europe*. Aldershot: Avebury, pp. 1–36.

Charnyavski M.M. 1979. *Nealit Ponyamonn'a* (*The Neolithic of the Neman area*). Minsk: Nauka i Tehnika.

Chernyagin N.N. 1941. Dlinnye kurgany i sopki (The long barrows and sopkis). *Materialy i issledovanija po arxeologii SSSR*, 6: 93–149.

Chernykh E.N. 1970. Drevneishaja metallurgija Urala i Povolzh'ja (The most ancient metallurgy of the Urals and Volga area). *Materialy i issledovanija po arheologii SSSR*, 172. Moscow: Nauka.

Chernykh E.N. 1992. *Ancient Metallurgy in the USSR. The Early Metal Age*. Cambridge: Cambridge University Press.

Chernykh E.N. and S.V. Kuz'minykh: 1987. Pamyatniki seiminsko-turbinskogo tipa v Evrazii (The sites of Ceima-Turbini type in Eurasia). In O.N. Bader, D.A. Krainov and M.F. Kozarev, (eds), *Epoha bronzy lesnoi polosy SSSR/ Arheologija SSSR./*Moscow: Nauka, pp. 84–105.

Chernysh A.P. 1973. *Paleolit i mezolit Pridnestrov'ya* (*The Palaeolithic and Mesolithic of the Dniestr Area*). Moscow: Nauka.

213

Childe V.G. 1952. *New Light on the Most Ancient East.* New York: Praeger.

Childe V.G. 1958. *The Dawn of European Civilization.* New York: A.A. Knopf.

Childe V.G. 1975. *The Dawn of European Civilization.* 6th edition, revised and reset. New York: A.A.Knopf.

Chvojka V.V. 1901. Polja pogrebenii v Srednem Podneprov'e (The urnfields in the Middle Dniepr area). *Transactions of the Russian Archaeological Society,* 12/1–2: 172–90.

Chvojka V.V. 1913. *Drevnie obitateli Srednego Podneprov'ja (The Ancient Inhabitants of the Middle Dneipr Area).* Kiev: Sinkevich Publishing House.

Clarke D.L. 1968. *Analytical Archaeology.* London: Methuen.

Coles J.M. and A.F. Harding. 1979. *The Bronze Age in Europe.* London: Methuen.

Comşa E. 1987. *Bertrachtungen über die Entwicklung der neolithischen Kulturen auf dem rumänischen Gebeit.* Slovenská Archeologia, 35 (1): 65–106.

Cook J.M. 1962. *The Greeks in Ionia and the East.* London: Thames and Hudson.

Daniel G. 1975. *150 Years of Archaeology.* London: Duckworth.

Danilenko V.N. 1955. Voloshskii epipaleoliticheskii mogilnik (The Voloshski epi-palaeolithic cemetery). *Sovetskaja etnografija,* 3: 56–61.

Danilenko V.N. 1969. *Neolit Ukrainy (The Neolithic of the Ukraine).* Kiev: Naukova Dumka.

Danilova E.I. 1979. Zatylochnaja kost' neandertal'ca iz transhei Zaskal'naja V vozle Ak-Kaja (A Neanderthal occipital from the trench at Zaskal'naya V, near Ak-Kaja). In Yu.G. Kolosov (ed.), *Issledovanie paleolita v Krymu.* Kiev: Naukova Dumka.

Davydova N.N. (ed.), 1992. *Istorija ozjor Vostochno-Evropeiskoi ravniny (The Story of Lakes in the East European Plain).* St Petersburg: Nauka.

Debets G.F. 1971. O fizicheskih tipah ljudei skifskogo vremeni (On the physical types of the Scythian-time population). In P.D. Liberov and V.I. Gulayev (eds), *Problemy skifskoi arheologii. Materialy i issledovanija po arheologii SSSR* 177: 8–10.

Demkin V.A., A.V. Lukashev and Yu.V. Lukashev. 1984. Kompleksnye pochvenno-arheologicheskie issledovanija istoricheskih pamjatnikov severnogo Prikaspija (The complex pedological-archaeological studies of the sites in the Northern Caspian area). In *Istorija razvitija pochv v golocene.* Pushchino: Centre for Biological Studies, pp. 221–2.

Denisova R.Ja. 1975. *Antropologija drevnih baltov (Anthropology of Ancient Balts).* Riga: Zinatne.

Denisova R.Ja. 1985. Kul'tura shnurovoi keramiki vostochnoi Pribaltiki i problema baltiiskogo etnogeneza (Corded Ware culture in the eastern Baltic area and the problem of Baltic ethnogenesis). In I.E. Ronis (ed.), *Problemy etnicheskoi istorii baltov.* Riga: Zinatne, pp. 12–14.

Dolukhanov P.M. 1979. *Ecology and Economy in Neolithic Eastern Europe*. London: Duckworth.

Dolukhanov P.M. 1986. Natural environment and the Holocene settlement pattern in the North-western part of the USSR. *Fennoscandia Archaeologica*, III: 3–16.

Dolukhanov. P.M. 1994. *Environment and Ethnicity in the Ancient Middle East*. Aldershot: Avebury.

Dolukhanov P.M. and D.I. Fonyakov. 1984. Modelirovanie kul'turno-istoricheskih processov (The modelling of cultural-historical processes). In V.M. Masson (ed.), *Kompleksnye metody izuchenija istorii s drevneishih vremjon do nashih dnei*. Moscow: Nauka, pp. 33–5.

Dolukhanov P.M. and A.M. Miklyayev. 1986. Prehistoric lacustrine pile dwellings in the north-western part of the USSR. *Fennoscandia Archaeologica*, III: 81–9.

Dolukhanov P.M. and E.N. Nosov. 1985. Paleolandshafty i zaselenie territorii Severo-Zapada v VI–X vv. (Palaeolandscapes and the settlement of the north-west in the sixth–tenth centuries AD). In V.M. Masson (ed.), *Novoe v arxeologii Severo-Zapada SSSR*. Leningrad: Nauka, pp. 19–23.

Dolukhanov P.M., N.A. Gey, A.M. Miklyayev and A.N. Mazurkiewicz. 1989. Rudnya-Serteya, a stratified site in the Upper Duna basin. *Fennoscandia Archaeologica*, VI: 23–6.

Donner J. 1984. Some comments on the pollen-analytical records of cereals and their dating in southern Finland. *Fennoscandia Archaeologica*, 1: 13–18.

Dubov I.V. 1994. The ethnic history of northwestern Rus' in the ninth to thirteenth centuries. In D.H. Kaiser and G. Marker (eds), *Reinterpreting Russian History. Readings, 860s–1860s*. New York–Oxford: Oxford University Press, pp. 14–20.

Dzhaparidze V., G. Bosinski, T. Bugianisvili, L. Gabunia, A. Justus, N. Klopotovkaja, E. Kuauadze, D. Lordkipanidze, G. Maisuradze, N. Mgeladze, N. Nioradze, E. Paulenišvili, H.- J. Schminke, D. Sologašvili, D. Tušabramišvili, M. Tulačrelidze, and A. Vekua. 1989. Der Altpaläolithische Fundplatz Dmanisi in Georgien (Kaukasus) *Jahrbuch des Römisch-Germanischen Zentralmuseum Mainz*, v. 36: 67–116.

Edgren T. 1970. *Studier över snörkeramiska kulturens keramik i Finland (Studies on Corded Ware Cultures in Finland)*. Helsinki: Suomen Muinaismuistoyhdistyksen Aikakauskirja.

Europaeus-Äyräpää A. 1930. Die relative Chronologie der steinzeitlichen Keramik in Finland (*Relative Chronology of Stone Age Pottery in Finland*). *Acta Archaeologica*, I: 165–200.

Fedorov P.V. 1978. *Pleistocen Ponto-Kaspiya (The Pontic-Caspian Pleistocene)*. Moscow: Nauka.

Fischer A. and H. Tauber. 1986. New C-14 datings of Late Palaeolithic cultures from north-western Europe. *Journal of Danish Archaeology*, 5: 7–13.

Foltiny S. 1958. *Velemszentvid, ein urzeitliches Kulturzentrum in*

215

Mitteleuropa. Vienna: Veröffentlichungen der Österreichischen Arbeitsgemeinschaft für Ur- und Frügeschichte, vol. 3.

Gaidukevich V.F. 1949. *Bosporskoe carstvo* (*The Bosporus Kingdom*). Moscow-Leningrad: Izd. AN SSSR.

Gamkrelidze T.V. and Ivanov V.V. 1984. *Indoevropeiskii yazik i indoevropeicy* (*The Indo-European Language and the Indo-Europeans*) vols 1 and 2. Tbilisi University Press.

Georgiev V.I. 1959. Balto-slavjanskii i germanskii (The Balto-Slavic and Germanic). *Slavia*, 28: 1–11.

Gerasimov I.P. (ed.), 1967. *Srednjaja polosa Evropeiskoi chasti SSSR. Prirpdnye uslovija i estestvennye resursy SSSR* (*The Middle Belt of the European Part of the USSR*). Moscow: Nauka.

Gerasimov I.P. (ed.), 1972. *Ukraina i Moldavia. Prirpdnye uslovija i estestvennye resursy SSSR* (*Ukraine and Moldavia. Natural environment and natural resources of the USSR*). Moscow: Nauka.

Gerasimova M.M. 1981. Paleantropologija verxnego paleolita Russkoi ravniny (Palaeoanthropology of the Upper Palaeolithic of the Russian Plain). In A.A. Velichko (ed.), *Arxeologija i paleogeografija pozdnego paleiolita Russkoi ravniny*. Moscow: Nauka, pp. 135–42.

Gimbutas M. 1963. *The Balts*. London: Thames and Hudson.

Gimbutas M. 1971. The beginning of the Bronze Age in Europe and the Indo-Europeans: 3500–2500 BC, *Journal of Indo-European Studies*, (1973, 1): 163–214.

Gladilin V.N. 1976. *Problemy paleolita vostochnoi Evropy* (*The Problems of the Palaeolithic in Eastern Europe*). Kiev: Naukova Dumka.

Gladilin V.N. 1985. Rannii paleolit (The Early Palaeolithic). In I.I. Artëmenko (ed.), *Arxeologija Ukrainskoi SSR*, t.1. Kiev: Naukova Dumka, pp. 12–53.

Gojda M. 1991. *The Ancient Slavs. Settlement and Society* (The Rhind Lectures 1989–1990). Edinburgh: Edinburgh University Press.

Gokhman I.I. 1966a. Iskopaemay neoantropy (The Fossil Neoanthrops). In V.V. Bunak (ed.), *Iskopaemye gominidy i proisxozhdenie cheloveka*. Moscow: Transactions of the Institute for Ethnography, vol 92, pp. 227–72.

Gokhman I.I. 1966b. *Naselenie Ukrainy v epoxu mezolita i neolita* (*The Ukrainian Population in the Mesolithic and Neolithic*). Moscow: Nauka.

Gokhman I.I. 1986. Antopologicheskie osobennosti drevnego naselenija severa evropeiskoi chasti SSSR (Anthropological features of the ancient and present population in the Russian north and the trajectory of their formation). In I.I. Gokhman and A.G. Kozintsev (eds), *Antropologija sovremennogo i drevnego naselenija evropeiskoi chasti SSSR i puti ix formirovanija*. Moscow-Leningrad: Nauka, pp. 216–22.

Gorodtsov V.A. 1901. Russkaja doistoricheskaja keramika (Russian prehistoric ceramics). *Transactions of the Eleventh Archaeological Congress*, 1: 577–672.

Gorodtsov V.A. 1908. *Pervobytnaja arxeologija* (*Prehistoric Archaeology*). Moscow: Snegireva Publishing House.

Goryunov E.A. and M.M. Kazanski. 1978. O priisxozhdenii shiroko-plastinchatyx fibul (On the origin of broad-plated brooches). *Kratkie soobshchenija Instituta arxeologii*, 155: 25–31.

Grakov B.N. 1971. *Skify (The Scythians)*. Moscow: Nauka.

Grakov B.N. 1977. *Rannii zheleznyi vek (The Early Iron Age)*. Moscow: Moscow University Press.

Graudonis J.J. 1967. *Latvija v epohu pozdnei bronzy i rannego zheleza (Latvia in the Early Iron Age)*. Riga: Zinatne.

Grekov B.D. 1949. *Kievskaja Rus (The Kievan Rus)*. Moscow: Izd. AN SSSR.

Gribbin J. 1978. *The Climatic Threat*. Glasgow: Fontana/Collins.

Grigor'ev G.P. 1993. The Kostenki-Avdeevo archaeological culture and the Willendorf-Pavlov-Kostenki-Avdeevo cultural unity. In O. Soffer and N.D. Praslov (eds), *From Kostenki to Clovis. Upper Palaeolithic-Paleo-Indian Adaptations*. New York/London: Plenum Press, pp. 51–66.

Gryaznov M.P. 1980. *Arzhan – carskii kurgan ranne-skifskogo vremeni (Arzhan, The Royal Barrow of Scythian Age)*. Leningrad: Nauka.

Gumilev L.N. 1980. *Etnos i biosfera Zemli (Ethnos and the Earth's Biosphere)*. Leningrad: Gidrometeoizdat.

Gurina N.N. 1956. Oleneostrovskii Mogil'nik (*The Oleni Ostrov Cemetery*). *Materialy i issledovanija po arheologii SSSR*, vol. 47. Moscow and Leningrad: Nauka.

Gurina N.N. 1961. Drevnjaja Istorija Severo-Zapada evropeiskoi chasti SSSR (Prehistory of the North West of the European USSR) *Materialy i Issledovanija po Arheologii SSSR*, vol. 87. Moscow-Leningrad: Izd. AN SSSR.

Gurina N.N. 1965. Novye dannye o kamennom veke severo-zapadnoi Belorussii (New data on the Stone Age of the northwestern Belorussia). *Materialy i Issledovanija po Arheologii SSSR*, 131: 141–203.

Gurina N.N. 1987. The main stages in the cultural development of the ancient population of the Kola peninsula. *Fennoscandia Archaeologica*, IV: 35–48.

Hajdu P. 1975. *Finno-Ugrian Languages and Peoples* (translated and adapted by G.F. Kushing). London: Andre Deutsch.

Harding A.F. and J. Ostoja-Zagórski. 1993. The Lausitz culture and the beginning and end of Bronze Age fortification. In J. Chapman and P. Dolukhanov (eds), *Cultural Transformation and Interactions in Eastern Europe*. Aldershot: Avebury, pp. 163–77.

Harrison S.P., I.C. Prentice and J. Guiot. 1993. Climatic control on the Holocene lake-level changes in Europe. *Climate Dynamics*, 8/3: 189–200.

Häusler A. 1974. *Die Gräber der älteren Ockergrabkultur zwischen Ural and Dnepr*. Berlin: Akademie-Verlag.

Heather P.-J. 1991. *Goths and Romans 332–489*. Oxford: Clarendon Press.

Hensel W. 1966. *La Naissance de la Pologne*. Wroclaw-Warszawa-Kraków: Wydawnictwo PAN.

Herrmann J. 1968. *Siedlung, Wirtschaft und gesellscahaftliche Verhlätnisse der slawischen Stämme zwischen Oder/Neisse und Elbe.* Berlin: Akademie-Verlag.

Herrmann J. 1982. *Wikinger und Slawen. Zur Frühgeschichte der Ostseevölker.* Berlin: Akademieverlag.

Herodotus. 1954. *The Histories* (translated by Auberey de Selincourt). London: Penguin Books.

Hodder I. 1982. *Symbols in Action.* Cambridge: Cambridge University Press.

Howe G.M. 1983. *The Soviet Union. A Geographical Survey.* 2nd edition. London: Longman.

Hubschmied J. 1960. *Mediterrane Substrate.* Geneva: Romanica Helvetica, 70.

Iessen A.A. 1950: K hronologii bol'ših kubanskih kurganov (To the chronology of the Great Kuban kurgans). *Sovetskaja arheologija,* 12: 157–202.

Iessen A.A. 1963: Kavkaz i Drevnii Vostok v IV–III tysjacheletii do n.e. (The Caucasus and the Ancient East in the 4th–3rd millenium BC). *Kratkie soobshchenija Instituta arheologii,* 93: 3–14.

Ilves E., A. Liiva and J.-M. Punning. 1974. *Radiouglerodnyi metod i ego primemenie v chatvertichnoi geologii i arheologii Estoni (The Radiocarbon Technique and its Applications to Quarternary Geology and Archaeology).* Tallinn: AN ESSR.

Indreko R. 1948. *Die mittlere Steinzeit in Estland.* Stockhlom: Kungliga Vitterhets Historie och Antivitets Akadermien.

Isaenko V.F., A.G. Mitrofanov and G.V. Shtykhov. 1970. *Ocherki po arheologii Belorussii (Essays on Archaeology of Belorussia).* Minsk: Nauka i tehnika.

Ivanov I.V. 1989. Evolucija pochv stepnoi zony kak indikator izmenenija klimaticheskih uslovii v golocene (The evolution of soils as an indicator of Holocene climate). In N.A. Khotinsky (ed.), *Paleoklimaty pozdnelednikov'ja i golocena.* Moscow: Nauka, pp. 68–75.

Ivanov V.V. 1965. *Obshcheindoevropeiskaja, praslavjanskaja i anatoliiskaja jazykovye sistemy* (The Common Indo-European, Pra-Slavic and Anatolian Language Systems). Moscow: Nauka.

Jaanits L. and K. Jaanits. 1975. Frühmesolithische Siedlung von Pulli. *Izvestija AN Estonskoi SSR,* XXIV: 64–70.

Jacobs K. 1992. Human population differentiation in the peri-Baltic Mesolithic: the odontometrics of Oleneostrovskii mogilnik (Karelia). *Human Evolution,* 7/4: 33–48.

Jacobs K. 1993. Human postcranial variation in the Ukrainian Mesolithic-Neolithic. *Current Anthropology,* 34: 311–24.

Jacobs K. 1994. Human dento-gnathic metric variation in Mesolithic/Neolithic Ukraine: possible evidence of demic diffusion in the Dnieper Rapids region. *American Journal of Physical Anthropology,* vol. 95: 1–26.

Jakobson R. 1985. O teorii foneticheskix sojuzov mezhdy jazykami (On the theory of phonological affinities of languages). In R. Jakobson *Izbrannye raboty*. Moskva: Progress, pp. 92–104.

Jakobson R. 1973. The place of linguistics among the sciences of man. In R. Jakobson (ed.), *Main Trends in the Science of Language*. London: Allen & Unwin, pp. 25–43.

Kaiser D.H. and G. Marker. 1994. *Reinterpreting Russian History. Readings 860s–1860s*. New York/ Oxford: Oxford University Press.

Kanivets V.I. 1976. *Paleolit krainego Severo-Vostoka Evropy* (*The Early Palaeolithic of Russian Extreme Northeast*). Moscow: Nauka.

Karlén W. 1982. Holocene glacier fluctuations in Scandinavia. *Striae*, 18: 26–34.

Kazansky M. 1991. *Les Goths (Ier–VIIs après. J.- C.)*. Paris: Errance.

Kazansky M. 1993. The sedentary elite in the 'empire' of the Huns and its impact on material civilisation in Southern Russia during the Early Middle Ages (5th–7th centuries AD). In J. Chapman and P. Dolukhanov (eds), *Cultural Transformations and Interactions in Eastern Europe*. Aldershot: Avebury, pp. 211–35.

Khalikov A.Kh. 1969. *Drevnjaja Istorija Srednego Povolzh'ja* (*Prehistory of the Middle Volga Area*). Moscow: Nauka.

Khodasheva K.S. 1966. O geograficheskih osobennostjah struktury naselenija nazemnyh zhivotnykh (On the geographical features of the population structure of terrestrial animals). In Yu.A. Isakov, (ed.), *Zonal'nye osobennosti neselenija nazemnyh zhivotnykh*. Moscow: Nauka, pp. 7–38.

Khotinsky N.A. 1977. *Golocen severnoi Evrazii* (*The Holocene of Northern Eurasia*). Moscow: Nauka.

Khotinsky N.A., Z.V. Alekshinskaya and V.A. Klimanov. 1991. Novaja sxema periodizacii landshaftno-klimaticheskix izmenenii v golocene (A new division of landscape-climatic changes during the Holocene). *Izvestiya AN SSSR, seriva geograficheskaya*, 3: 30–42.

Kirpichnikov A.N. 1988. Ladoga i ladozhskaja zemlja v VIII–XIII v (The Ladoga and Ladoga Area in the 8th–13th centuries). In A.N. Kirpichnikov (ed.), *Istoriko-arxeologicheskoe izuchenie drevnei Rusi: itogi i osnovnye problemy*. Leningrad: Nauka.

Klejn L.S. 1991. *Arxeologicheskaja tipologija* (*An Archaeological Typology*). Leningad: Academy of Sciences.

Klejn L.S. 1993. *Fenomen Sovetskoi arxeologii* (*The Phenomenon of Soviet Archaeology*). St Petersburg: Farn.

Klyuchevsky V.O. 1919. *Bojarskaja duma Drevnei Rusi* (*The Boyard Duma in the Ancient Rus*). St Petersburg: Synodal Publishers.

Kol'tsov L.V. 1989. *Mezolit SSSR* (*The Mesolithic of the USSR*). *Arxeologija SSSR*. Moscow: Nauka.

Kolosov Yu.G. 1979. Akkaiskie stojanki i nekotorye itogi ih izuchenija (The Ak-Kaya sites and several results of their investigations). In Yu.G. Kolosov (ed.), *Issledovanie paleolita v Krymu*. Kiev: Naukova Dumka.

Konduktorova T.S. 1972. *Antropologiya drevnego naseleniya Ukrainy* (*The Anthropology of the Population of Ancient Ukraine*). Moscow: Nauka.

Konduktorova T.S. 1973. *Atropologija naselenija Ukrainy mezolita, neolita i epoxi bronzy* (*The Anthroplogy of the Ukrainian Population in the Mesolithic, Neolithic and Bronze Age*). Moscow: Nauka.

Kopytin V.F. 1979. Mezolit poselenija Gorki v Posozh'e (The Mesolithic site of Gorki in the Sozh area). *Kratkie Soobshchenija Instituta Arhehologii AN SSSR*, 157: 27–32.

Kossina G. 1911. *Die Lerkunft der Germanen zur methode der siedlungsarchäologie.* Mannus – Bibliotek 6. Würzburg: Kaibitzsch.

Kozarski J. 1991. Warta, a case study of a lowland river. In L. Starkel, K.W. Gregory and J.B. Thorns (eds), *Temperate Palaeohydrology. Fluvial Processes in the Last 15,000 Years.* Chichester: John Wiley and Sons, pp. 189–216.

Kozlova G.I. 1978. Rastitel'nost' i geobotanicheskie raiony (The vegetation and botanical regions). In N.V. Razumikhin (ed), *Prirodnoe raionirovanie Novgorodskoi oblasti.* Leningrad: Leningrad University Press, pp. 156–91.

Kozłowski J.S. and S.K. Kozłowski. 1979. *Upper Palaeolithic and Mesolithic in Europe. Taxonomy and Palaeohistory.* Wroclaw: Państwowe Wydawnictwo Naukowe.

Krainov D.A. 1972. *Drevneishaja istorija Volgo-Okskogo mezhdurech'ja. Fatjanovskaja kul'tura* (*Prehistory of the Volga-Oka interfluve. The Fatyanovo Culture*). Moscow: Nauka.

Krainov D.A. 1978. Hronologicheskie ramki neolita verhnego povolzh'ya (The Chronological Frameworks of the Neolithic in the Upper Volga Area). *Kratkie Soobshcheniya Instituta Arheologii AN SSSR*, 153: 57–61.

Krainov D.A. and N.A. Khotinsky 1977. 'Verhnevolzhskaja arheologicheskaja kul'tura' (The Upper Volga archaeological culture). *Sovetskaja arheologija*, 3: 42–68.

Krasnov Yu.A. 1971. *Rannee zemledelie i zhivotnovodstvo v lesnoi polose Vostochnoi Evropy* (*Early Agriculture and Animal Husbandry in the Boreal Eastern Europe*). Moscow: Nauka.

Kremenetsky K.V. 1991. *Paleoekolgija drevneishih zemledel'cev i skotovodov Russkoi raviny* (*The Palaeology of Prehistoric Farmers and Stock-breeders of the Russian Plain*). Moscow: Nauka.

Krichevsky E.Yu. 1940. Tripol'skie ploshchadki (The Tripolye plattforms). *Sovetskaja arheologija*, 6: 20–45.

Kropotkin V.V. 1967. *Ekonomicheskie svjazi Vostochnoi Evropy v I tysjacheletii n.e.* (*Economic Links in Eastern Europe during the First Millennium* AD). Moscow: Nauka.

Kruglov A.P. and G.V. Podgaetsky. 1935. *Rodovoe obshchestvo stepei Vostochnoi Evropy* (*The Clan Society in the East European Steppe*). Moscow-Leningrad: IGAIMK.

Kryzhitsky S.L. 1985. *Olvija. Istoriograficheskoe issledovanie arhitekturno-stroitel'nyh kompleksov (Olbia. A Historiography of the Studies of Architectural Complexes).* Kiev: Naukova Dumka.

Kukharenko Yu.V. 1961. *Pamyatniki zheleznogo veka Belorussii (Iron Age Sites in Belorussia). Svod arxeologicheskix istochnikov, D1–29.* Moscow. Nauka.

Kukharenko Yu.V. 1964. *Zarubinetskaja kul'tura (The Zarubintsy Culture). Svod arxeologicheskix istochnikov, D1–19.* Moscow: Nauka.

Kukla G. 1989. Long continental records of climate: an introduction. *Palaeogeography, Palaeoclimatology, Palaeoecology,* 72: 1–9.

Kuza A.V. 1989. *Malye goroda Drevnei Rusi (The Smaller Cities of Ancient Rus).* Moscow: Nauka.

Kvasov D.D. 1975. *Pozdnechetvertichnaja istorija krupny ozër i vnutrennix morei Vostochnoi Evropy (The Late Quaternary History of Large Lakes and Inner Seas of Eastern Europe).* Leningrad: Nauka.

Lamb H.H. 1977. *Climate: present, past and future,* vol. 2. London: Methuen.

László, Gy. 1961. *Östörténetunk legégibb szakaszai. (The Oldest Parts of Our Prehistory).* Budapest: Acadèmiai Kiado.

Lebedev G.S. 1985. *Epoxa vikingov v Severnoi Evrope (The Age of the Vikings in Northern Europe).* Leningrad: Leningrad University Press.

Lebedev L.S. 1992. *Istorija otechestvennoi arxeologii 1700–1917 gg (The History of Russian Archaeology, 1700–1917).* St Petersburg: St Petersburg University Press.

Lehr-Splawinski T. 1946. *O pochodzeniu i praojczyznie Slowian. (On the Origin and Motherland of the Slavs).* Poznan: Wydawnictwo Instituto. Zachodnego.

Leroi-Gourhan Arl. 1981. Diagrammes polliniques des sites archéologiques au Moyen-Orient. *Beiträge zum umweltgeschichte des Vorderen Orients,* 130. Wiesbaden.

Levasheva V.P. 1994. Agriculture in Rus (tenth–thirteenth centuries). In D.H. Kaiser and G. Marker. (eds), *Reinterpreting Russian History. Readings, 860s–1860s.* New York/Oxford: Oxford University Press, pp. 39–44.

Lieberman, Ph. 1984. *The Biology and Evolution of Language.* Cambridge MA and London: Cambridge University Press.

Loze I.A. 1979. *Pozdnii neolit i rannjaja bronza Lubanskoi ravniny (Late Neolithic and Early Bronze Age of the Lubana Lowland).* Riga: Zinatne.

Lumley de, M.-A. 1973. *Anténéanderthaliens et Néanderthaliens du bassin Mediterranéen Occidental Européen.* Marseille: Études Quaternaires; Université de Provence.

Lyubin V.P. 1989. Paleolit Kavkaza (The Palaeolithic of the Caucasus). In P.I. Boriskovsky (ed.), *Paleolit Kavkaza i Severnoi Azii.* Leningrad: Nauka, pp. 9–142.

Lyubin V.P. 1993. Evrazija iznachal'naja – poslednie otkrytija na Kavkaze (The initial Eurasia: the latest finds in the Caucasus). *Vestnik Drevnei Istorii,* 1: 173–4.

Machnik J. 1979. Kręg kultury keramiki sznurowej (*The area of the corded ware culture*). *Prahistoria Ziem Polskich*, t. 2. Warsaw: PAN, pp. 337–412.

Malachovsky D.B. and K.K. Markov. 1969. Geomorfologija i chetvertichnye otlozhenija Severo-Zapada evropeiskoi chasti SSSR (*Geomorphology and Quaternary Deposits in the North-west of the European USSR*). Leningrad: Nauka.

Malmer M.P. 1962. *Jungneolithische Studien*. Lund: Acta Archaeologica Ludensia.

Mallory J.P. 1989. *In Search of Indo-Europeans. Language, Archaeology and Myth*. London: Thames and Hudson.

Mann M. 1986. *The Sources of Social Power*. Cambridge: Cambridge University Press.

Mark K. 1970. *Die Herkunft der finnisch-ugrischen Volker vom Standpunkt der Archaeologie*. Tallinn: Academy of Sciences of the Estionian SSR.

Mark K. 1972. Anthropologische Eigenschaften der Bevölkerung Finnlands. *Annales Academiae Scientiarum Fennicae*. Series A.V. Medica, 152: 3–68.

Markevich V.I. 1974. *Bugo-Dnestrovskaya kul'tura na territorii Moldavii* (*The Bugo-Dniestrian Culture on the Territory of Moldavia*). Kishinev: Shtiinţa.

Martin P.S. and R.G. Klein, (eds). 1984. *Quaternary Extinctions – A Prehistoric Revolution*. Tucson, AZ: University of Arizona Press.

Masanov N.E. 1970. La dispersion comme loi générale de l'activité nomade. In H.-P. Francfort (ed.), *Nomades et sédentaires en Asie centrale*. Paris: Éditions du CNRS, pp. 193–210.

Mel'nikova E.A. and V.Ya Petrukhin. 1989. Nazvanie 'Rus' v rannei etnokul'turnoi istyorii Russkogo gosudarstva (The term of 'Rus' in the early ethno-cultural history of the Russian state). In I.I. Peiros (ed.), *Lingvisticheskaja rekonstrukcija i drevneishaja istorija Vostoka*. Moskva: Nauka, pp. 42–55.

Melyukova A.I. (ed.). 1989. *Stepi evropieskoi chasti SSR v skifo-sarmatskoe vremya* (*The Steppe in the European USSR during the Scythian-Sarmatian Age*). *Arheologija SSSR*. Moscow: Nauka.

Merpert N.Ya. 1968: *Drevneišaja istorija naselenija stepnoi polosy Vostochnoi Evropy* (*The Ancient History of the Population in the Steppe Belt of Eastern Europe*). Moscow: Nauka.

Mikic Z. 1986. Die Ethnogenese der Südslawen under Berücksichtigung von West- und Ostslawen aus der Sicht der Anthropologie. In B. Kandler-Pálsson (ed.), *Ethnogenese europäischer Völker*. Stuttgart/New York: Gustav Fischer.

Miklyayev: A.M. 1977. O svajnyh poselenijah III-II tys. do n.e. v Pskovskoi i Smolenskoi oblastjah' (On the pile-dwellings of the 3rd–2nd millennia BC in the Pskov and Smolensk districts). In B.B. Piotrovsky (ed.), *Drevnie pamjatniki kul'tury na territorii SSSR*. Leningrad: Hermitage.

Mitrofanov A.G. 1978. *Zheleznyi vek srednei Belorussii, VII–VI vv.do n.e.–VI v.n.e.*(*The Iron Age of the Middle Belorussia*). Minsk: Nauka i tehnika.

Mörner N.-A. 1969. *The Late Quaternary History of the Kattegat Sea and the Swedish West Coast*. Sveriges Geologiska Undersökning, series C No 640.

Munchaev R.M. 1970: *Kavkaz na zare bronzovogo veka* (*The Caucasus on the eve of the Bronze Age*). Moscow: Nauka.

Nazarenko V.A. 1982. Normanny i a pojavlenie kurganov v Priladozh'je (The Normans and the emergence of barrows in the Ladoga area). In A.D. Stolyar (ed.), *Sevennaja Rus' i eje sosedi v epoxu rannego srednevekov'ja*. Leningrad: Leningrad University Press, pp. 142–6.

Nieminen E.K. 1957. K voprosu o vlijanii praslavjanskogo jazyka na pribaltiisko-finskie jazyki (On the impact of the Pra-Slavonic on the Baltic-Finnic languages). In K. Tarnovski (ed.), *Beogradski Mezhdunarodni slavisticki sastanak*. Beograd: Izdanie Organizacionog Odbora.

Niewiarowski W.B., Noryśkiewicz, W. Piotrowski and W. Zajaczkowski. 1992. Biskupin fortified settlement and its environment in the light of new environmental and archaeological studies. In B. Coles (ed.), *The Wetland Revolution in Prehistory*. Exeter: WARP – The Prehistoric Society, pp. 81–92.

Nikonov V.A. 1964. *Etnogenez mordovskogo naroda i toponimika* (*The Ethnogenesis of the Mordovial People and Place Names*). Saransk: Mordovan Book Publishers.

Noble M. 1973. Social networks: its use as a conceptual network in family analysis. In J. Boissevain and J.C. Mitchell (eds), *Network Analysis: Studies in Human Functions*. The Hague: Mouton, pp. 3–13.

Nosov E.N. 1981a. Nekotorye obshchie voprosy izuchenija pogrebal'nyx pamjatnikov vtoroi poloviny I tysjacheletija n.e. (Several general problems in the study of burial sites of the second half of the first millennium AD). *Sovetskaja arxeologija*, 1: 42–56.

Nosov E.N. 1981b. Volxov – vodnyi put' i poselenija konca I tysjacheletija n.e. (The Volkhov and a major waterway for the settlements of the final first millennium AD). *Kratkie sobbshchenija Instituta arxeologii AN SSSR*, 164: 18–23.

Nosov E.N. 1981c. Poselenie i mogil'nik kul'tury dlinnyx kurganov na ozere S'ezzhee (The settlement and the cemetery of the Long Barrow Culture on the lake of S'ezzhee). *Kratkie soobshchenija Instituta arxeologii AN SSSR*, 166: 64–8.

Nosov E.N. 1990. *Novgorodskoe (Rurikovo) gorodishche* (*The Novgorod (Rurik's) Hill-Fort*). Leningrad: Nauka.

Nosov E.N. 1993. The problem of the emergence of early urban centres in Northern Russia. In J. Chapman and P. Dolukhanov (eds), *Cultural Transformations and Interactions in Eastern Europe*. Aldershot: Avebury, pp. 236–56.

O'Shea, J. and M. Zvelebil. 1984. Oleneostrovski Mogilnik: reconstructing social and economic organization of prehistoric foragers in northern Russia. *Journal of Anthropological Archaeology*, III: p. 1–40.

Oshibkina S.V. 1987. Eneolit i bronzovyi vek Severa evropeiskoi chasti SSSR (The Eneolithic and Bronze Age of the North of European USSR). In O.N. Bader, D.A. Krainov and M.F. Kosarev (eds), *Epoha bronzy lesnoi polosy SSSR/Arheologija SSSR*. Moscow: Nauka, pp. 147–56.

Paaver K. 1965. *Formirovanie teriofauny i izmenchivost' mlekopitajushchih Pribaltiki v golocene.* (*The Formation and Variability of the Mammalian Fauna in the Peribaltic Area during the Holocene*). Tartu: Tartu University Press.

Pankrushev G.A. 1978. *Mezolit i neolit Karelii (The Mesolithic and Neolithic of Karelia)*. Moscow: Nauka.

Pashkevich G.A. 1982. Paleobotanicheskaja harakteristika poselenija Mirnoe (The palaeobotanic characteristics of the site of Mirnoe). In V.N. Stanko (ed.), *Mirnoe. Problema mezolita stepei Severnogo Pricheromor'ja*. Kiev: Naukova Dumka.

Pashkevich G.A. 1991. *Paleoetnobotanicheskie nahodki na territorii Ukrainy (Neolit-bronza). Katalog (Palaeoethnobotanical Finds in the Territory of Ukraine (Neolithic-Bronze Age). Catalogue)*. Kiev: Institute of Archaeology.

Petrov V.P. 1968. *Podsechnoe zemledelie (Swidden Agriculture)*. Kiev: Naukova Dumka.

Pleiner R. 1980. Early iron metallurgy in Europe. In T.A. Wertime and J.D. Muhly (eds), *The Coming of the Age of Iron*. New Haven, CT: Yale University Press, pp. 375–415.

Pobol' L.D. 1970. Zheleznyi vek (The Iron Age). In V.F. Isaenko, A.G. Mitrofanov and G.V. Shtykhov (eds), *Ocherki po arxeologii Belorussii*. Minsk: Nauka i texnika, pp. 136–84.

Popov A.I. 1948. K voprosu o mordovskoi toponimike (To the problem of Mordovian toponimics). *Sovetskoe finno-ugrovedenie*, 2: 202–30.

Praslov N.D. 1984. Rannii paleolit Russkoi Ravniny (The Early Palaeolithic of the Russian Plain). In P.I. Boriskovsky (ed.), *Paleolit SSSR/Arxeologija SSSR*. Moscow: Nauka, pp. 42–4.

Price D.T. and K. Jacobs. 1990. Olenii Ostrov: first radiocarbon dates from a major Mesolithic cemetery in Karelia, USSR. *Antiquity*, 64: 849–53.

Pryakhin A.D. and A. KH. Khalikov. 1987. Abashevskaya kul'twa (The Abashevian culture). In O.N. Bader, D.A. Krainov and M.F. Kosarev (eds), *Epoha Bronzy Lesnoi Polosy SSSR (The Bronze Age of the Boreal USSR)*. Moscow: Nauka, pp. 124–30.

Randsborg K. 1980. *The Viking Age in Denmark*. London: Duckworth.

Ranov V.A. 1993. Tout commence au Paléolithique. *Les Dossiers d'Archéologie*, 185: 4–13.

Rauner Ju.L., A.N. Zolotokrylin and V.V. Popova. 1983. Kolebanija vlazhnosti klimata evropeiskoi chasti SSSR za poslednie 4000 let (The fluctuation of precipitation in the European USSR over the past 4,000 years). *Izvestija AN SSSR, seriya geograficheskaya*, 1: 50–9.

Renfrew A.C. 1987. *Archaeology and Language. The Puzzle of Indo-European Origins*. London. Jonathan Cape.

Richards J.D. 1991. *Viking Age England*. London: Batsford/English Heritage.

Rimantiene R.K. 1971. *Paleolit i mezolit Litvy (The Palaeolithic and Mesolithic of Lithuania)*. Vilnius: Mintis.

Rimantiene R. 1980. *Šventoji. Pamariu kulturos gyvenvietes. (Šventoji: Excavations of the Sites of Pomorian Culture)*. Vilnius: Mokslas.

Roberts N. 1994. *The Changing Global Environment*. London: Blackwell.

Roerich N.K. 1903. Nekotorye drevnosti pjatin Derevskoi i Bezhitskoi (Antiquities of Derevsk and Bezhitsk counties). *Zapiski Otdelenija russkoi i slavjanskoi arxeologii Russkago arxeologicheskogo obshchestva*, 1: 14–43.

Rogachev A.N. and M.V. Anikovich. 1984. Pozdnii paleolit Russkoi ravniny i Kryma (The Late Palaeolithic of the Russian Plain and the Crimea). In P.I. Boriskovsky (ed.), *Paleolit SSSR/Arxeologija SSSR*. Moscow: Nauka, pp. 162–271.

Rostovtseff M.I. 1922. *Iranians and Greek in South Russia*. Oxford: Clarendon Press.

Rostovtseff M.I. 1927. *A History of Ancient World*, vol. II. *Rome*. London: Clarendon Press.

Rudenko S.I. 1962. *Sibirskaya kollekciya Petra I (The Siberian Collection of Peter I)*. Moscow: Nauka.

Rudenko S.I. 1970. *Frozen Tombs of Siberia*. London: Dent.

Ryabinin E.A. 1990. Xarakter mezhetniciskix kontaktov na severe Rusi (sovremennoe sostojanie problemy) (Intraethnic contacts in the Russian North; the present-day aspects). *Kratkkie Soobshcmeniya Instituta arxeologii AN SSSR*, 205: 3–9.

Rybakov B.A. (ed.), 1966. *Istorija SSSR (The History of the USSR)* vol. 1. Moscow: Nauka.

Rybakov B.A. 1948. *Remeslo Drevnei Rusi (The Crafts of Ancient Rus)*. Moscow: Academy of Sciences of the USSR.

Rybakov B.A. 1979. *Gerodotova Skifija (The Scythia of Herodotus)*. Moscow: Nauka.

Rybakov B.A. 1981. *Yazychstvo drevnix slavjan (The Paganism of Early Slavs)*. Moscow: Nauka.

Rybakov B.A. 1982. *Kievskata Rus' i Russkie knyazhestva* XII–XIII w. Moscow: Nauka.

Ryndina N.V. 1971. *Drevneishee metalloobrabatyvajushchee proizvodstvo Vostochnoi Evropy (The Oldest Metal-working in Russia)*. Moscow: Moscow State University Press.

Sarmela M. 1987. Swidden cultivation in Finland as a cultural system. *Suomen Antropologi* (Special issue on swidden cultivation), 4: 241–62.

Schild R. 1975. Pózni paleolit (The Late Palaeolithic). In W. Chmielewski and W. Hensel (eds), *Prehistorija Ziem Polskich*, (*The Prehistory of Polish Lands*) t.1. Warsaw/Wroclaw: PAN.

Schild R. 1984. Terminal Palaeolithic of the North European Plain. *Advances in World Archaeology*, 3: 193–274.

Schwitetzky I. 1986. Die Ethnogenese der Finno-Ugrier aus der Sicht der Anthropologue. In B. Kandler-Pálsson (ed.), *Ethnogenese europäischer Völker*. Stuttgart/New York: Gustav Fischer, pp. 357–89.

Sedov V.V. 1970a. *Novgorodskie sopki* (*The Novgorod Sopkis*). *Svod arxeologicheskix istochnikov*, E1–8. Moscow: Nauka.

Sedov V.V. 1970b. *Slavjane Verhnego Podeprov'ja i Podvin'ja* (*The Slavs in the Upper Dniepr and Upper Dvina Areas*). Moscow: Nauka.

Sedov V.V. 1974. *Dlinnye kurgany krivichei* (*The Krovichian Long Barrows*). *Svod adxeologicheskix istochnikov*, E1–6. Moscow: Nauka.

Sedov V.V. 1982. *Vostochnye slavjane v VI–XIII vv.* (*The Eastern Slavs in the 6th–13th centuries* AD). *Arxeologija SSSR*. Moscow: Nauka.

Sedov V.V. 1987. Nachalo gorodov na Rusi (The early cities in the Rus). In *Trudy Mezhdunarodnogo kongressa slavjanskoi arxeologii*, vol. 1. Moscow: Nauka, pp. 12–31.

Sedov V.V. 1989. Stanovlenie evropeiskogo rannesrednevekovogo goroda (The emergence of early medieval cities). In V.V. Sedov (ed.), *Stanovlenie evropeiskogo srednevekovogo goroda*. Moscow: Nauka, pp. 6–55.

Senn A. 1954. Die Beziehungen des Baltischen zum Slavischen und Germanischen. *Zeitschrift fur vergleichende Sprachvorschung auf dem Gebiete der indoeuropaischen Sprachen*, 71: 162–88.

Serebrennikov B.A. 1957. O nekotoryh sledah ischeznuvshego indoevropeiskogo jazyka v centre Evropeiskoi chasti SSSR blizkogo baltiiskim yazykam (On the traces of an exitict Baltic-related language in the centre of the European USSR). *Lietuviu Mokslu Akademijos Darbai*, ser. A, 1/2. Vilnius: pp. 69–72.

Sergeev G.P. 1963. Rannetripol'skii klad u sela Karbuna (An early Tripolye hoard near the village of Karbuna). *Sovetskaya arheologija*, 1: 135–51.

Service E.R. 1962. *Primitive Social Organisation: an Evolutionary Perspective*. New York: Random House.

Shapiro A.L. 1977. *Problemy social'no-ekonomicheskoi istorii Rusi XIV–XVI vv.* (*The Problems of Socio-Economic History of Russia in the 14th–16th Centuries*). Leningrad: Leningrad University Press.

Shakhmatov A.A. 1947. Kievskii nachalnyi svod 1095 goda (The Kievan initial chronicles of 1095 AD). In A.A. Shakhmatov (ed.), *Sbornik statei i materialov*. Moscow-Leningrad: Izd. AN SSSR.

Shaposhnikova O.G. 1985. Jamnaja kul'turno-istoricheskaja obshchnost (The Yamna cultural-historic entity). In D.Ya. Telegin (ed.), *Arheologija Ukrainskoi SSR*. Kiev: Naukova Dumka, pp. 336–53.

Shcheglov A.N. 1978. *Severo-zapadnyi Krym v antichnuju epohu* (*The North-western Crimea in Ancient Times*). Leningrad: Nauka.

Shchelinsky V.E. 1989. Some results of new investigations at the Kapova cave in the southern Urals. *Proceedings of Prehistoric Society,* 55: 181–91.

Shchukin M. 1989. *Rome and Barbarians in Central and Eastern Europe, First Century* BC – First Century AD. Oxford: BAR, International Series, 542.

Shchukin M.B. 1994. *Na rubezne er. Opyt istoriko – arkeologicheskoi rekonstrukci i politicheskih cobytii IIIv. do n.e. – IV.n.e.v. vostochnoi i central'noi Evrope (On the Turn of Erae. An Attempt at the Reconstruction of Political Events in Eastern and Central Europe during the 3rd Century BC – 1st Century AD).* St Petersburg: Farn.

Shennan S.J. 1982. Ideology, change and the European early Bronze Age. In: I. Hodder (ed.), *Symbolic and Structural Archaeology.* Cambridge: Cambridge University Press, pp. 155–61.

Sherratt A.G. 1981. Plough and pastoralism: aspects of the Secondary Products Revolution. In I. Hodder, G. Isaac and N. Hammond (eds), *Pattern of the Past.* Cambridge: Cambridge University Press, pp. 261–306.

Sherratt A.G. Social evolution: Europe in the later Neolithic and Copper Ages. In J. Bintliff (ed.), *European Social Evolution. Archaeological Perspectives.* Bradford: University of Bradford, pp. 123–34.

Shvets G.I. 1978. *Mnogovekovaja izmenchivost' stoka Dnepra (Long-term Variability of the Dniepr Discharge Pattern).* Leningrad: Gidrometeoizdat.

Siiriäinen, A. 1973. Studies relating to shore displacement and Stone Age chronology in Finland. *Finkst Museum,* 1973/1: 5–22.

Siiriäinen, A. 1980. Recent studies on the Stone Age economy in Finland. *Fennoscandia Antiqua,* I: 17–26.

Siiriäinen A. 1982. Shore displacement and archaeology in Finland. *Annales Academiae Scientiarum Fenniciae,* series A III. 134, 173–84.

Soffer O. 1985. *The Upper Palaeolithic of the Central Russian Plain.* Orlando, FL: Academic Press.

Soffer O. 1993. Upper Palaeolithic adaptations in Central and Eastern Europe and Man-Mammoth interactions. In O. Soffer and N.D. Praslov (eds), *From Kostenki tos. Upper Palaeolithic-Paleo-Indian Adaptations.* New York/London: Plenum Press, pp. 31–50.

Sokal R.R., N.L. Oden and C. Wilson. 1991. Genetic evidence for the spread of agriculture in Europe by demic diffusion. *Nature,* 351: 193–5.

Spitzyn A.A. 1899. Rasselenie drevnerusskih plemjon po arxeologicheskim dannym (The settlement of Old Russian tribes based on the archaeological evidence). *Zhurnal ministerstva narodnogo prosveshchenija,* 7: 301–40.

Stalin I.V. 1950. *Marksizm i voprosy jazykoznanija (Marxism and the Problems of Linguistics).* Moscow: Politizdat.

Stankevich Ya.V. 1960. *K istorii naselenija verhnego Podvin'ja v I i nachale sjacheletija n.e. (On the History of the Population of the Upper Dvina Area in the Early First Millennium* AD). *Materialy i issledovanija po arheologii SSSR*, vol. 76. Moscow-Leningrad: Academy of Sciences of the USSR.

Stanko V.N. 1982. *Mirnoe. Problema mezolita stepei Severnogo Pricheromor'ja (Mirnoe. The Problem of Mesolithic in the North Pontic Steppe)*. Kiev: Naukova Dumka.

Strabo. 1918–27. *The Geography of Strabo* (with an English translation by H.L. Jones). Cambridge, MA.: Harvard University Press.

Straus G.S. 1990. The early upper Palaeolithic of south-western Europe, Cro-Magnon adaptations in the Iberian peripheries, 40000–20000 BP. In P. Mellars (ed.), *The Emergence of Modern Humans*. Edinburgh: Edinburgh University Press, pp. 274–302.

Sulimirski T. 1970. *Prehistoric Russia. An Outline*. London: John Baker Humanities Press.

Symons L. (ed.). 1983. *The Soviet Union. A Systematic Geography*. London: Hodder & Stoughton.

Tallgren A.M. 1911. *Die Kupfer- und Bronzezeit in Nord- und Ostrussland* (The Copper and Bronze Ages in Northern and Eastern Russia). Helsingfors: Suomen Muinaismuistoydistyksen Aikakauskirja, vol. 25.

Tallgren A.M. 1926. La Pontide Préscythique après l'introduction des métaux. Helsinki: Eurasia Septentrionalis Antique.

Telegin D.Ya. 1986. *Dereivka, A Settlement and Cemetery of Copper Age Horse-keepers on the Middle Dniepr*. Oxford: BAR International Series, S267.

Telegin D.Ya. 1973. *Sredn'ostogis'ka kul'tura epohi midi (The Sdedni Stog Culture of the Copper Age)*. Kiev: Naukova Dumka.

Telegin D.Ya. 1981. *Mezolitichni pam'jatki Ukrainy (Mesolithic Sites of the Ukraine)*. Kiev: Naukova Dumka.

Telegin D.Ya. 1968. *Dnipro-Donec'ka kul'tura (The Dniepr-Donetsian Culture)*. Kiev: Naukova Dumka.

Terenozhkin A.I. 1955. K voprosu ob etnicheskoi prinadlezhnosti lesostepnyx plemjon severnogo Prichernomir'ja v skifskoe vremja (On the ethnic affiliation of Forest-Steppic tribes during the Scythian Age). *Sovetskaja arxeologija*, XXIV: 7–28.

Terenozhkin A.I. 1976. *Kimmeriicy (The Cimmerians)*. Kiev: Naukova Dumka.

Terenozhkin A.I. and V.A. Il'inskaya. 1986. Skifija (The Scythia). In S.D. Kryzhitsky (ed.), *Arheologija Ukrainskoi SSR*, vol. 2. Kiev: Naukova Dumka, pp. 43–169.

Tikhomirov M.N. 1956. *Drevnerusskie goroda (Old Russian Cities)*. Moscow: Izd. AN SSSR.

Tolochko P.P. 1983. *Drevnii Kiev (Ancient Kiev)*. Kiev: Naukova Dumka.

Tolochko P.P. 1989. *Drevnerusskii feodal'nyi gorod (Old Russian Feudal Cities)*. Kiev: Naukova Dumka.

Toporov V.N. and O.N. Trubachev. 1962. *Lingvisticheskii analiz gidronimov Verxnego Podneprov'ja. (The Linguistic Analysis of Upper Dnieprian Hydronimics).* Moscow: Izd. AN SSSR.

Trautmann R. 1923. *Baltisch-Slavisches Wörterbuch.* Göttingen: Vandenhoek.

Tretyakov P.N. 1959. *Chaplinskoe gorodishche (Chaplino Hill-Fort). Materialy i issledovanija po arxeologii SSSR,* vol. 70. Moscow: Izd. AN SSSR.

Tretyakov P.N. 1966. *Finno-ugry, balty i slavjane na Dnepre i Volge (The Finno-Ugrians, Balts and Slavs on the Dniepr and Volga).* Moscow-Leningrad: Nauka.

Tretyakov V.P. 1990. *Volosovskie plemena evropeiskoi chasti SSSR v III – II tys. l. do n. e. (The Volosova Tribes of the European USSR in the Third and Second Millennia BC).* Leningrad: Institute of Archaeology.

Trofimova T.A. 1946. Krivichi, vyatichi i slavjanskie plemena Podneprov'ja po dannym antropologii (The Krivichians, Vyatichians and Slavic tribes in the Dniepr area according to the anthropological evidence). *Sovetskaja etnografija,* 1: pp. 91–136.

Trubetskoy N.S. 1939. Gedanken über das Indogermanenprobleme. *Acta Linguistica,* 1: 81–9.

Urtans J.T. 1994. *Latvian Hillforts: The Originality of the Archaeological Reality.* Amsterdam: Zeisiende Kroon-voordacht.

Vasmer M. 1932. *Über die Ostgrenze der baltischen Stämme. Beiträge zur historischen Völkerkunde Europas.* Berlin: Sitzberichte der Preussischen Akedemie der Wissenschaften. Philosophisch-historische Klasse.

Velichko A.A., G.V. Antonova, E.M. Zelikson, A.K. Markova, M.M. Monoszon, T.D. Morozova, M.A. Pevzner, M.B. Suleimanov and T.A. Khalcheva. 1980. Paleogeografija stojanki Azyx – drevneishego poselenija pervobytnogo cheloveka na territorii SSSR (The Palaeogeography of the Azykh, the oldest Hominid site in the USSR). *Izvestija AN SSSR, seriya geograficheskaya,* 3: 20–35.

Velichko A.A., O.K. Borisova, A.G. Doskach, T.D. Morozova, I.I. Spasskaya and M.A. Faustova. 1993. Russkaja Ravnina (The Russian Plain). In A.A. Velichko (ed.) *Razvitie landshaftov i klimata Severnoi Evrazii,* vol. 1. Moscow: Nauka, pp. 11–20.

Vuorela T. 1964. *The Finno-Ugric Peoples.* Bloomington, IN: Indiana University Press.

Wells P.S. 1981. *The Emergence of an Iron Age Economy.* The Mecklenburg Grave Groups from Halstatt and Stična. Bulletin 33. Cambridge MA: American School of Prehistoric Research, Peabody Museum of Archaeology and Ethnology, Harvard University.

Wells P.S. 1983. *Rural Economy in the Early Iron Age.* Bulletin 36. American School of Prehistoric Research. Peabody Museum of Archaeology and Ethnology. Harvard University.

Whittle A. 1985. *Problems in Neolithic Archaeology.* Cambridge: Cambridge University Press.

Wiślański T. 1980. *The Neolithic in Poland*. Warsaw: PAN.

Wolfram H. 1988. *History of the Goths*. Berkeley, CA/London: University of California Press.

Yakimov V.P. and V.M. Kharitonov. 1979. K probleme krymskix neandertal'cev (The problem of Crimean Neanderthals). In Yu.G. Kolosov (ed.), *Issledovanie paleolita v Krymu*. Kiev: Naukova Dumka.

Zagwijn W.H. 1975. Variations in climate as shown by pollen analysis, especially in the Lower Pleistocene in Europe. In A.E. Right and F. Moseley, (eds), *Ice Ages: Ancient and Modern. Geological Journal*, 6: 137–52.

Zaibert V.F. 1993. *Eneolit Uralo-Irtyshskogo mezhdurech'ya* (*The Eneolithic of the Ural-Irtysh Interfluve*). Petropavlovsk: Nauka.

Zakharuk Yu.M. 1964. Proelemy arzeologicheskoi kul'tury (The problems of the concept 'archaeological culture'). *Arxeologija*, 17: 12–24.

Zaliznyak L.L. 1979. *Ohotniki na severnogo olenja Ukrainskogo Poless'ja epoxi final'nogo paleolita* (*Late Palaeolithic Reindeer Hunters of the Ukrainian Polessye*). Kiev: Naukova Dumka.

Zarrina E.I. and I.I. Krasnov. 1983. Detal'naja xronostratigraficheskaja shkala pozdnego pleistocena Evropeiskoi chasti SSSR (The detailed chrono-stratigraphic division of the Late Pleistocene of the Russian Plain). *Sovetskaja geologija*, 6: 52–60.

Zavernyaev F.M. 1978. *Khotylevskoe paleoliticheskoe mestonaxozhdenie* (*The Palaeolithic Site of Khotylevo*). Leningrad: Nauka.

Zbenovich V.G. 1974. *Pozdnetripol'skie plemena Severnogo Prichernomor'ja* (*Late Tripolye Tribes in the North Pontic Area*). Kiev: Naukova Dumka.

Zbenovich V.G. 1989. *Ranii etap tripol'skoi kul'tury na territorii Ukrainy* (*The Early Tripolian Stage in the Ukraine*). Kiev: Naukova Dumka.

Zinkjavičus Z. and P. Gaučas. 1985. Vostochnaja granica rasprostranenija litovskogo jazyka v proshlom po dannym toponimiki (The eastern boundary of the Lithuanian language based on the toponimic evidence). In I.E. Ronis (ed.), *Problemy etnicheskoi istorii baltov*. Riga: Zinatne, pp. 174–6.

Zubakov V.A. 1986. *Global'nye klimaticheskie processy pleistocena* (*Global Climatic Processes of the Pleistocene*). Leningrad: Gidrometeoizdat.

Zubakov V.A. and I.I. Borzenkova. 1983. *Klimaty pozdnego Kainozoja* (*Late Cainozoic Climates*). Leningrad: Gidrometeoizdat.

Zubrow E. 1989. The geographic modelling of Neanderthal extinction. In P. Mellars and C. Stringer (eds), *The Human Evolution: Behavioural and Biological Perspectives on the Origin of Modern Humans*. Edinburgh: Edinburgh University Press, pp. 123–54.

Zvelebil M. and P. Dolukhanov. 1991. The transition to farming in Eastern and Northern Europe, *Journal of World Prehistory*, vol. 5 (3): 233–78.

Zvelebil M. and P. Rowley-Conwy. 1984. The transition to farming in northern Europe: a hunter-gatherer perspective. *Norwegian Archaeological Review*, v. 17 (2): 104–27.

Index

Abashevian culture, 100, 108
Abayev, V.I., Russian linguist, 125
Acheulean, 26, 28
Agriculture, 6, 61, 62, 64, 65, 68, 75,
    99, 110, 111, 114, 129, 132, 134,
    152, 165, 173
Ahrensburgian, 42
Alexeyev, V.P., Russian anthropologist,
    31, 34
Alexeyeva, L.I., Russian anthropologist,
    140
Alleröd, 30
Altantic period (Alti-thermal or Climatic
    optimum), 47, 48, 50, 61, 70, 71,
    73, 146, 198
Anatolian languages, 96
Ancylus Lake, 49
Anetovka Upper Palaeolithic site, 36
Anikovich, M.V., Russian archaeologist,
    38
Animal style, 125, 126
Anthony, D.W., 70
Antrea-Korpilahti, 53
Apsheronian transgression, 24
Arabs, 172, 174, 195
Arbman, H., 173, 174
Archaeological culture, 3, 38, 41, 42,
    57, 60, 62, 64, 65, 70–4, 83, 84, 86,
    89, 115
Arslanov, Kh.A., Russian expert in
    geochronology, 29
Artamonov, M.I., Russian
    archaeologist, 121, 125

Artëmenko I.I., Ukrainian archaeologist,
    99, 100
Arzhan, Scythian-time barrow, 127
Asbestos or network pottery, 103
Attila, 159
Avdeevo, Upper Palaeolithic site, 36, 38
Azykh Cave, 26, 27, 28, 32
Azykhanthropus, 28, 31

Bader, O.N., Russian archaeologist, 39,
    98, 105, 106
Baltic Ice Lake, 49
Baltic Sea, 10, 49–51, 58, 59, 96, 135,
    141
Baltic Shield, 8, 9, 11
Balto-Slavic (-Germanic) linguistic
    entity, 90, 135, 199
Balts, Baltic languages, 20, 21, 135,
    139, 141–2, 180
Basque–Caucasian linguistic entity, 49
Batai site, 70
Bear cave, 36
Belorussians, 20, 21, 170
Berezanskaya, S.S., Ukrainian
    archaeologist, 99, 117
Bibikov, S.N., Russian archaeologist,
    39, 65
Bintliff, John, 112
Birka, 174, 175
Biskupin hill-fort, 113
Black Sea, 2, 13, 28, 30, 51, 58, 70,
    93, 118, 120, 129, 130, 131, 133,
    155

231